About this book

Guide to Baby Products comes to you from CONSUMER REPORTS, the testing and consumer-information source best known for product Ratings and buying guidance. We are also a comprehensive source of unbiased advice about services, personal finance, autos, health and nutrition, and other consumer concerns. Since 1936, the mission of Consumers Union has been to test products, inform the public, and protect consumers. Its income is derived solely from the sale of CONSUMER REPORTS magazine and its other publications and services, and from nonrestrictive, noncommercial contributions, grants, and fees. Only CONSUMER REPORTS has 150 secret shoppers who buy all the products it tests to be sure that they're the same products you buy. Consumer Reports accepts no ads from companies, nor does it let any company use our reports or Ratings for commercial purposes.

Other books from Consumer Reports

- Best Buys for Your Home
- Consumer Reports Buying Guide
- Travel Well for Less
- New Car Buying Guide
- Used Car Buying Guide
- Home Computer Buying Guide
- Consumer Drug Reference
- Consumer Reports Money Book

Consumer Reports®

Guide to Baby Products

Consumer Reports®

Guide to Baby Products

Sandy Jones
and the Editors of Consumer Reports

CONSUMER REPORTS SPECIAL PUBLICATIONS, YONKERS, NEW YORK

A Special Publication from Consumer Reports

Director, Special Publications Andrea Scott
Managing Editor Bette LaGow
Project Editor Dennis Fitzgerald
Contributing Editors Kristin Godsey, Maggie Keresey
Design Manager Kim Adis
Art Director Alison Wilkes
Medical Editor Marvin Lipman, M.D.
Pediatric Consultant Herbert Newman, M.D.
Copy Editor Amy Borrelli
Production Jennifer Dixon
Illustrations Ted Burn (products and babies), Tatjana Krizmanic (tips)
Special Publications Staff Joan Daviet, Jay Heath, Merideth Mergel

Consumer Reports

Vice President and Editorial Director Julia Kagan
Editor/Senior Director Margot Slade
Executive Editor/Associate Editorial Director Eileen Denver
Design Director George Arthur
Managing Art Director Tim LaPalme
Director, Publishing Operations David Fox
Associate Director, Retail Sales Geoffrey D. Baldwin
Retail Trade Sales Carol Lappin
Manufacturing & Distribution Ann Urban
Senior Vice President and Technical Director R. David Pittle
Vice President, Technical Operations Jeffrey A. Asher
Director, Consumer Sciences and Public Service Geoffrey Martin
Testing Director, Recreation and Home Improvement John Galeotafiore
Project Leader Werner Freitag
Senior Marketing Analyst Karin Weisburgh

Consumers Union

President James A. Guest
Executive Vice President Joel Gurin

Guide to Baby Products

Reference

Welcome to baby world

**Congratulations! You're expecting.
Now plan to make a multitude of buying decisions
to get ready for your baby.**

There are few events in life more exciting than having a baby. And expectant parents want to welcome their new addition not just with joy and love, but also with the most secure and nurturing environment they can create. That's why baby stores all over the country are filled with future parents test-driving strollers, cuddling stuffed toys, and tracking down the most secure cribs and car seats.

Baby-product choices are heartfelt and personal. What you buy should be functional and safe, too. CONSUMER REPORTS can help by letting you know what's out there. The knowledge of its baby-products experts, based on the results of unbiased, side-by-side testing, can guide you as you gauge quality. CONSUMER REPORTS can also help you discern value, scanning the marketplace and telling you when quality is connected to the price tag, when you need to buy new, and when used is OK.

How this book can help

As you decide on your own individual selections, consider "Guide to Baby Products" your personal shopping consultant. It covers a wide range of essential baby products, consolidating the very latest information on quality, safety, product features, and cost to assist you in making smart, informed buying decisions. It's designed to familiarize you with the broad array of baby merchandise, pointing you toward the best products and away from the less than best.

"Guide to Baby Products" is divided into two parts. The first delivers the big-picture advice you'll need on cribs, car seats, strollers, high chairs, baby-monitors, all those enticing toys, and more. There is also information on feeding products such as bottles, breast pumps, and formula, as well as diapering and bathing essentials and those cute clothes. To help you record key milestones such as baby's first steps, there's a chapter on cameras, camcorders, and baby books, old-style and online.

The second part of the book is a Reference section designed to make it easy to find information when you are ready to buy or simply need to check a fact. The product guide gives you a quick look at your shopping choices, listing major brands and models and their features in an easy-to-use table format. You'll also find manufacturers' phone numbers and web addresses as well as a list of retail oulets. Toward the back of the book are the latest CONSUMER REPORTS Ratings of key equipment such as car seats and play yards; a selection of parenting organizations, publications, and web sites; tips on babyproofing your home; facts on drugs commonly prescribed for children; and a list of product recalls. There are also checklists and worksheets to help you organize your shopping efforts.

Baby-product ABCs

Hard-to-resist goodies such as huggable bears, multicolored mobiles, jazzy sports strollers, and attaché-style diaper bags can turn a shopping trip into a spending spree. But a newborn doesn't really need much besides a place to sleep, comfy clothes to keep warm, and diapers to stay dry. So our very first piece of advice is to start with the basics. You can then decide which extras you really want and need. There are some items you simply must have: a crib, a car seat (required by law in all states), basic clothing, diapers, some type of diaper bag, and, for most parents, a stroller. (See "The basics to have before baby arrives," page 12.)

Soft carriers, backpacks, breast pumps, changing tables, and bottle warmers help make caring for your baby easier—but you can do just fine without them. Items such as crib mobiles, baby swings, and toys can add a little fun and stimulation to the daily routine.

Products marketed specifically for babies are generally safe, partly because of government safety regulations. The Consumer Product Safety Commission regulates baby equipment and oversees recalls. It enforces general rules that apply to most categories as well as mandatory standards for a few specific categories such as cribs and clothes. The National Highway Traffic Safety Administration oversees mandatory safety standards related to the crash performance of car seats. The U.S. Food and Drug Admininistrations is responsible for baby formula and most baby food. The U.S. Department of Agriculture monitors baby food containing meat.

Manufacturers of a product that poses hazards or fails to comply with mandatory safety standards may be ordered to issue a recall. When this happens, the manufacturer must take steps to remove the offending product from store shelves and warn consumers. Sometimes it may be forced to offer remedies to consumers, such as offering free product replacements or retrofit kits. And when it imports products that don't comply with federal regulations, or when it fails to report to the CPSC injuries caused by its products that have been reported to it by consumers, it may be fined. For a list of recent product recalls, see page 257.

In addition, the CPSC advises in the development of voluntary standards administered by the Juvenile Products Manufacturers Association, an industry trade group. Such standards exist for about a dozen categories including cribs, car seats, high chairs, strollers, play yards, gates, and toddler beds. They're written under the oversight of the American Society for Testing and Materials, an independent, nonprofit organization, and ratified by manufacturers and consumer groups including Consumers Union, publisher of CONSUMER REPORTS. Once a voluntary standard has been adopted, manufacturers that choose to have their products certified submit samples to independent testing laboratories approved by the ASTM.

Products are constantly redesigned, and safety standards may change.

Because baby goods are always evolving, a product that has initially been deemed safe may turn out to pose a safety problem later. For instance, recent tests of toddler/booster seats by CONSUMER REPORTS turned up problems with shoulder belt guides that could make these seats less effective in a crash. One way to make sure you're avoiding old problems is to get new models that meet the most recent safety guidelines.

Parenting magazines and product-advice publications such as CONSUMER REPORTS (and Consumer Reports Online, *www.consumerreports.org)* can help you keep up, as can conversations with experienced parents. The Reference section in the back of this book can point you to baby-product and product-safety web sites. You should also look at merchandise with your own common sense.

Your primary buying goals right now are safety, reliability, convenience—and getting your money's worth.

1

Buying for your baby

Today's baby products reflect the latest design trends and a continuing concern with safety.

Kids born in this day and age—and their parents too—have it made when it comes to choices for baby products. You'll find strollers for babies whose parents jog, cribs that rival the finest furniture, and full-color video baby monitors. But with choice comes confusion. You can save yourself some time and energy if you have an idea of what's out there before you begin. Several key trends are influencing what you'll see in the store, in catalogs, and on the web.

Baby product trends

FUNCTIONAL DESIGN. Manufacturers, studying the preferences of young parents, have decided that functionality is a key to sales success.

Strollers may have comfort features such as cup holders for both baby and parent and boldly colored, "outdoorsy" looks with rugged, fat tires and high-profile frames. Many high chairs have a height-adjusted seat as well as trays that can be removed and adjusted with one hand. Products such as big-wheel sports strollers and framed backpack carriers appeal to those

Contents

Show off

"Stall" visitors who come to see the baby so that the older child can be the center of attention for a few minutes. Show pictures of the child as well as the baby. Then let the child help you show off the baby.

with an athletic lifestyle. Parental careers are a given, and some diaper bags and breast-pump carriers can pass for briefcases.

You'll also see equipment that "grows with baby," such as car seats that serve two or even three age ranges, cribs that convert to loveseats or toddler beds, and high chairs that turn into play tables and chairs. Such multi-use products may seem particularly practical, but there is a downside. CONSUMER REPORTS has found that dedicated, single-purpose products, such as age-specific and size-specific car seats, often perform better than those designed for several different uses.

LICENSING FAMILIAR CHARACTERS. Marketers have sold popular cartoon creations to manufacturers of merchandise since the early days of Mickey Mouse. Current sources of inspiration include Looney Tunes, Precious Moments, Sesame Street, and Winnie the Pooh. Increasingly, adult-oriented brands and themes such as Eddie Bauer, Jeep, Martha Stewart, and NASCAR are making their way into the baby realm. You'll find names and figures on just about every type of baby product, from strollers to sleepers.

IMPACT OF SAFETY CONCERNS. Products are routinely approved for safety through a system of standards, some mandated by federal regulation, some followed on a voluntary basis by manufacturers. Federal regulators, industry groups, and consumer groups such as Consumers Union, publisher of CONSUMER REPORTS, work to refine those standards on a regular basis. Uncertainty over how child car seats should be installed has led to a federal rule requiring by September 2002 that all automakers and child car seat manufacturers follow a simpler, standardized system for attaching seats in cars and light trucks. Some safety experts expect Congress to call for a tighter standard for booster seats and state legislation requiring their use. A voluntary standard for walkers—baby seats with wheels on the base that have been involved in tens of thousands of infant injuries—has been updated so new designs that meet the standard don't fall down stairs easily. A voluntary standard for cribs has been strengthened and now includes rigorous structural tests to make sure slats don't separate from side rails.

In addition, CONSUMER REPORTS regularly tests key items of baby equipment, often to more rigorous standards than the government requires. You'll find results of our car-seat tests, which turned up design problems with toddler/booster seats, in Chapter 3.

Baby products that prove unsafe are subject to safety recalls. You'll find a guide to typical problems and a list of recent actions in the section starting on page 257.

Shopping options

Whatever type of shopper you are—diligent researcher, casual browser, or determined time-saver—the baby-products shopping scene holds plenty of options. You can visit every variety of store, leaf through catalogs, and surf web sites. You'll find details on shopping venues on page 181. Here's an overview.

AT THE STORES. The hands-on environment of a store allows you to see an item, pick it up, and get a sense of how it works. Besides, it can be fun to browse the aisles and imagine your little one using all those cute things. Little wonder that, despite the rise of baby catalogs and online shopping, stores are still the consumer's first choice.

• **Megastores and discount chains.** Big specialists such as Baby Superstore, Babies "R" Us, and Toys "R" Us, as well as mass merchandisers such as Kmart, Sears, Target, and Wal-Mart, generally have the lowest prices. The theme at these giants can be summed up as "cute and conservative." Strollers mostly come in navy, cribs are simply constructed and streamlined, infant seats and bedding are splashed with fun patterns, and cartoon characters and familiar cuddly pals cover just about everything else. Small convenience items, clothing, and toys are mounted on pegs for quick selection. Sometimes big stores offer "lowest price" guarantees, which means they'll match the prices of competitors. But there are often restrictions, such as requirements that discounts apply only to the *exact* products advertised. Most also operate computerized gift registries (see "Baby-product registries," page 11). Close-out sales and promotions using loss leaders—deeply discounted car seats or other big-ticket items—are common enticements.

The pivotal advantage of shopping in a baby megastore is a broad selection of baby products at very competitive prices. The downside is the possibility you'll get lost in all the thousands of pieces of baby paraphernalia. Sales help can be hard to find, and associates may not be very well informed about what's safe or even useful.

• **Regional specialty chains and baby boutiques.** A number of chains operate regionally, such as Babyland, Baby 2 Teen, Bellini, Bergstrom's, Buy Buy Baby, Lewis of London, Once Upon a Child, the Right Start, Small Fry World, and USA Baby. There are also independent boutiques—smaller "stork" stores that have to offer something besides low prices to compete with the big chains.

All of these stores tend to cater to upscale parents who want to buy the best for their baby, no expense spared. The merchandise, a mix of domestic and imported lines, includes high-end car seats and cribs as well as accessories including babyproofing products, diaper bags, and toys.

A hallmark of these places is personalized service. Ideally, knowledgeable salespeople will answer your queries with carefully tailored buying advice. They'll go to some trouble to see that you are satisfied—going out with you to your car to try out a safety seat, for instance, or offering exchanges or refunds for unsatisfactory products.

Some salespeople, however, have product biases, and you may be led to unnecessarily expensive product choices. You could end up paying more —a lot more—for a car seat or high chair that's also available through a baby-product web site or in a big discount chain.

• **Traditional department stores.** Stores such as Bloomingdale's, Lord & Taylor, Macy's, Meier & Frank, and Nordstrom devote a relatively small amount of space to baby products and focus more on top-priced garments and soft accessories than on space-grabbing hard goods such as cribs, car seats, and high chairs. You can find well-constructed, fashionable baby shirts, sleepers, coats, and clothing sets in a variety of styles. The best time to shop is during end-of-season sales, when prices are typically reduced by half or more.

IN CATALOGS. Catalog merchants provide extensive selection, convenience, and often an excellent record of customer service. Many let you makes purchases online. The catalog-web fusion can give you the best of both worlds. You can often use the printed catalog to make selections and then enter item numbers online. Catalog web sites frequently feature product lines not available in the printed catalog, as well as online-only sales and product-selection tips.

ON THE WEB. Internet stores for baby products are trying to make online shopping as easy as possible for parents. As with catalogs, they include product photos, specifications, prices, and sizes. You'll also find reviews from experts and other parents.

Given the shakeout in the world of e-tailing, no one can say which baby-product sites are likely to remain in business for the long term. Some sites that have gone under have left customers with unfilled orders. Because established catalog merchandisers and bricks-and-mortar stores or chains have more than a virtual business, their sites seem more likely to survive than "pure-play," online-only sites.

CONSUMER REPORTS recommends that before you buy from any online site, you should check to see that it has complete contact information—including a toll-free number, and e-mail and postal addresses—and 24-hour customer service. You'll also want a 100 percent satisfaction guarantee. Take a moment to read the site's privacy policy, which should tell you which type of information is collected and who gets to use it.

You may find the Internet more useful as a research tool than a shopping tool. Information that in the past would have taken many hours and many

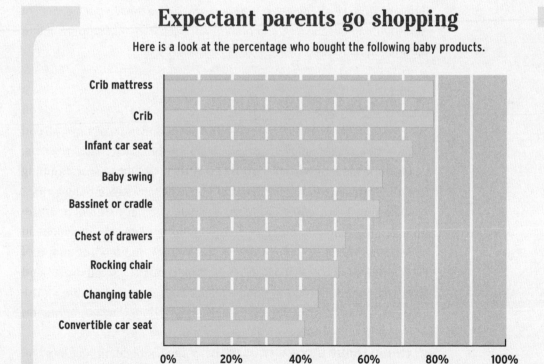

Expectant parents go shopping

Here is a look at the percentage who bought the following baby products.

Source: American Baby Group survey in 2000 of 1,309 expectant or new mothers. Coordinated by Bruno and Ridgeway Research Associates Inc.

phone calls—if it could be found at all—is now available through a few clicks of a mouse. To check out what's available and to compare prices, surf the major baby-products sites. You can find them through search engines, which scour the Internet with varying degrees of success, and metasearch sites—search engines that query search engines. Or use the shopping guide, page 181. It gives web addresses and more details on a selection of baby-gear sites.

BABY FAIRS. Baby expos, held in many cities across the country, give manufacturers, retail stores, and local nonprofit agencies a chance to show their wares to a select audience—you and hundreds of other expectant and new parents. They let you compare notes with other parents about their product preferences or question experts on the scene.

The best time to snag bargains is the last day of the fair. Arrive early, bring some cash, and prepare for old-fashioned haggling. You may be able to carry away your desired product for half price or less. If you find a stroller or high chair that's already on your shopping list and you've researched the retail price, make an offer to the sales rep. You have the advantage, since a rep would rather sell you the product than pack it up and ship it back to the store or factory.

A shopping strategy

You can shop most efficiently—and avoid extras and impulse buys—if you create a shopping strategy in advance. Here are things to consider:

MAKE A LIST OF WHAT YOU NEED FIRST. Organize your shopping to get the crucial purchases out of the way first. Before your baby arrives, you'll want these essentials: a car seat, crib or bassinet, mattress and bedding, diapers, diaper pail, diaper bag, clothing, bathing supplies, medical necessities, formula (if you're not breastfeeding), and feeding supplies. Once you have the essentials, you can think about items you don't need right away: a stroller, carrier, changing table, high chair, and pacifiers. (The chart on page 12, "The basics to have before baby arrives," gives an overview of shopping issues for each type of product.)

THINK ABOUT BUYING IT USED. Baby clothes, bedding, and toys can sometimes be found in thrift stores and yard sales at a small fraction of their original retail prices. But some items—such as a car seat—should always be purchased new to ensure that they comply with updated safety requirements and have no hidden flaws. When buying anything used, check to see if the product has been recalled. (See Recalls, page 257.)

COMPARISON SHOP. Prices can vary from one shopping venue to another, sometimes dramatically. Check ads and sales circulars for store information and set aside some time to browse. Online, you can use a comparison-shopping site, sometimes called a shop bot (short for "shopping robot"), to check prices. The major shop bots include Dealtime.com, MySimon.com, Smartshop.com, and Webmarket.com. They cover a broad range of consumer goods, including brand-name strollers and other baby products. Be as specific as possible in your search, detailing the type of product, model, and manufacturer, if you can. Note that these sites usually have a commercial relationship with the merchants they recommend. So it's a good idea to use several bots and compare their findings.

BE WILLING TO BARGAIN. Sometimes, small stores are so eager to make a sale, they'll let you negotiate a discount. The best time to bargain is late in the afternoon or evening, when the store will soon be adding up its sales for the day.

CONFIRM RETURN POLICIES. A store's return policies can make the difference between being a satisfied customer and being stuck with something you don't want or can't use. Inquire about returns at the information desk before you start shopping in a store. It's not unusual for a store to allow returns only within 30 days after a purchase, which won't help if you're shopping long before baby arrives.

Continued on page 14

Baby-product registries

Many baby specialty shops and some chains offer a computerized wish-list registry. Smaller shops may simply offer to save information in a notebook. Big chains use huge databases to store parents' names and addresses, babies' due dates, and gift choices. Data can then be accessed and printed in any store branch.

Signing up with a registry can help you avoid duplicate or unwanted gifts (provided gift givers check the registry) and may get you coupons and other money-saving offers. The price: your privacy. Information you might want to keep private is readily exposed to the world. And it can be sold to other companies for marketing purposes.

The basics to have before baby arrives

Car seat
Pages 31-40

[handwritten: Infant w/ Stroller & convertable]

Never buy used. The seat may be a defective, damaged, or recalled model. An infant or convertible car seat must securely fasten in a rear-facing position to your car's back seat, preferably in the middle. Infant car seat/stroller combinations, called travel systems, are also available. If you have a preemie, you may be able to exchange the seat you bought for a special design that allows a preemie to recline completely.

Crib
Pages 16-21

Avoid using a crib more than a few years old. Components and hardware could be worn and weakened. New designs offer the latest safety features. When shopping, test bars to make sure they can't be moved or rotated, and try drop sides for ease of handling. Look for a sticker indicating a certified manufacturer.

Crib mattress
Pages 21-24

Choose the firmest foam or innerspring mattress you can find. Mattresses are made to fit cribs, but you still should check for gaps between the mattress and crib. If you can insert two fingers side-by-side between the mattress and any one side of the crib, there may be a suffocation hazard. **SPECIAL ADVICE:** A store's return policy is more important than a manufacturer's warranty, which may cover only minor flaws.

Crib bumpers
Page 27

Crib bumpers, which keep baby's arms and legs from getting captured in the crib bars, should fit snugly and tie or snap into place. To avoid a strangulation risk, ties should be no more than 7 inches long.

Bedding
Pages 26-29

Stock up with two to three crib sheets, four or more lightweight cotton blankets (receiving blankets), and a mattress pad. Sheets must be elasticized all around so they don't slip off the mattress and entrap baby. The fabric should be soft. Layered sleepwear is a safer option than covering baby with blankets.

Diapers
Pages 76-80

Disposables: Get at least one small package in newborn size, a large package in size 1, plus one or two dozen cloth diapers as backups and milksops. **Cloth:** Buy two to three dozen, plus four small snap-on, waterproof outer pants and two to three sets of diaper pins, or buy several sets of pinless diaper covers with inserts.

Diaper pail
Pages 80-81

Disposables: Get a pail with several boxes of liner refills, or use a garbage can with easy-to-seal liners. **Cloth:** Choose a diaper pail for soaking cloth diapers. It should have a locking lid to eliminate a potential drowning hazard.

Diaper-changing table Pages 81-82

Look for a stable, sturdy model that has a safety belt and a raised edge on all sides to keep baby from rolling off. If it's light, make sure it has a wide stance. You can also use the crib with one side dropped down or a changing pad on the floor. Fold-down adapters for the top of a nursery chest may tip the whole chest if a baby's weight is placed on the fold-down lid. Some structures may pose a hazard to older siblings who may want to climb on them.

Diaper bag
Pages 82-84

Consider size and carrying comfort. Look for heavy-duty, moisture-resistant material, such as vinyl or moisture-resistant nylon, plus reinforced seams and secure handles, separate compartments, a changing pad, and bottle pockets. **SPECIAL ADVICE:** You can adapt other carriers, such as a small overnight satchel or a backpack, for carrying baby gear.

Clothing
Pages 91-94

You'll need six to eight nightgowns or one-piece sleepers, the same number of side-snap T-shirts, a small baby cap (the hospital will probably give you one), several pairs of socks, and at least a couple

Clothing continued~	of soft, comfortable daytime outfits. Get only a few items in newborn size. Go for clothing in the 6-month size—your baby will grow into it quickly. But don't let baby wear sleepwear that's too big—it's a fire hazard.
Feeding supplies Pages 98-108	**Breastfeeding:** Buy two or three nursing bras, a box of washable or disposable breast pads for leaks, and four small baby bottles for storing expressed breastmilk. Wait until breastfeeding is well established before deciding about a breast pump. Ask the lactation specialist at the hospital for advice or visit the web sites of the International Lactation Consultant Association *(www.ilca.org)* or La Leche League *(www.lalecheleague.org).* **Bottle feeding:** Get 8 to 12 bottles, plus nipples, rings, and a dishwasher basket. Boil bottles and nipples at least five minutes before first use to remove any chemical residue. Stay with a single major formula type and brand recommended by your doctor. Plain soy milk and off-brand formula can cause malnutrition.
Bathing/grooming Pages 89-90	Have two to four soft towels; a package of baby washcloths; fragrance-free cleansing bars, such as Basis, Dove, or Neutrogena; and a pair of blunt-tip scissors or baby-sized fingernail clippers. Any soap can irritate a newborn's skin, so stay with plain warm water for the first 4 weeks. A zinc-oxide-based diaper rash cream may help protect baby's bottom during diaper rash outbreaks. Avoid other creams, lotions, and powders—their chemicals and fragrances may irritate or cause an allergic reaction. **SPECIAL ADVICE:** It's easiest to trim nails while baby is sleeping.
Medicine chest essentials Page 90	Ask your baby's doctor to recommend a pain-and-fever reducing formula, such as Infant's Tylenol. Choose a thermometer: rectal, axial (armpit), or ear type; digital or mercury. Consider buying a nasal aspirator—a bulb-shaped device for suctioning mucus from a baby's nose when congested. Talk to your pediatrician for further medical recommendations.
Stroller Pages 41-53	New is better. With an older model, brakes or folding mechanisms may be worn, or it may have been recalled. A newer model may be easier to handle. When shopping, take a "test drive" to check brakes, folding mechanism, and ease of handling and lifting.
Pacifiers Page 107	If you go this route, buy several in infant size, preferably made of silicone, which lasts longer than latex. Boil pacifiers five minutes before first use to remove any chemical residue. Some recent studies have linked pacifier use with recurrent ear infections. Some babies who are breastfeeding may not take to a pacifier.
Night-lights Page 220	Use plug-in night-lights for your bedroom and the nursery in out-of-reach outlets only. An alternative is installing a dimmer switch. Or use a lamp with a low-wattage bulb.
Sling or strap-on soft carrier Pages 55-56	A sling forms a wearable hammock for a young baby that can be handy when breastfeeding. Slings can be hard to figure out at first, so talk with another mother who has used one, or consult an organization such as La Leche League *(www.lalecheleague.org).* A soft carrier leaves your hands free, and some models let you breast-feed. Check leg holes in a soft carrier to make sure baby can't shift and fall through.
Optional equipment	You may want a rocker or glider and a footstool for late-night feedings. Avoid a glider with sharp metal hardware on the front or the base, or with "X" joints that could crush small fingers.

Continued from page 11

ASSESS WARRANTIES. Manufacturers and retailers often replace returned goods that are clearly flawed or have obviously failed. Hold on to warranty information so you can refer to it easily if there's a problem.

You may find a warranty being used as a sales tool. Some less expensive but adequately firm baby mattresses, for example, offer no warranty, while top-of-the-line models may have "a lifetime guarantee." That may be protection you don't need to pay for, considering that the typical use of a baby mattress is about two years per baby.

AVOID SPECIAL ORDERS. Specialty shops and boutiques often take special orders on cribs, furniture, or other items, but it's not uncommon for orders to arrive months late, maybe even after your baby is born. Also, special orders may be difficult to return should they have flaws.

TAKE ADVANTAGE OF FREEBIES AND COUPONS. If you don't mind getting your name on mailing lists, call the the toll-free customer-service lines of formula, baby-food, and disposable-diaper companies and sign up for their new-mother programs. Join grocery stores' or drugstores' baby clubs for more coupons and discounts. Check the ads and display racks of giant baby retailers for product coupons. Toys "R" Us stores routinely display in-store baby-product catalogs with savings of up to 20 percent for featured name-brand baby items.

2

Furnishing baby's room

Safety, budget, and personal taste will be your main concerns as you set up a place for baby to sleep.

One of the most exciting and fun aspects of preparing for the birth of a child is setting up a nest for the little one. The centerpiece of the nest, of course, is the crib. You'll also need a mattress, which is usually sold separately. Crib alternatives such as a bassinet or cradle may be useful to you during the first months.

Once your baby has a secure, comfortable place to sleep, you're ready to assess other furnishings—which may or may not match the crib. These include an armoire, a chest, and a changing table. They need not be elaborate. You may also want a baby monitor, so you can keep an ear out when you're away from baby's room.

After you've picked out the furnishings, you can turn your attention to paint, wallpaper, window treatments, and accessories such as rugs and lamps. Many home stores have introduced lines of decorator paint, fabric, and accessories for babies' rooms.

Contents

Full-sized cribs

You'll find a broad variety of styles and prices. We suggest that you buy new to ensure that the crib adheres to the latest safety standards.

A crib is generally seen as a "must-have" item of baby equipment. If you're like most parents, you'll opt for a full-sized one. Deciding exactly which crib to buy can be a little daunting. Baby superstores and mass merchandisers are filled with rows and rows of economy and midpriced models. Upscale baby boutiques sell cribs that have the look of expensive furniture. Manufacturers also offer full-sized cribs that convert to a toddler bed, a loveseat, or even a twin or double bed.

What's available

A crib is basically a box with a mattress support on legs with wheels. The sides and sometimes the endboards are made of bars or slats so you can see inside—and baby can see you. One or two sides can be lowered with a lift-and-press, foot-release, or latch mechanism.

Most cribs are constructed of wood, from porous and easily dented pine in lower-priced cribs to strong and durable hardwoods such as ash, beech, oak, and hard maple in top-of-the-line cribs. As a rule, use of a harder wood produces a heavier crib.

Most cribs are constructed of wood, but steel, brass, or molded plastic are also used.

Cribs may also be constructed of other materials such as steel, brass, or molded plastic. Some manufacturers are experimenting with "engineered wood," such as medium-density fiberboard, which can be hard to distinguish from natural wood.

Federal regulations and a voluntary industry standard apply to crib design and safety, so your selection can largely focus on your own furniture preferences and how much you wish to spend. You can create a showpiece nursery suite for thousands of dollars. Or you can simply buy a well-constructed crib—the option most parents take.

There are three major price segments:

ECONOMY CRIBS. Models at the low end of the price scale are perfectly adequate. Prices are low because manufacturers use cheaper materials and simpler finishes and designs. These models tend to be small compared with top-of-the-line models. White or pastel paint or shiny lacquer-like finish may be used to cover wood defects, such as knots and variations in wood shading. You may notice minor finishing flaws, such as poorly sanded rough spots, uneven patches of paint, and the heads of metal brads or glue residue at the base of the bars, which are made of wooden dowels or flat slats.

On a low-priced model, typically only one side can be released—the more stable approach. Casters are disk-shaped and may not lock. "S"-shaped hooks hold the painted-metal mattress support at each corner. The springs making up the mattress support are thinner and appear springier than those in pricier models. When you shake the crib, it may seem rattly rather than sturdy. Jenny Lind cribs—a style with dark finishes and spooled dowels on the sides and ends—often fall into this price category.

Price range: $60 to $100.

MIDPRICED CRIBS. At this price level, it becomes increasingly difficult to discern quality differences from brand to brand. These models are sturdier and more decorative than economy models. They come in an array of wood finishes, from Scandinavian-style natural, to golden maple and oak shades, to reddish-brown cherries and deep mahoganies. Endboards are

Safe sleeping do's and don'ts

- Do keep the crib away from windows.

- Do place a baby on his back in the crib, with nothing around the head or body.

- Do dress baby in layers instead of using blankets. If you do use a blanket, it should be tucked under the mattress and only reach baby's underarms.

- Don't use any bedding that can bunch up around a baby's face and head, including quilts, comforters, lambskin, pillows, and overly soft mattresses.

- Don't use an electric blanket, heating pad, or even a warm water bottle to heat your baby's crib. An infant's skin is highly heat-sensitive and can be burned by temperatures comfortable to an adult.

- Don't put baby down to sleep on a futon, waterbed, beanbag chair, or sofa cushion. Like all soft surfaces, they pose a suffocation risk to a baby.

- Do keep baby's room relatively cool—68° to 72° F.

- Do keep all toys out of the crib.

solid and smoothly finished, and many models have slats on all sides. The gentle curves of the endboards are well finished with rounded edges. Dowels are thicker than those of economy models and may be spooled or flat with rounded edges.

The mattress supports on these models tend to be sturdy, the springs thick, firm, and exposing no sharp edges. These cribs have single or double drop sides. Locking wheels or casters provide stability. There may be a stabilizer bar or two running underneath. The best-made cribs in this category have no exposed brads or glue residue where the slats are fastened to the rails, and staining is uniform. There may be high posts, canopies, or a storage drawer underneath the unit.

Price range: $100 to $400.

UPSCALE CRIBS. These models—many of them imported from Europe —have the heavyweight look of expensive furniture. Finishes are burnished and very smooth. You'll see huge Victorian sleigh-bed styles with curved endboards, cribs with sumptuous, hand-painted scenes of gardens or jungles, and high-tech metal styles. Matching armoires, chests, and changing tables create a coordinated nursery.

Upscale cribs have single or double drop sides. The drop-side hardware may be so well hidden that it's difficult to tell whether the side lowers or not. Mattress supports use heavyweight metal frames and springs. Practical touches, such as multidirectional casters and storage drawers, may be absent.

Price range: $400 to $700.

Features to consider

As you assess crib features, think about your own taste and budget as well as safety and durability.

STRUCTURAL INTEGRITY. Sturdiness is a sign of construction quality. Use of one or more stabilizer bars—metal rods fastened to both endboards beneath the crib—help to steady the frame, providing an advantage over cribs that offer no additional stabilization.

DROP SIDES. Most cribs have only a single side that lowers, which is the more stable approach. Some cribs, including expensive heavyweight models, have double drop sides. Nylon-sleeved, lift-and-press mechanisms have largely replaced metal, foot-release hardware. These newer designs have silent releases that require you to lift the rail while you press the release with your knee. The older design requires you to lift the side while pressing a metal lever or tab under the railing with your foot. The foot maneuver is awkward, and your shins may be bruised when the railing falls. Metal components often rattle and squeak. A third, rare type of release mechanism uses latches at each end of the top rail that must be pulled out at the same time. Federal regulations require that lowering mechanisms be built to prevent accidental release by a baby or sibling.

TEETHING RAILS. These are smooth, plastic coverings for the top of the side rails to protect the crib and a gnawing baby's gums. But there's nothing covering the endboards. The voluntary industry standard says teething rails should be built to stay in place, and not crack or break.

FINISH. The "natural look" of pale wood stain is currently the most popular, although you'll also see deeper wood stains, from maples and cherries to mahoganies. The lowest-priced cribs are typically painted white, allowing manufacturers to cover mixed wood grains, knots and flaws, and variations in wood tones. Other painted shades include off-whites, washed whites (revealing the wood's grain), and green, blue, or yellow pastels. A little roughness in the finish isn't a problem as long as there are no serious defects such as splintering or peeling paint.

MATTRESS SUPPORTS. Most mattress supports consist of a metal frame with coiled springs attached. They're adjustable so the mattress can be raised or lowered depending on the size of the child. Springs give the mattress an extra bounce that may encourage toddlers to jump on it as if it were a trampoline, increasing the chance of a fall. With some cribs, the mattress support is a height-adjustable one-piece board,

All full-sized cribs offer mattress supports with at least two or three height positions. To prevent a baby from falling out of the crib, adjust the mattress to its lowest height position when the baby is able to sit or pull up, usually between 6 and 8 months.

The metal assemblies that adjust mattress supports vary. One type is a series of movable, connected metal components. Another uses simple "S"-shaped hooks. In tests, CONSUMER REPORTS has found that the former does a better job at holding the support frame in place.

SIDES AND RAILINGS. Crib sides are constructed by fitting bars (sometimes called spindles or slats) into mortised holes in the top and bottom rails, then securing each bar with glue and one or two metal brads. The small holes made by the brads are usually filled and covered with a finish so they're invisible.

Quick change

Make up your baby's crib sheets and pads in layers so all you need to do is pull off a top sheet and pad to "change" sheets.

WHEELS. Made of plastic or metal, a crib's wheels can be standard rollers or round, multidirectional, ball-shaped casters. Lockable wheels or casters prevent your tot from "walking" the crib across the room when shaking it and help keep siblings and other children from rolling the crib when your back is turned.

DRAWERS. Some models incorporate a drawer or two under the mattress. Drawers are not usually attached to the crib frame but are freestanding and roll out from under the crib on casters. Before buying, pull any drawer all the way out to inspect its construction. You may find that it has a thin, cardboard-like floor that could bow and give way when loaded with linen or clothing. A drawer floor made of a harder material, such as fiberboard, is more likely to hold up over time.

How to choose

KEY DIFFERENCES. All crib manufacturers must adhere to the uniform federal safety standard, and most meet the voluntary industry standard. So you can be reasonably assured that a crib bought as new is as safe as it can be. Differences between what you'll find on the market tend to be related to features and sturdiness.

RECOMMENDATIONS. Buy a new crib. That way you'll be assured that your crib conforms with the latest safety standards. A used crib given to you from someone you trust may be fine as long as it's only a few years old. But avoid buying a used crib unless you know its history. Drop sides, slats, and hardware may have been weakened as a result of rough use or excessive dampness or heat during storage. Joints and screws may have loosened during disassembly and reassembly.

• **Check construction and workmanship.** The simplest in-store test is to give the crib a slight shaking and see if the frame seems loose rather than solid. Without applying excessive pressure, try rotating each bar to see if it's well secured to the railings. You shouldn't find loose slats on a new crib.

• **Try out the drop sides.** Try lowering the sides of the crib you're considering. Models that open with a lift-and-knee-press action or those with a foot-release mechanism can usually be opened with one hand—an advantage. Most parents only raise and lower the sides of the crib during the first few months, when a baby has little postural support. When babies get bigger and stand up in the crib, many parents pick the baby up without lowering the side. Thus a crib that doesn't have the best drop-side mechanism but is satisfactory in other ways may still be a livable option.

• **Think twice about convertible cribs.** A model that can morph into, say, a loveseat or toddler bed may turn out to be less useful than it seemed in the store. Be sure it can perform each of its multiple functions the way it's supposed to.

• **Ask for store assembly.** Most stores sell cribs sealed in the carton. But rather than coping with the hassle of assembly, see if the store will put it together in your home—in the baby's room—free or for a fee. Besides saving tempers and fingers, having the store assemble it allows you to inspect the assembled crib on the spot—and reject it if you discover flaws in the crib's finishing and frame. If you do choose to assemble the crib, carefully follow the instructions. Assemble the crib in the baby's room. Once put together, it may not fit through the door.

CERTIFICATION. The Consumer Product Safety Commission requires that a crib's lock-release mechanism be beyond a child's capability and that its slats be spaced no more than 2⅜ inches (the diameter of a soda can). Interior dimensions have been standardized. The crib must measure 28 inches in interior width, plus or minus ⅝ inch, and 52⅜ inches in interior length, plus or minus ⅝ inch. Mattress supports must be low enough in their lowest position so a child can't easily climb out when the sides or ends are in their highest position. The federal rules don't cover mattresses, but there is a voluntary standard addressing size. (Gaps between the crib and the edge of the mattress can pose a suffocation hazard.)

Located somewhere on the crib frame should be a certification sticker that shows that the crib meets the minimum requirements of the American Society for Testing and Materials' voluntary standard and that its manufacturer participates in the certification program administered by the Juvenile Products Manufacturers Association. The key tests are for drop sides, teething rails, and safety from protrusions at the corner posts.

Crib mattresses

Mattresses are generally purchased separately from the crib. Firmness and the quality of the mattress covering are your main concerns.

Buying a baby mattress can be a lot like buying an adult mattress. A store may sometimes sell a crib with a promotional mattress as a giveaway—an

Shopping checklist

CRIBS

○ **Buy new to ensure safety.**

○ **Check for the certification sticker.**

○ **Request delivery and assembly.**

○ **Inspect the assembled crib carefully.**

incentive to get you into the store so it can sell you a more expensive combination. It may also try to get you to buy more warranty protection than you need.

What's available

Like adult mattresses, baby mattresses can be foam or innerspring. The major brands are Colgate, Evenflo, Kolcraft, Sealy, and Simmons.

FOAM. Low-priced models tend to be mushy and flimsy, with a thin vinyl covering and vinyl edging. Higher-priced models tend to be firmer, with thicker, laminated vinyl coverings. You can get an idea of foam density (and firmness) by comparing the weight of different foam models. The heavier the mattress, the denser the foam. You can also give the mattress a squeeze test by pressing your palms into both sides of the mattress at once. A dense mattress won't let you press your palms very far.

Foam is relatively lightweight. The densest foam mattress is usually no more than 7 or 8 pounds, compared with 20 to 25 pounds for an innerspring mattress, so changing baby's sheets is relatively easy. Foam is also less springy and therefore less apt to encourage your baby to use the mattress as a trampoline.

Price range: $30 and up.

INNERSPRING. The quality of an innerspring mattress mainly depends on the number of springs (also called coils) and the thickness of the steel used to make them. Springs may be individually pocketed or interconnected. Babies are light, so either type can give good support.

The cheapest innerspring baby mattresses have about 80 coils; the most

'Breathing' mattresses

Avoid 'breathing' mattresses. Recently the Consumer Product Safety Commission required a handful of small companies to withdraw "breathing" crib mattresses and pads that were supposed to prevent Sudden Infant Death Syndrome because it said the companies didn't give adequate scientific backing to their claims. Some models were made of mesh attached to wooden frames. Others used air pumps to provide ventilation. Such mattresses are no longer being manufactured or distributed but you may find them being sold secondhand. There are much better choices.

expensive, 600 coils. A high spring or coil count doesn't always mean a firmer mattress—a model with 150 coils can be firmer than one with 600. The number of layers of padding, what it's made of, and the quality of the covering add to the price. As long as the metal springs and side supports are well shielded, the thickness of a mattress' padding is not that important. Steel border rods added at the top and bottom of the mattress give extra edge support.

The cheapest innersprings, like low-end foam mattresses, have thin vinyl coverings and edgings. As prices go up, coverings become thick, puncture-resistant double or triple laminates, and edgings have fabric binding. Price: Several hundred dollars at the high end.

How to choose

KEY DIFFERENCES. With any mattress, the key factors are firmness and the quality of the mattress covering. Cheaper, low-density foam may soften with use. A high-density foam mattress should keep its shape as well as a good innerspring mattress. The least expensive innersprings may feel mushy. Pricier mattresses tend to have thicker coverings. All mattresses have some sort of waterproofing built into the surface.

RECOMMENDATIONS. Go for the firmest mattress you can find, whether you choose foam or innerspring. The mattress must fit snugly in the crib. If you can fit two fingers between the mattress and any side of the crib, the mattress is too small. A baby's body or head could get trapped between the mattress and the crib—a potentially fatal danger.

• **Measure thickness.** Most mattresses are 6 inches thick. If you opt for a 4- or 5-inch mattress, try to buy appropriately sized sheets.

• **Assess workmanship.** Quality mattresses will use a fabric binding rather than vinyl, and the stitching will be even, with no loose threads. Pinch the ticking to test for thickness. Vents on the side or end of the mattress (small, metal-lined holes or a pocket at each end) help keep the mattress ventilated and may keep seams from splitting when a tot inevitably starts jumping. A vent should be securely attached so it won't pose a swallowing hazard.

• **Confirm store return policies.** A store's return policy is more important than a mattress maker's warranty, which may be encumbered with fine-print exclusions or provisions. The store should be willing to exchange a mattress that doesn't fit. Don't be impressed by a 5- or 10-year warranty. A baby typically uses a crib no more than about two years.

CERTIFICATION. While no federal certification program exists for crib mattresses, California law requires that baby mattresses be fire-resistant. Most major manufacturers meet that requirement, regardless of where they sell their mattresses. A voluntary standard addresses mattress size.

Crib alternatives

A bassinet, bedside sleeper, cradle, or miniature crib may come in handy for very young babies, but such products have a limited useful lifespan.

Crib alternatives—bassinets, bedside sleepers, cradles, and miniature cribs—offer a cozy nest near a parent's bed for a newborn. A small baby may seem more at home in a compact space than in a large, airy crib. And there's something to be said for keeping your baby close by for nighttime feedings and diaper changes.

Once your baby begins to move around more and seems uncomfortable (or nears the upper weight limit recommended by the manufacturer), it's time to move to a crib. So think of these options as short term.

What's available

BASSINETS. These compact, wheeled baby beds are made of wicker or woven wooden splints. Most have a rigid hood that can be attached on one end. They take up little space and can be rolled easily from room to room.

Sudden Infant Death Syndrome

Sudden Infant Death Syndrome (SIDS), also known as crib death, typically happens to babies under 6 months of age, peaking at 2½ months. Boys are slightly more prone to SIDS, and deaths are two-thirds more likely during winter months.

The cause of SIDS is not completely understood, although recent research suggests that some SIDS babies may have had unusual heart rhythms or brain-signaling abnormalities.

Stomach sleeping doubles the likelihood of SIDS. That's why placing baby on her back is recommended by the American Academy of Pediatrics. Breastfeeding appears to offer a baby some protection from SIDS.

Overheating may also be a contributor to SIDS. Keep the temperature in baby's room between 68° and 72° F. Also ban smoking around your baby. Exposure to cigarette smoke increases the risk of SIDS.

Some may convert into another piece of furniture, such as a changing table, when baby has outgrown a bassinet.

Bassinets present some safety issues. Some models have relatively rough, sharp inside edges. Models with soft sides may present entrapment dangers. The soft, thin mattress found in many models can pose a suffocation hazard. Bassinets are not as inherently stable as portable cribs. The hinged legs on collapsible models have been known to fold accidentally. Your baby will outgrow a bassinet after about three months. Price: about $100.

BEDSIDE SLEEPERS. These are so compact they could be called "cribettes." They fit flush against the side of a bed, at the same height as the adult mattress, with an open side next to the bed. Bars or a high, padded rim enclose the other three sides. The bridge between your mattress and the sleeper is usually a length of fabric secured between the mattress and the bedsprings. A safety issue: If a bedside sleeper is not completely joined with your bed or doesn't match it in height, a gap or ridge could form that can capture a baby's head or neck. Your baby will outgrow a bedside sleeper after two months or so. Price range: $100 to $200.

CRADLES. Although a cradle has a charming, old-fashioned look about it, we suggest that you resist buying one. Babies do love rhythmic motion, but experts advise that the most effective rocking direction is a head-to-toe motion, similar to what a baby experiences when held on a parent's shoulder in a rocking chair. The side-to-side motion of a cradle can press a tiny baby against the side of the unit. Cradle frames suspended on hooks have a gentler motion but can still cause the baby to roll from side to side. Babies should never be left unattended in freely rocking cradles. Locking pins should be bolted in place so the cradle can't tilt at an angle greater than 5 degrees. Your baby will outgrow a cradle after four to six months.

MINIATURE CRIBS. Sometimes called "grandma cribs" (not to be confused with play yards, see page 70), these are small, rectangular wooden or metal baby beds that mimic full-sized cribs but are compact enough to roll through doorways. Some have legs that lower, so the bed portion can sit close to the floor. Miniature cribs are safer than bassinets and fold compactly for traveling. Your baby will outgrow a miniature crib as soon as she is able to push up on all fours—usually between 4 and 6 months. Price range: about $80.

Hush!

Apply petroleum jelly or spray nonstick vegetable oil to the side rails of the crib to keep them from squeaking when they're raised or lowered. Or rub them with waxed paper.

Familiar

To help the family dog or cat adjust to the new baby, bring home one of the baby's diapers or blankets the day before the baby is brought home, and give it to the pet to play with and sniff. The baby's odor will then be a familiar one.

How to choose

KEY DIFFERENCES. The ability to keep baby in a cozy space near where you're sleeping is the primary attraction. The main drawback is their relatively brief period of usefulness since babies grow so fast.

RECOMMENDATIONS. View any crib alternative with some caution. Evaluate construction, looking for a model with a sturdy bottom and a wide, stable base. Make sure the mattress and padding are smooth and extra firm, and fit snugly.

• **Follow guidelines.** Always adhere to the manufacturer's weight and size specifications. They are usually printed on the product's carton, or you may need to consult the instructional materials that come with the unit.

• **Measure spacing between slats.** If the model has slats, the spacing should be no more than a regular crib's standard spacing of 2⅜ inches.

• **Assess folding mechanisms.** If legs fold for storage, make sure that effective locks are provided by pressing down. Otherwise, legs could accidentally fold while the crib is in use.

CERTIFICATION. Programs are pending for bassinets and cradles. Some crib alternatives may fall into the non-full-sized crib category and be subject to a federal standard similar to the one for full-sized cribs.

Bedding needs

Complete your baby's sleeping space with sheets, mattress pads, crib bumpers, and some light blankets.

The color scheme and design theme of your nursery often revolves around the bedding you select. For many, this is where preparing for baby's arrival really gets fun. Colors of sheets and bumpers range from muted tones, pastels, and gingham to sophisticated burgundy and navy. Beyond traditional bedding fabrics, you'll also find piqué, velours, fake suede, corduroy, chenille, and country quilting. Licensed characters adorn not only sheets and bumpers, but also curtains, wallpaper, rugs, laundry bags, and wall hangings as part of nursery "ensembles."

You'll still see large, puffy quilts and stuffed bedding products in stores, even though the Consumer Product Safety Commission has deemed them unsafe for use in cribs. A small number of companies have introduced lighter-weight coverlets, but it's best to forgo stuffed bedding until the child is at least a year old.

What's available

BLANKETS. Receiving blankets can be used for layering (see "Safe sleeping do's & don'ts," page 17), mopping up spit-ups, protecting a car seat from summer heat, discreet nursing, or covering both baby and car seat in cold weather. Get a half-dozen large blankets made of 100 percent cotton for good absorbency.

CRIB BUMPERS. These pads tie onto crib rails around all sides to keep baby's arms and legs safely inside. Use bumpers only until a baby can pull up to a standing position, about 6 months or so. Once on her feet, a child might use bumpers to climb out of the crib. Bumpers should fit around the entire crib, tying or snapping into place in at least six locations. Bumper ties should be 7 inches or less in length.

MATTRESS PADS. Quilted pads, usually made of cotton or synthetic material, should cover the mattress securely. Some are like fitted sheets, while others cover the entire mattress, front and back, or fasten with elastic on the bottom side of the mattress. You'll want at least two. There are also moisture-proof pads, but all mattresses have some form of waterproofing.

SHEETS. Most crib sheets come with fitted corners or are elasticized all the way around. Sheets that completely encase the mattress are harder to find, but they're also less likely pull loose from the mattress. Fabrics range from woven cottons and cotton blends to knitted sheets (which cost a little more but fit the mattress better) and even lightweight flannel.

How to choose

KEY DIFFERENCES. Bypass puffy bedding. Quilts, pillows, comforters, sheepskin, stuffed toys, and all other soft products do not belong in a crib. A baby may accidentally pull them over his head while tossing about in his sleep. Plastic is also a suffocation hazard, so do not use any type of plastic bag as a mattress protector. Waterbeds and beanbag chairs are dangerous sleeping places for babies.

RECOMMENDATIONS. Whatever the variations in design, your main criteria is safety. Purchase tightly fitting sheets, then recheck the fit after each laundering, since washing can weaken the elastic. Check for loose threads or ties that could catch a baby's head or neck.

Plan to launder sheets twice before the first use to remove any chemical residue left over from the fabric-treatment process and to ensure correct fit. Use a fragrance-free, dye-free liquid or powder laundry detergent. Avoid liquid fabric softener or dryer sheets.

CERTIFICATION. Sheets that meet a voluntary standard have a warning that says, "Prevent possible strangulation or entanglement. Never use crib sheet unless it fits securely on crib mattress." The standard also covers other bedding products.

Nursery furniture: The basics

Armoires, chests, and changing tables made expressly for use in a nursery do offer some advantages. Usually drawers have stops in the back to keep them from being pulled out and dumped—a favorite tot activity. Some pieces have rounded edges and recessed drawer pulls to minimize cuts and scrapes.

But nursery furniture is often overpriced for the quality offered. Scrutiny reveals that individual chests of drawers within a manufacturer's line are virtually the same except for the various wooden overlays. Wood veneers are often glued on to the front of units. The back of what looks like a well-made piece of furniture may be only thin fiberboard attached with staples.

Consider shopping in regular furniture stores, especially during seasonal sales, for storage units and rockers. A thrift or antiques store may yield a top-quality chest for hundreds of dollars less than a poorly constructed unit designed for nursery use.

Look for well-glued drawers and a smooth finish that won't peel off. Stay away from any item with sharp edges or protruding decorative details. Beware of drawers on roller tracks—they slide in and out so fast that they can pinch little fingers as they close.

In the store, test for tipping by pulling out all of the drawers. Avoid pieces any higher than three drawers. To revamp a chest that you already have, install drawer stops and replace sharp or protruding drawer pulls with flattened ones.

When setting up a nursing area, get a rocker or some other kind of comfortable chair with side arms as well as a footstool. Or use a daybed with high endboards. Include a side table with a small lamp. You may want to add a tape player and earphones, a bottle warmer if you're using formula, and other creature comforts.

Bolt all nursery units to the wall with angle braces or "L" brackets. Store toys on low shelves, or crates or baskets rather than in chests, whose lids can close unexpectedly.

Some models of nursery furniture have been recalled in recent years. Problems included furniture that could tip over and toy chests that could entrap and suffocate a child.

Baby monitors

Baby monitors allow you to keep tabs on your sleeping baby when you're not in the the same room.

Thanks to technology, you can turn on a baby monitor and listen to or watch your baby even if you're in the kitchen or out in the yard. Audio monitors use a selected radio frequency to send sound from the baby's room to the receiver, which usually looks like a walkie-talkie. Video monitors have a small wall- or table-mounted camera that transmits images to a monitor.

What's available

The major brands are Evenflo, First Years, Fisher-Price, Graco, and Safety 1st. Audio baby monitors are downsizing into small, sleek, and sometimes easy-to-misplace units. Most manufacturers have switched to a 900-MHz frequency to increase range. It may still be possible to pick up a neighbor's cordless phone conversation or even police communications. Most audio baby monitors have more than one channel. If you're picking up interference on one channel, try switching to the other.

Pager and cellular technologies have been incorporated into some new designs, including models with an "out-of-range" alarm or vibration signal for the belt-clip receiver. Intercom systems allow two-way (parent-baby and parent-parent) communication.

A video system lets you watch your baby's every move. A few video monitors have a VCR connection that lets you record images.

Price range: audio, $20 to $70; video, $90 to $200.

Simple baby monitors are lightweight and sensitive to baby's every cough and coo.

Features to consider

ON AUDIO MONITORS. Audio baby monitors usually run on household current or 9-volt or AAA batteries. Monitors can exhaust a set of batteries after a few days of continual use, and they usually feature a low-battery indicator. Some models are rechargeable—a potential money-saving option.

All models have an on/off switch, and some also offer a volume-control knob, so you can decide whether you want to hear baby's every breath or only when she is crying.

Some transmitters have built-in night-lights with on/off switches. Others include computer-chip lullabies or even alarm clocks. Receivers may have lights that turn on when baby makes noise.

Most parent units are equipped with a clip to fasten to your waistband or pocket. Antennae, usually flexible and covered with a cushioned sleeve, are fragile and should not be gripped. (Some "U"-shaped antennae resemble carrying handles.)

ON VIDEO MONITORS. With small black-and-white or color screens, these units can also function as regular, albeit small, TV sets. With many models, light-emitting diodes on either side of the camera's lens are designed to provide enough illumination to monitor a baby in a dark room.

How to choose

KEY DIFFERENCES. More money gets you more extras, not necessarily greater safety and security for your child. With an audio monitor, useful features include a 900-MHz frequency instead of 49-MHz for wider reception, out-of-range indicator lights, a low-battery indicator, a rechargeable capacity, and a volume-control knob. In past tests of video monitors, CONSUMER REPORTS found that the picture wasn't clear enough to determine if a baby's eyes were open.

RECOMMENDATIONS. Test an audio baby monitor in the store to see how it fits in your hand and how it feels when you clip it on. Video monitors continue to be pretty pricey. If you buy one, you may discover that an audio monitor is all you really need.

CERTIFICATION. Although as electrical products they're Underwriters Laboratories-listed, no specific certification program exists for these products. A few models have been recalled in recent years. Problems have included faulty wiring that could pose a fire hazard.

3

Traveling with baby

The one truly indispensable piece of equipment for your baby is a car seat. Correct installation is key.

Gone are the days when Mom would have to throw an arm across her little one's chest whenever the car came to a sudden stop. Every state now requires that small children, usually up to 4 years of age, ride in a car seat. Hospitals and birthing centers won't let you leave by car with your newborn if you don't have one. Correct use greatly reduces the odds that a child will be injured or killed in a car crash. So this essential piece of equipment should be one of your first purchases.

Car seats

Match the seat with your child's weight and age and make sure that the seat is anchored securely in the car.

A child car seat—also called a child-safety seat or a child restraint—is usually a hard, molded-plastic shell covered with fabric that can be removed for washing. With an infant or a toddler, an adustable harness is used to keep the child in the seat. A car seat is usually secured to a vehicle with an adult seat belt, but a new system of anchors is being phased in.

Because infants are extremely vulnerable to neck and other injuries, it's

Contents

recommended that they ride in a semireclined, rear-facing position, with full support of the head, neck, and back, from birth until at least 1 year old. Infant-only car seats require the infant to face the rear. Other seats— so-called convertible models—have infants ride facing the rear and toddlers at least 1 year old *and* weighing at least 20 pounds ride facing forward. Toddlers can also ride facing forward in a toddler/booster seat.

Most parents quit using car seats when their child reaches 40 pounds or so. But because adult seat belts don't fit small children properly and can cause serious damage to the spinal cord, head, and internal organs in a crash, a toddler/booster seat or a plain booster seat should be used until a child is tall enough to use the car's seat belts correctly. That means the child's knees bend comfortably at the seat's edge when the child is sitting up straight against the seatback, the car's shoulder belt crosses between the neck and arm, and the car's lap belt touches the thighs. In many cases, children don't reach that point until about age 8. But 9 out of 10 children in the U.S. who should use a booster don't, according to the National Highway Traffic Safety Administration. The U.S. Senate has held hearings on child car seats with a focus on the need for state legislation requiring the use of booster seats.

A car seat can't properly protect its occupant unless it's installed correctly. But studies of car-seat use have shown that anywhere from 50 to 85 percent of all child car seats were installed incorrectly. Part of the difficulty

How the LATCH system works

The LATCH installation system, shown here as typically installed, is already appearing with some forward-facing car seats for children up to 40 pounds. With LATCH (Lower Anchors and Tethers for Children), no safety belts are required to install a seat. The seat attaches directly to lower anchors and a top-tether anchor in the car. The goal is to simplify installation and improve compatability with different vehicles. The system is not used with booster seats.

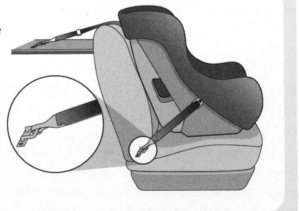

ILLUSTRATION BY GREG MAXSON

stems from the wide variety of child car seats, vehicle seats, and seat belts (used to secure the child car seats). Addressing that confusion, NHTSA is phasing in a system of attaching car seats to vehicles, known as LATCH (Lower Anchors and Tethers for Children).

Under the first phase, stricter requirements went into effect on Sept. 1, 1999, for front-facing car seats for children up to 40 pounds—convertible seats in the front-facing toddler configuration and toddler/booster seats in toddler mode. To meet these requirements, virtually all of these seats have a top tether, which attaches to an anchor behind the car's back seat to help stabilize the seat and to reduce the child's head movement in a crash. The car's seat belt is used to secure the lower part of the seat. All new passenger vehicles except convertibles must have tether anchors as of Sept. 1, 2000. Tethering retrofit kits are available for older car seats and vehicles.

With an infant car seat, the child rides facing the rear. A handle allows the seat to double as an infant carrier.

The second phase of the system—required for all infant and toddler seats and vehicles as of Sept. 1, 2002—uses direct attachments such as metal hooks at the end of a webbed belt to attach the car seat to small "U"-shaped metal bars, sometimes called lower anchors or ISOFIX anchors, in the crease of a vehicle's rear seat. (The system is not meant for booster seats.) Some models of vehicles and convertible seats already comply. The use of lower anchors eliminates the need to struggle with seat belts and should allow simpler, more secure installation of seats. Car seats are ideally installed in the center of the back seat—the safest place according to accident statistics. But many vehicles that have lower anchors lack them in the center rear position.

If a car has no back seat, or a child has a medical condition that requires monitoring, parents can have an on/off switch installed for the front-passenger air bag so the child's car seat can be placed next to the driver. A letter of authorization from NHTSA is required.

What's available

Car seats are categorized by the child's weight, height, and the direction the seat faces inside the car. The major brands are Britax, Century, Cosco, Evenflo, and Graco. Fisher-Price is getting out of the car-seat business. Offering built-

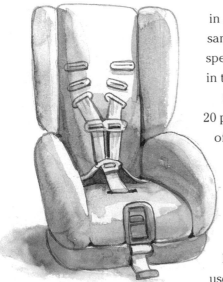

A convertible seat can face forward or backward depending on your child's age and weight.

in seats in select cars and minivans are Daimler-Chrysler, Ford, GM, Nissan, Subaru, Toyota, and Volvo. There are also car beds for preemies and special seats for children with disabilities. Every model of car seat sold in the U.S. must pass government crash-test standards.

INFANT SEATS. These are designed to hold infants weighing up to 20 pounds or so. The infant lies in them semireclined and faces the rear of the vehicle. All models come with a handle, and most have a base secured with a seat belt, allowing a sleeping baby to be lifted as if in a basket and removed from the car without being disturbed. An infant seat can be strapped into a car without the base, though. Some bases can be adjusted to compensate for the slope of auto seats. Manufacturers have gradually increased the maximum weight limits of infant seats. Right now, only a handful of infant car seats can be used for babies heavier than 20 pounds, but some babies younger than 1 year weigh more than that. A few car seats claim a maximum limit of 22 or even 35 pounds. Some infants under 1 year have to quit using an infant seat not because of weight but because of height. Taller infants, whose legs can hit against the vehicle's seat, are better accommodated in a convertible seat used rear-facing. In the past, most infant seats had a three-point harness—two adjustable shoulder straps and a lock between the child's legs. But now most have the superior adjustable five-point system—two straps over the shoulders, two for the thighs, and a crotch strap. An infant seat's handle usually swings from a horizontal position behind the seat's shell when in the car to an upright position for carrying. Slots underneath most seats help them attach to the frame of a shopping cart.

As of this writing, no infant seat is compatible with the LATCH system of lower anchors. Price range: $30 to $140.

TRAVEL SYSTEMS. Most manufacturers of car seats offer combination strollers/infant car seats, called travel systems. The snap-on car seat is generally positioned atop the stroller so the infant rides facing the person who is pushing. Toddlers ride in the stroller seat. See page 42 for more on travel systems' configurations as strollers. There are also lightweight strollers and stroller frames with no seat that accommodate various brands of infant seats. Price range: $40 (stroller frame only) to $400.

CONVERTIBLE SEATS. Convertible seats face forward or backward. Like infant seats, convertible seats have varying weight ranges. They function as a rear-facing seat for infants up to 20, 22, or 35 pounds, depending on the model, and as a forward-facing seat for toddlers, up to 40 pounds. Models typically have an adustable five-point harness system—two straps over the shoulders, two for the thighs, and a crotch strap between the legs. Some models have a tray shield that lowers over the baby's head and fastens with a buckle between the legs. But our tests have shown that such a design may make a child more vulnerable to injuries in a crash. All convertible seats can be used with a tether. As of this writing, a couple are compatible with the LATCH lower-anchor system. Price range: $40 to $225.

TODDLER SEATS. Typically made by European manufacturers, these are used forward-facing for toddlers 20 to 40 pounds. Models typically have an adjustable five-point harness system—two straps over the shoulders, two for the thighs, and a crotch strap between the legs. All toddler seats can be used with a tether. A few conform with the LATCH lower-anchor system. Price range: $170 to $200.

TODDLER/BOOSTER SEATS. Looking like large versions of convertible seats, these front-facing seats are used with an internal harness for toddlers 20 to 40 pounds; a top tether and the lap portion of the car's safety belt secure the seat. For children between 40 and 80 pounds who aren't tall enough to use a car's seat belt correctly, they convert to a booster seat and use the car's seat belt as a restraint. (The harness and top tether aren't used.) To help position the shoulder belt over the chest for children weighing between 40 and about 60 pounds, belt guides are used. But during recent tests by CONSUMER REPORTS, some belt guides prevented the vehicle's shoulder belt from retracting properly. With taller children, the belt position should be fine without the guide. Price range: $50 to $290.

BOOSTER SEATS. Sometimes called belt-positioning boosters, these also use the car's seat belt to restrain a child weighing between 40 and 80 pounds who isn't tall enough to use a car's seat belt correctly. Many boosters resemble convertible seats but are taller and have guides for the shoulder belt. Boosters with a high back should be used if your vehicle's seat back is short. Backless booster seats are simple platforms with a guide for the vehicle's safety belts. They're suitable for vehicles with tall seat backs. Price range: $30 to $120.

BUILT-IN SEATS. Some models of cars and minivans offer a forward-facing built-in seat as an option. Some built-in

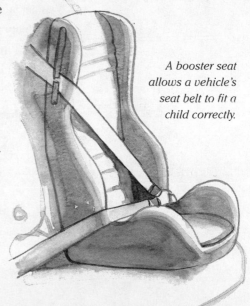

A booster seat allows a vehicle's seat belt to fit a child correctly.

seats have a harness and accommodate toddlers more than 20 pounds. Others are boosters that use the vehicle's lap and shoulder belts. Built-in seats generally work well, but they offer little or no side protection. They're usually located next to a door, instead of in the center—the safer position.

Features to consider

TOP TETHER. This webbed strap is used with virtually all forward-facing seats for children up to 40 pounds to meet stricter head-excursion rules. It's located on the back of a convertible or toddler seat and hooks into an eye bolt in a vehicle's rear deck, floor, roof, or seatback. New passenger vehicles have the anchors in place, but older models may need to have the hardware added. The tether is not used with cars that lack a top-tether anchor, with infants facing the rear, or with booster seats.

LOWER-ANCHOR ATTACHMENTS. All car seats for infants and toddlers will be required by Sept. 1, 2002, to have lower anchor attachments that connect to small "U"-shaped metal bars between a vehicle's seat cushion and seat back. Car seats that conform with the LATCH system of lower anchors must also be able to be secured with a vehicle's seat belt so they can be used in older vehicles.

LEVEL INDICATOR. All infant seats and convertible seats have a level indicator on the side to help you install them facing the rear at a safe angle.

UPHOLSTERY AND COMFORT FEATURES. Upholstery quality varies by manufacturer and price. Babies tend to be messy, so stain resistance and washability are important. Most coverings snap on or are held in place with elastic so they can be removed for laundering. Add-on seat covers can be found in large baby stores. Thicker padding, extra reclining options, or adjustable head-support cushions offer additional comfort. Some models offer elastic side pockets for toys, bottles, or snacks.

SEAT SHELL. Typically manufacturers use the same shell, molded from rigid plastic, for all seats in a particular brand line.

How to choose

KEY DIFFERENCES. All seats must pass government-standard requirements, and most seats do fine when tested to the standard. CONSUMER REPORTS tests seats to a somewhat more rigorous standard. Dummies of various sizes are strapped into seats placed on a rig that is run through a simulated head-on collision. High-speed cameras show if a dummy's head moved so far that in real life a child might be injured.

Infant seats usually do a little better without a base than with one, but all were fine in recent tests. With front-facing convertible seats, the tests showed that five-point restraints were superior to overhead tray/shield harnesses, which could leave children vulnerable to injuries to the head in a crash. We tested both types of systems when they were available from the same brand. Forward-facing seats tested with a top tether performed consistently better than when the tether was not used. The tethers of a few models broke, absorbing some of the energy of the impact in doing so.

We encountered problems when we tried to use a vehicle's seat belt with some combination toddler/boosters used as a booster seat. They worked fine when the shoulder belts were threaded through their guides properly and left alone, but in our opinion they could become slack if kids fiddled with them. Slack in a shoulder belt could expose a child to an increased potential for injury in a crash. The problem doesn't affect all booster seats. Some of the toddler/booster combinations and plain boosters we tested offered very good or excellent protection. Even the problematic toddler/booster seats were fine when tested with a harness for toddlers and when the shoulder belt guide was not used. But we don't recommend these seats for children in the 40-to-60-pound range, who need the shoulder belt threaded through the guides.

In the past, handles that released accidentally were a problem with some models of infant seats when used as carriers outside the car. Notable was Evenflo's recall in 2001 of 3.4 million infant seats sold between 1988 and 1998 after dozens of reported problems with the carrier-handle locks. A new voluntary industry standard has been credited with improving the safety of infant car seats' handles.

RECOMMENDATIONS. Start with an infant seat for a newborn. If your baby outgrows it before age 1, use a convertible seat rear-facing, up to the seat's weight limit. Then use it forward-facing (after your child is age 1 and at least 20 pounds) until your toddler is about 40 pounds. Finally, use a booster seat until your child is tall enough to use the car's safety belts. Buying three seats instead of two may cost more, but it can pay off in protection and peace of mind.

• **Try before you buy.** Put similar-looking models side by side to com-

○ Buy a new seat—never use a second-hand one.

○ Shop sooner, not later.

○ Try in your car before buying.

pare features. Try out handles and buckles. Recline the convertibles and measure how much space they'll need.

If possible, bring the seat out to your car to see whether it fits. Some rear seats are simply too shallow or too indented to correctly support a child seat, especially with sportier cars. With some cars, the armrests can't be moved out of the way, or the seat belts may not fit. If the store won't let you take the seat out to your car to try it, make sure you can return it.

When shopping for an infant car seat, try holding it in the store, keeping in mind that toting a car seat with a baby in it won't be comfortable for very long. Although a new voluntary standard addresses problems with handles of infant car seats that accidentally release, consider using both hands when carrying a baby in an infant seat—one for each end of the seat—and use the harness.

• **Never buy a secondhand seat.** There are just too many possible dangers and disadvantages. The seat may have been in a crash or recalled. The manufacturer's instructions may be missing.

• **Check for recalls.** You'll find an up-to-date recall list on NHTSA's web site *(www.nhtsa.gov)*. Recalls of infant car seats whose handles may accidentally release may be found on the Consumer Product Safety Commission's web site *(www.cpsc.gov)*.

CERTIFICATION. Car seats are subject to a mandatory standard regulated by NHTSA, which crash-tests models, but not on a routine basis. The CPSC provides oversight with respect to the use of infant seats as carriers outside the car. A new voluntary standard administered by the American

Booster giveaway

The Ford Motor Co. recently announced it will give away 1 million booster seats—half to customers at participating dealerships, and half to families through the United Way. The giveaway is part of Boost America!, a highway-safety campaign created by 24 government and private organizations to promote the use of booster seats.

Among the seats being offered is the Evenflo Right Fit, a CR Best Buy that we judged to be excellent. Dealers offer another option: a $23 voucher toward the purchase of any booster sold at Toys "R" Us.

For details of the booster giveaway, visit *www.boostamerica.org*.

Society for Testing and Materials and the Juvenile Products Manufacturers Association addresses the handle-failure problem.

Installation tips

Surveys show that as many as 85 percent of car seats are installed incorrectly. The most common problems are loose harness straps, harness straps in the wrong harness-slot positions, and loose car safety belts. When installing a seat for the first time, give yourself a good half-hour. If you can recruit a helper, even better.

• **Read the instructions.** In addition to the instructions that come with the seat, check your car's owner's manual for information on how to use your car's seat belts with car seats. Some car manufacturers have a free how-to brochure or video that can help with installation.

• **Position the seat.** The center rear seat is the safest spot. You may have to place the seat next to a door if you have more than one small child, if there is no shoulder belt in the center, if your LATCH-compatible vehicle lacks lower anchors in the center rear position, or if using the center rear seat would make the child car seat unstable.

• **Secure the seat.** Use your weight to push it into the vehicle's seat (you may have to kneel on the seat) while pulling the slack out of the vehicle's seat belt. With a rear-facing seat, adjust the angle as directed by the manufacturer, using the level indicator. With a front-facing seat for a toddler up to 40 pounds, use the top tether. If the top tether is not in use, such as with a toddler/booster seat used as a booster, the top-tether strap should be removed or secured so it doesn't fly around and injure a child in a collision. When you're securing an infant or toddler seat with a car's seat belt, you may need a locking clip so the lap belt remains tight. See the manufacturer's instructions.

• **Adjust the harness.** When your baby or toddler is in the safety seat, all the harness straps should be in the proper slots and should fit snugly across the "strong" parts of the body—the shoulders and thighs—not the soft belly. The harness should lie flat when buckled. If the harness straps have a chest clip to hold them together, make sure the clip is fastened level with your child's armpits.

• **Check the seat every time you use it.** Whenever you buckle your child in, try shifting the car seat from side to side and back to front. It shouldn't move more than an inch. The harness straps should fit snugly.

The shoulder straps should feed through the rear slots slightly below the shoulders for an infant facing the rear, and at or slightly above the shoulders for a child facing the front.

• **Get expert advice.** Installation tips are available on NHTSA's web site *(www.nhtsa.gov)*. At the National Safe Kids Campaign site *(www.safekids.org)*, you'll find similar information, plus details on about 300 local organizations. Other web sites worth a visit: *www.carseat.org, www.childsafety.org, www.safechild.net,* and *www.saferidenews.com.*

Communities have trained experts or clinics to teach parents how to correctly install car seats. Try your local police or sheriff's department first. You can also try your state's highway department.

Tips for plane travel

A child car seat fastened to the airline seat with the aircraft's seat belts makes a comfortable seat for your baby and can protect in the event of turbulence or an accident. The Federal Aviation Administration strongly recommends— but does not mandate—car seats' use for babies and toddlers. The agency has established guidelines for the type of restraint, based on the child's size and weight: A rear-facing seat should be used for infants weighing less than 20 pounds. Use a forward-facing seat for toddlers weighing 20 to 40 pounds. Heavier children should use the airplane's seat belt as an adult would. Boosters aren't allowed—commercial airplanes lack the shoulder harness needed to hold them in place.

Most car seats are approved for use in airplanes. Check for a label somewhere on the seat's shell that reads, "This restraint is certified for use in motor vehicles and aircraft." The label may also contain the letters FMVSS, standing for Federal Motor Vehicle Safety Standard. If the seat lacks this approval sticker, airline personnel may not allow you to take it on the plane and you will have to check it as luggage. Also check the width of your child's safety seat. If it's wider than 16 inches, it may not fit in a coach seat. Call the airline to confirm that your seat is acceptable.

Ask a flight attendant to help install the car seat. It may be easier to belt down if you first recline the airplane seat. Once the seat is installed, you return the airplane seat to its upright position.

4

Getting around

When you're on the go, strollers and baby carriers offer convenience for you and comfort for your baby.

Sooner or later, you're going to want to get out of the house. That's where the stroller comes in. You'll want a model that fits your baby's stage of development and your own lifestyle. Multiseat strollers make it possible to take two or more children along. Jogging strollers and bicycle trailers let you exercise outdoors with baby in tow.

Baby carriers are a great way to keep baby close and cozy even when you're mobile. Slings form a comfy, portable nest for infants and can be adjusted to tote toddlers. Strap-on soft carriers are good for toting a baby during the first few months. Framed carriers, which come into play after your little one learns to sit up, offer a brand-new view of the world.

Strollers

For visits to the mall or park, or just a walk around the block, you'll need a stroller. You may end up needing more than one.

Thanks to design changes during the past decade or so, strollers have become smaller, lighter, and easier to maneuver. Increasingly, manufacturers

Contents

are forgoing steel for aluminum, making for lighter frames. It can reduce stroller weight 5 to 10 pounds, though it raises the price substantially.

Navy is still the main color. You'll also see some plaid upholstery in colors such as beige and forest green; splashes of bright, outdoorsy red, blue, or yellow; and images from cartoon land. Some frames are painted in pastels—green, yellow, or blue—while others feature finishes such as gray, burgundy, and polished steel.

What's available

The biggest-selling brands are Cosco, Evenflo, Graco, and Kolcraft. High-end import brands include Aprica, Combi, Maclaren, and Peg Pérego. Your baby's size and your own preferences will determine what you use and how you use it. Because newborns can't sit up without support, they can't ride in a standard stroller. You'll find three basic choices for young babies:

A carriage/stroller provides a place for an infant to sleep and converts to a standard stroller for older babies.

TRAVEL SYSTEMS. With an infant seat/stroller combination, known as a travel system, you create a carriage by snapping an infant car seat into a stroller or a frame. A travel system with a stroller saves you from having to buy another piece of equipment. A frame is less bulky to transport. A frame and some strollers can accommodate various brands of infant car seats. If you use a frame, you'll have to buy a stroller after baby outgrows the infant seat. For more on infant seats, see page 34. Price range: travel systems, $100 to $400, stroller frames, $40.

CARRIAGE/STROLLERS. These models have seats that fully recline, providing sleeping space for infants. Once your child can sit up—at about 6 months —this type can convert to a stroller configuration. Some units have large, spoked wheels and compartments that can be removed and used as a bassinet. Price range: $50 to $600.

CARRIAGES. Carriages, the classic way to go, have a springy, rocking motion that can soothe a fussy baby— even indoors. The big, spoked, nonswiveling wheels make for easy rolling on level ground but can hamper movement in tight spaces. With some models, a removable compartment can be used as a bassinet. Sometimes weighing more than 30 pounds, carriages can be bulky and heavy.

Once a baby can sit up, you can use a regular stroller. You'll find three basic types:

MIDWEIGHT STROLLERS. Think of these as the minivans of the stroller world—ubiquitous and practical. Weighing from 17 to 35 pounds, they are somewhat heavy and bulky but are quite stable. Interiors are relatively deep and roomy. Even the least expensive models have padded seat coverings that can be removed for laundering. A reclining seatback offers two to three positions, from upright to almost fully reclined. Dual front wheels that swivel allow smooth rolling and cornering and can usually be locked into a forward-only position for rough terrain. Some models have hard, plastic tires, but most tires are made of foam. Front-wheel assemblies typically have built-in shock absorbers. (Higher-end models may have shock absorbers on rear-wheel assemblies as well.) Handlebars are a single crossbar. Seat belts are a given, and most include a crotch strap to further keep baby from slipping out.

For folding, many strollers use a one-handed release embedded in the stroller's handlebar. You flip a lock switch or move the casing of the latch mechanism to one side, then push the handlebar forward until the frame begins to fold. Other strollers require you to simultaneously squeeze release mechanisms on the sides of the frame. Some models balance upright on their wheels when folded—handy when you have to hold baby while standing in line.

Price range: $40 to $150.

UMBRELLA STROLLERS. Named after their curved, umbrella-like handles, these units usually weigh less than 12 pounds. With the baby on board, they can be maneuvered in tight spots—into a store fitting room, for example. They can be rolled behind you in a folded position, an advantage when you're boarding an airplane or a bus or are on an escalator.

No-frills umbrella strollers are made with metal tubing, a pouchlike seat suspended in the frame with two straps attached at either side as seat belts, and rear-wheel brakes. Step-up features include a canopy (a piece of fabric strung between two wires), an adjustable seat, and padding.

Durability is often poor. You may need several to get through a baby's

A travel system joins an infant seat with a stroller or a frame, making it easier to move baby from the car to the stroller.

stroller phase. An umbrella stroller may also be unstable. Looping a purse or shopping bag on the handles (or simply pressing down too hard) can tip one backward. And some frames have dangerous "X" joints, where metal tubes cross each other, which could capture and bruise a child's hands if they happen to get in the way when you're folding the stroller.

Price range: $20 to $40.

LIGHTWEIGHT STROLLERS. These models, often expensive European or Japanese imports, are the most sophisticated strollers on the market. Often with aluminum frames, they weigh 12 pounds or less. Some have umbrella-like handles, but the similarity with inexpensive umbrella strollers pretty much ends there. They typically have an easy-to-use spring-action folding mechanism. To fold, you simply release the safety locks and squeeze the frame. To open, release the locks and jerk back on the handles. Other typical features include thick padding, a reclining seat, an adjustable sun canopy, a safety belt with a crotch strap, easy-to-operate brakes, and maybe a snap-on plastic weather shield. Wheel assemblies typically have built-in, spring-action shock absorbers. Dual wheels swivel in front for quick turns and can be locked into a forward-facing position for uneven terrain.

There are a few drawbacks to models of this type. Small wheels don't perform well on uneven sidewalks or rough terrain. The compact size of this type of stroller may cramp preschoolers, especially when they're dressed in winter clothes.

Price range: $50 to $450.

An umbrella stroller is an inexpensive way to maneuver baby around tight spots, such as at a mall.

Features to consider

Generally, paying more gets you options such as extra padding, more reclining positions, or a sophisticated suspension.

SAFETY BELTS. Get a model with a sturdy seat belt and crotch strap, which help keep a baby or toddler from slipping out. Thick nylon webbing is the typical material used. Look for well-mounted buckles that are easy for you to operate but difficult for small hands to unfasten. While most standard strollers offer only waist and crotch straps, some top-of-the-line models offer an adjustable five-point harness (two straps over the shoulders, two for the thighs, and a crotch strap), much like those found in car seats.

BRAKES. Over the years, stroller brakes have become increasingly reliable and easy to use. Most are activated either by a single bar in the rear of the stroller frame or by foot-operated tabs above the rear wheels. When brakes are engaged, plastic cogs engage with the sprockets of the rear wheels. Some pricier strollers have brakes on the front as well as the rear wheels, which keep the front of the stroller from swiveling sideways. Avoid models with metal bars that press directly into the tires instead of locking into the spokes. They could release unexpectedly when a stroller is pushed or pulled.

WHEELS. The larger the wheels, the easier it is to negotiate curbs. But big wheels eat up trunk space. Most strollers offer double wheels on the front to make steering easier. Front wheels often offer two positions: full swivel for smooth surfaces, or locked in the forward-facing position for rough terrain. Misaligned and loose wheels are a chronic stroller problem. One sign of good construction is that the wheels of a stroller contact the floor uniformly when there is a baby inside. Stroller wheels that give the smoothest ride and the best handling are filled with air or made of dense foam. Some manufacturers have created wheel assemblies that can be completely slipped off the frame for easy replacement, which is a plus.

SHOCK ABSORBERS. Tires molded from foam can help give baby a smoother ride. So can shock absorbers—covered springs or rubber pads above the wheel assemblies. A few expensive imports instead have a loose, nonrigid frame that is supposed to reduce jarring.

HANDLES. Handles may be padded, even thickly cushioned, on more expensive models. Adjustable handlebars can be extended or angled to accommodate parents of different heights. Reversible handles allow you to swing them over the top of the stroller, then lock them into a front position so baby rides facing you. A single crossbar not only allows for one-handed steering, but generally makes the stroller more stable and controllable. Umbrella strollers and other models with two independent handles require two hands to maneuver.

CANOPIES. These range from a fabric square strung between two wires to deep, pull-down canopies that shield almost the entire front of the stroller. Before you pay extra for a fancy canopy, think about how often you and baby will be out in glaring sunlight or inclement weather. Some canopies have a clear vinyl window on top so you can keep an eye on baby.

Lightweight strollers are often sophisticated imports with spring-action folding mechanisms.

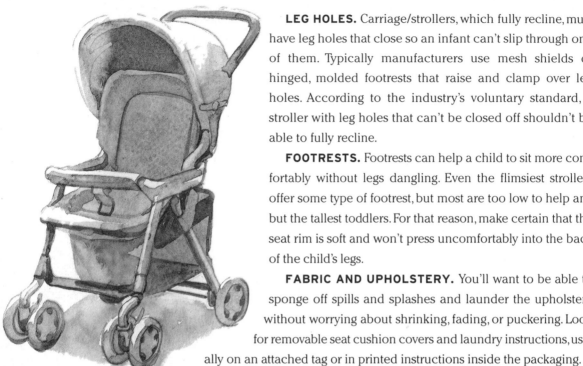

Midweight strollers are deep and roomy but also somewhat heavy and bulky.

LEG HOLES. Carriage/strollers, which fully recline, must have leg holes that close so an infant can't slip through one of them. Typically manufacturers use mesh shields or hinged, molded footrests that raise and clamp over leg holes. According to the industry's voluntary standard, a stroller with leg holes that can't be closed off shouldn't be able to fully recline.

FOOTRESTS. Footrests can help a child to sit more comfortably without legs dangling. Even the flimsiest strollers offer some type of footrest, but most are too low to help any but the tallest toddlers. For that reason, make certain that the seat rim is soft and won't press uncomfortably into the back of the child's legs.

FABRIC AND UPHOLSTERY. You'll want to be able to sponge off spills and splashes and launder the upholstery without worrying about shrinking, fading, or puckering. Look for removable seat cushion covers and laundry instructions, usually on an attached tag or in printed instructions inside the packaging.

PLAY TRAY. Strollers may have a tray where baby can play, dribble milk, and drop crumbs. If the tray comes with attached toys, check their size. Some strollers have been recalled because small parts on their play trays' toys pose choking hazards. (No toy part, removable screws included, should be smaller than the diameter of a toilet-paper roll.) Instead of a tray, other models have a front bar to help keep baby safely inside. To make it easier to get a squirming baby or toddler seated, the bar should be removable rather than permanently attached.

STORAGE AREAS. A big, easily accessible storage bin underneath the stroller makes errands with baby a lot easier. Sizes of bins vary. Try to choose one that's at least big enough to accommodate a diaper bag. When shopping for a stroller, press on the storage-bin floor—it shouldn't drag on the ground when loaded. Some strollers also offer storage pouches with elastic lips in back. With other strollers, you can buy a net bag that fastens onto the handle—good for storing snacks, but nothing much heavier than that.

BOOTS. A few strollers offer protective leg coverings, or "boots," made of a matching fabric that can snap over baby's legs for added warmth.

CUP HOLDERS. Some strollers have a cup holder for the pusher as well as one for the small passenger.

How to choose

KEY DIFFERENCES. High price and good quality don't always match up. CONSUMER REPORTS tests have shown that some economical strollers can perform as well as or even better than models priced hundreds of dollars higher. Even the more sophisticated models can suffer typical stroller flaws: malfunctioning wheels, frames that bend out of shape, locking mechanisms that fail, seat belts that come loose, or buckles that break.

RECOMMENDATIONS. A stroller is a key item of baby equipment—you may well end up with more than one. To take a small baby for a stroll, you'll need something big enough to accommodate her while she is lying down, since in the early months, a baby lacks the back and neck strength to sit up. Only carriages and carriage/strollers allow a baby to fully recline, but these units are rather weighty. Another option is to buy a travel system, in which the infant is partially reclined. Or you can postpone using a stroller until your baby can sit up, relying instead on a sling or soft carrier in the early months.

For babies who can sit up, a small stroller is fine. A lightweight model that is easy to fold and carry and has good shock absorbers is an excellent, if often expensive, choice for traversing crowded shopping malls and city streets. A midweight stroller, typically less expensive than a lightweight stroller, is fine when space isn't at a premium. Inexpensive umbrella strollers—while lightweight and maneuverable—are often not very durable. But they're perfectly adequate to take along on vacation or other jaunts in which compactness is a prime concern. An alternative is using a sports stroller with wheels small enough for the unit to be used indoors.

When shopping for strollers, here are things to consider:

• **Test-drive the stroller.** A stroller should fit the baby and the person pushing it. When shopping, take the models you're considering for a test-drive. Make sure that you're not hunched over when you push and that your feet don't hit the frame as you walk. If you're tall, look for a model with adjustable handle height. Try pushing with one hand as well as two.

• **Check sturdiness.** Shake the stroller. The frame should feel solid, not loose. The axle connecting the rear wheels should be thick and sturdy to allow you to press down on it with your foot while raising the front to get over curbs. Check how easy it is to fold the stroller, remembering that you'll often be

Spotless

Carry a stain remover stick in a diaper bag (or keep one on hand near your changing area) to apply to spots before they set.

Shopping checklist

S T R O L L E R S

○ Look for a certification sticker.

○ Test-drive the stroller.

○ Judge steering and handlebar height.

○ Check ease of folding and reclining.

○ Heft the stroller to assess weight.

○ Verify the retailer's return policy.

holding your baby and folding the stroller at the same time.

• **Consider weight.** Strollers weigh anywhere from 7 to 35 pounds. Frame and seat size, plus extras such as a play tray or canopy, all affect weight. Aluminum is generally lighter than steel but more expensive.

Manufacturers set weight limits, and they should be taken seriously. Too much weight loaded into the stroller can cause the frame to bend, the wheels to loosen, or the safety catches to accidentally release, maybe leading to injuries. Never try to put two kids in a stroller meant for one.

• **Evaluate warranties and return policies.** Most stroller manufacturers and retailers have warranties that protect you from poor workmanship and inherent flaws. But they won't necessarily take the unit back if it malfunctions in some way. Manufacturers may either refer you back to the store for a replacement or insist you ship the stroller back for repair—at your expense—leaving you stranded without baby wheels. Your best bet is to purchase the stroller from a store, catalog, or web site that offers a 100 percent satisfaction guarantee.

CERTIFICATION. Located somewhere on a stroller's frame or carton, a certification sticker shows that the stroller meets the minimum requirements of the American Society for Testing and Materials' voluntary standard and that its manufacturer participates in the pass/fail certification program administered by the Juvenile Products Manufacturers Association. The key tests are for safety of seat belts, brakes, leg openings, and locking mechanisms that prevent accidental folding, and for stability and the presence of sharp edges. The program is voluntary, and uncertified models may be as safe as certified ones. But all things being equal, go for a certified model.

Multiseat strollers

Similar to other strollers, these give you a relatively efficient means of taking your twins or closely spaced siblings for a ride.

Most companies that manufacture strollers for one also make a version with two or more seats. Multiseaters offer the same features as strollers for a single rider, just a larger-scale construction. Alternatives include multiseat sports strollers with wheels small enough for indoor use and strollers and travel systems with a standing bench or small seat in the rear that lets a toddler hitch a ride.

What's available

The major brands are Aprica Cosco, Graco, and Kolcraft, as well as high-end imports such as Combi, Maclaren, and Peg Pérego. Multiseat strollers come in one of two configurations. Tandem models have one seat directly behind the other. Side-by sides are two seats attached to a single frame or a unit resembling two strollers bolted together. You can also join two umbrella strollers with a set of screw-on brackets—available at baby discount chains and specialty stores. Features of multiseat strollers are similar to what you'll find on single-passenger models.

Tandem strollers are good for carrying children of different weights.

TANDEMS. The same width as single-passenger strollers, tandems are the best choice for carrying children of two different weights, with the heavier one in front and the lighter one in back. They're the most common type of multiseat stroller. While the back seat can recline, the front seat can't without infringing on the space of the rear passenger. Tandems easily go through standard doorways. But steering can be difficult, and it can be hard getting them over a curb. Some models offer limited leg support and very little legroom for the rear passenger.

"Stadium seating," with the back seat raised higher than the front seat, is a tandem design that offers the rear passenger more comfort, more legroom, and more room to recline than a plain tandem stroller. Some tandems have moveable seats that allow children to face forward, backward, or each other.

Price range: $100 to $450.

SIDE-BY-SIDES. This type works best for children about the same weight, such as twins. Manufacturers may promise that the stroller is slender enough to go through a standard doorway, but measure for yourself from side to side on the frame and from wheel hub to wheel hub. Any stroller more than 29 inches may run into trouble. Most side-by-sides have a single large sunshade that pulls overhead. Each of the seats has independent reclining mechanisms. Price range: $100 to $450.

How to choose

KEY DIFFERENCES. A tandem is easier to maneuver (particularly with one hand) than a side-by-side and will do a better job steering with only one child inside. A folded tandem takes up just a little more space than a folded standard midweight stroller. A side-by-side model goes over curbs more easily than a tandem, but when children of different weights ride in the unit, it may veer. A folded side-by-side requires twice as much space as a standard midweight.

RECOMMENDATIONS. Evaluate a multiseater the same way you would a standard stroller: Size up individual features, test-drive the model in the store, check folding ease, assess the weight, and purchase from a retailer that offers a 100 percent satisfaction guarantee.

CERTIFICATION. As with single-occupancy strollers, a certification sticker shows that a multiseat stroller meets the minimum requirements of the American Society for Testing and Materials' voluntary standard and that its manufacturer participates in the pass/fail certification program administered by the Juvenile Products Manufacturers Association. While many uncertified multiseat strollers may be quite safe, it's better to buy a certified model if you can find one.

Side-by-sides are good for toting children of the same weight, such as twins.

Sports strollers

Sports strollers let you take your child or children along for the ride when you're jogging—or just walking.

A sports stroller, or jogging stroller, lets you push a child semireclined in a canvas pouch while jogging or walking. The larger the wheels, the easier it is for the parent pushing the unit to run. Smaller wheels are mostly suited for walking.

Like a bicycle, a sports stroller is made of metal tubing and has wheels with spokes and rubber tires. It has three large wheels 12 to 20 inches in diameter—two in the rear and one in front. The long, high handlebar is designed to help keep the runner or walker's feet and legs away from the stroller's frame and legs, but you may still have to adjust your gait to avoid bumping into the unit.

All-terrain strollers imitate the look of their bigger cousins but are really not much more than oversized strollers with bicycle-like spoke or molded-plastic wheels. The wheel diameter measures 12 inches or less, which makes these units maneuverable indoors. Most all-terrain strollers have four wheels, although some have three. Some parents use an all-terrain stroller as their main stroller.

The appropriate age for children to ride in a sports stroller is a matter of debate. Some manufacturers suggest 8 weeks, but our medical consultants say a baby should be at least 6 months, able to sit up, and have some head support to withstand a jogging stroller's jarring ride. A sports stroller has a longer useful life than a plain stroller, with some models able to accommodate a child as heavy as 75 pounds. Several brands offer double and triple sports strollers with a total weight limit of up to 100 pounds.

What's available

Arriving on the scene some 15 years ago, jogging strollers are now offered by virtually every stroller manufacturer. Brands that started by selling only sports strollers included Baby Jogger (which originated the concept) and InStep. Manufacturers have made jogging strollers easier to store than in the past, but they still require more space than other strollers and their wheels may have to be removed to fit the stroller in the trunk. Price range: $100 to $600, depending on the size of the wheels (the bigger, the more expensive) and the number of seats.

Features to consider

WHEELS. Most sports strollers have rubber, air-inflated, bicycle-type tires with inner tubes, although some smaller sports strollers may have molded-plastic wheels. Bicycle-type tires can go flat, requiring patching and reinflating with a bicycle pump or a gas-station hose. Wheels may go out of alignment, but can be taken to a bike shop for service.

BRAKES. Most sports strollers have two

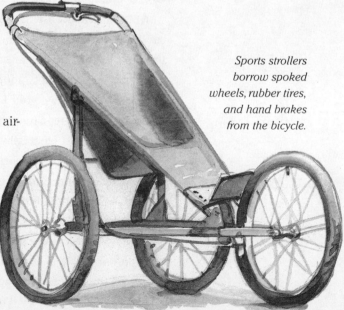

Sports strollers borrow spoked wheels, rubber tires, and hand brakes from the bicycle.

types of brakes: a bicycle-style hand brake for quick stops when you're in motion, and a foot-applied brake, which uses calipers that press into the air-filled rubber tires when the unit is standing still. Foot-applied brakes lose their effectiveness as tires and wheels become uneven. You'll probably have to have them adjusted periodically at a bicycle-repair shop.

SEAT AND SEAT BELTS. Unlike standard strollers, jogging strollers use stitched, semireclined canvas pouches as seats. Seat belts are usually an adjustable five-point harness (two straps over the shoulders, two for the thighs, and a crotch strap). Some models have individual seating for two or three children.

HANDLEBAR. This is a single bar connected to the stroller's frame. It usually has thick, slip-resistant foam padding for a comfortable grip. A strap that connects the wrist to the handlebar prevents "runaways."

ACCESSORIES. A canopy, storage pouch, and weather shield—a thick plastic shield that encloses the front of the stroller—are standard equipment on some models and optional extras on others.

How to choose

KEY DIFFERENCES. You'll see differences in the construction of the frame. The more expensive models use aluminum instead of steel. Sports strollers also vary in terms of wheel size, handlebar height, seat cushioning, ease of folding, and number of storage pockets.

RECOMMENDATIONS. Consider delaying the purchase of a sports stroller until you know you can return to your former fitness routine. Around-the-clock baby demands can sap more energy than you may have expected.

Even with big wheels, sports strollers don't permit total running freedom. You have to keep your hands on the handle and adjust your gait to avoid kicking the rear frame. And they don't provide a truly cushioned ride. In fact, some subject baby to quite a few bumps and bounces. Because of their bulkiness and nonswiveling wheels, the larger sports strollers are for outdoor use only. Serious runners will probably find all-terrain strollers more of an impediment than a convenience, but their smaller wheels do make them an option for indoor use.

• **Check child safety and comfort.** Look for a deep seat with a sturdy, five-point seat belt. The seat should be at a comfortable angle for young passengers and offer adequate leg support without cutting into the back of a baby's or child's legs. You'll also want a sun-shielding canopy and a wrist strap to hold the stroller if you accidentally let go of the handlebars.

• **Test-drive the model.** When taking a jogging stroller out for a trot, you may discover that the handlebar height is too low or too close to the back wheels for jogging comfort. Be sure you won't kick the rear of the unit when in full stride, and see that the overall weight is light enough for fast movement. Try out the brakes, and be sure wheels are easily removable and handlebars can be adjusted for height.

CERTIFICATION. While no certification program exists for these products, some four-wheel all-terrain strollers meet the voluntary standard for regular strollers. Some models of sports strollers have been recalled in recent years because of brake problems.

Bicycle trailers

Although they appear to be a secure nook for a baby or toddler while you're bicycling, trailers have real safety problems.

Bicycle trailers are designed for towing a child big enough to sit up— usually 6 months or so. They have two bicycle-type wheels and a long hitching arm that fastens onto the bicycle's chain assembly or seat posts. Some can carry two kids, and others are designed for kids with disabilities.

The trailers may give the impression of being safer than bicycle-mounted baby seats, since the passenger or passengers are seated, strapped in, and enclosed in a zippered compartment. (Bicycle-mounted child seats can make a bike unstable and hard to mount and dismount.) But a trailer's low profile makes it hard for motorists to see, especially in limited light. Trailers have a tendency to tip over, especially when turning abruptly or turning when one wheel goes over a bump. As a bike speeds up, braking becomes harder, even more so on wet surfaces. Trailers may also be snagged as the bike is pedaled past bushes or other objects.

For safety's sake, trailers should be considered off-road vehicles, used only in parks and on safe, smoother trails where there is no risk of encounters between bicycles and cars. Each

The low profile of a bicycle trailer can pose dangers on the highway.

Blankie

Cut a favorite blanket in half as soon as the child becomes attached to it, and whisk the dirty half away for laundering when the child's not around. With luck, the child will never realize there are two blankets.

child passenger should wear a well-fitting helmet. You should follow the manufacturer's recommendations regarding weight and size limitations.

What's available

The major brands are Burley and Kool-Stop. All trailers have a rigid frame designed to protect the young passenger in the event that the unit rolls over. Price range: $150 to $400.

Features to consider

The interior of the trailer should offer comfortable seating for the child, with adequate legroom, good back support, and storage for toys or snacks. There should be an adjustable five-point harness (two straps over the shoulders, two for the thighs, and a crotch strap), much like a car seat's. The hitching arm should have a backup to prevent the trailer from accidentally breaking loose. Check the wheel mounting to be sure that it will hold securely.

Frames are generally steel, but more expensive models may be made of aluminum, which is lighter. The frame should be firmly welded or bolted.

A canopy offers sun protection, and a zippered front shield can keep mud from splattering onto the baby. But if the shield encloses the entire cabin, make certain there is some form of ventilation.

You'll want clear instructions—assembly can be a challenge.

How to choose

KEY DIFFERENCES. The better bicycle trailers have sturdy construction and an interior that is comfortable.

RECOMMENDATIONS. First, decide if you will use the trailer enough to justify the price. Consider how much weight you can tow. When the weight of the bicycle trailer plus the passenger or passengers exceeds 50 pounds, you may start to think of yourself as a beast of burden. With fewer than a dozen trailer manufacturers, you may find it hard to locate models in the store to assess them before purchase. For safety's sake, avoid buying a used bicycle trailer or one you are not able to examine carefully. Remember that bicycle trailers are for off-road use only.

Although some manufacturers have conversion kits for turning one of their heavier strollers into a trailer, we don't recommend trying to rig a stroller to your bike.

CERTIFICATION. No certification program exists for these products. Standards do exist in other countries.

Baby carriers

Baby carriers offer the close physical contact and gentle walking rhythms that soothe babies, and leave your arms and hands free.

A sling or a strap-on soft carrier can be especially useful during the early weeks and months after birth. Fussy babies can often be calmed by riding in one. A framed carrier, like a backpack for baby, can be used later, after your baby can sit up.

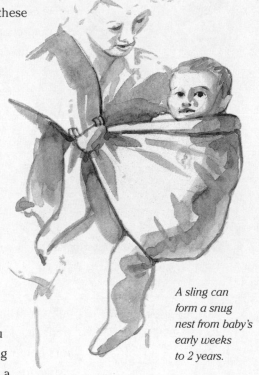

A sling can form a snug nest from baby's early weeks to 2 years.

You may feel somewhat awkward the first few times you use any type of carrier. First you have to figure out how to put it on. Then you have to adjust straps or fabric so the carrier will fit your body comfortably. Last—and this is the fun part—you have to get your baby inside the carrier without generating a fuss. Some manufacturers recommend that you practice with a teddy bear or doll until all steps become natural.

Learning how to move with a carrier may take some practice. You can't lean over, and your back, shoulders, and legs must adjust to the extra weight. And you'll have to be mindful of your extra dimensions when you go through doorways and around corners so baby won't bump into anything.

You'll probably find your child too heavy to use a carrier before his weight reaches the upper limit of most models. A simple rule is to stop using a carrier when you sense you're approaching your own limitations.

What's available

NoJo Over-the-Shoulder Baby Holder and Prince Lionheart are among the brands of slings. The major brands of soft carriers are Baby Björn, Fisher-Price, Graco, Infantino, Kelty K.I.D.S., KidCo, Snugli (Evenflo), Theodore Bean, and Weego. Evenflo, Kelty K.I.D.S., and L.L. Bean make framed carriers.

SLINGS. Made of pleated fabric, a sling forms an over-the-shoulder "hammock" for holding a young baby across your front in a semireclined position. The sling's length typically adjusts with two "O" or "D" rings worn over one shoulder. For maximum comfort, a baby should ride above the waist and below the bustline. (Babies can remain in the sling for discreet nursing.) As baby grows into a toddler, you can use the sling to carry her upright against your body, facing out, or on your hip.

Mastering the adjustment of rings and pleats so everything fits correctly takes time, even with clear, printed directions. You may experience some back and neck discomfort from carrying most of a baby's weight on one side. When that happens, put the sling on with the strap on the opposite shoulder. Once your baby can sit up on her own, you may prefer a backpack carrier or a strap-on soft carrier.

Price range: $35 to $40.

STRAP-ON SOFT CARRIERS. The human answer to marsupial pouches, strap-on soft carriers are designed for babies weighing as little as 6 or 8 pounds and toddlers weighing as much as 35 or 40 pounds. The range varies by model. Some models specify only a maximum weight, but CONSUMER REPORTS has found soft carriers that aren't safe for use with infants under 2 months of age. They fasten to a parent's front with adjustable shoulder straps, waist straps, or both. Most have a strap for each shoulder, with the two crisscrossing in back. Other straps fasten around the parent's waist. Some soft carriers are relatively easy to buckle or tie on, but others require practice. A soft carrier holds a young baby in an upright position (facing outward or inward), which he may like less than the curled position promoted by a sling. Some soft carriers can also be worn on the back.

Two leg holes and a crotch piece between them are designed to protect against slipping out or falling. (With some recalled models, the leg openings were big enough to let a child slip out through one of them.) The system of shoulder or waist straps helps distribute a baby's weight.

A soft carrier offers less structural support for babies over 6 months—and less for the parent, too—than framed backpack carriers provide. Your baby will probably become too heavy and uncomfortable being in a soft carrier before you reach the upper limits specified by most.

Price range: $20 to $100.

FRAMED CARRIERS. These are basically backpacks with a fabric baby seat. They're intended for children old enough to sit up independently—

A backpack carrier is designed to tote a baby big enough to sit up—usually 6 months or older.

usually at least 6 months old. They can be used for children up to 20 to 40 pounds, depending on the model, and until they're about 3 years old.

The metal or plastic frame, together with the waist or hip belt, distributes a baby's weight along the parent's back and waist, rather than putting it all on the shoulders and neck as some soft carriers do. Most framed packs come with built-in stands that help make loading and mounting easier, but these carriers are not stable enough to be used as baby seats. Seats and shoulder harnesses are made of moisture-resistant fabric. Many models have multiple positions for the wearer.

High-end framed carriers are usually found through camping outlets and catalogs rather than baby stores. They have densely padded shoulder straps and hip belts, as well as extra storage compartments, vinyl weather shields, and toy loops.

Framed carriers can be more cumbersome and expensive than soft carriers. And some have safety drawbacks, including leg openings that are big enough to let a child slide through.

Price range: $50 to $250.

Features to consider

Your baby's comfort and safety (not to mention yours) are the most important issues when evaluating carrier features.

FABRICS. Slings and carriers are usually made of cotton, corduroy, flannel-like materials, or moisture-resistant nylon, and come in a variety of colors and patterns. When shopping, test for softness to make sure the carrier doesn't chafe baby's skin. Slings and front carriers should be completely washable. Launder them a few times before use to soften them and remove chemical odors.

Framed-carrier fabrics are likely to be thick nylon similar to that used in backpacks or suitcases, and they come in subdued colors such as navy or dark green. The fabric should be sturdy and moisture-resistant and cleanable by wiping with a mild detergent. Allow framed carriers a few days to air out after you unpack them.

SEAT AND SEAT BELTS. With framed carriers, look for a seat that adjusts to different baby sizes, with strong snaps or

Soft carriers allow babies and small toddlers to ride kangaroo-style.

closures that will hold tight. A seat belt or other type of harness is needed to keep baby from scrambling out. Check all buckles and other securing hardware to be sure seams won't tear and straps won't slip.

SHOULDER AND WAIST STRAPS. Shoulder-strap padding for the parent should be firm and thick. Putting the baby in and strapping the carrier on should be fairly simple. Straps should be positioned so they won't slip off your shoulders or chafe your neck, and they should be adjustable even while you're carrying baby.

PADDING. Straps should be padded for the parent's comfort. Packs for younger babies should offer firm, padded head and neck support that adjusts to a baby's size. The metal frame of a framed carrier must be padded around the baby's face.

LUMBAR SUPPORT. Well-made framed carriers may have a special padded waist strap for adults that helps to distribute the stress of carrying a baby's weight from your shoulders to your hips and pelvic area. This is a definite comfort advantage. Fasten the belt to test that it's long enough and neither too high nor too low when the carrier is in place. Padding should be dense rather than mushy.

FASTENERS. Carriers use a variety of buckles and fasteners for shoulder

The art of the sling

There is an art to adjusting a sling so both you and your baby are comfortable. Its rings may look like simple fasteners, but they actually allow you to tighten various parts of the sling and loosen others, so baby is comfortably positioned and the sling doesn't pull on your neck and shoulders. The foam-padded section at one end isn't for the baby (as some might assume) but for cushioning the mother's neck and shoulders.

Because a sling requires you to carry most of a baby's weight on one side, you may experience neck and back discomfort. When that happens, try switching sides. You may want to cradle your baby with your arm when she is inside the carrier until both of you become used to how it feels. Walking around and talking to baby may calm her if she gets fussy.

Coaching from an experienced sling wearer can help. Talk to a friend who has used one or get in touch with an organization such as a local parenting group or La Leche League (www.lalecheleague.org) to find someone to give you pointers. Some models of slings include a video to help you get started.

and waist straps and babies' seats. Buckles that hold shoulder and waist straps should be easy to adjust and not allow straps to work loose when the carrier is in use. The most effective buckles are the squeeze-release type that must be pressed by adult hands to unlatch. Snaps should be sturdy and take a lot of force to unfasten.

KICKSTAND. If a framed carrier has one, it should lock firmly in the open position and have hinges with spacers to prevent finger entrapment. When the pack is on the stand, it should be hard to tip over. Never use a framed carrier with a stand as a baby seat.

LEG HOLES. Leg holes should be wide enough not to bind baby's legs, but not so wide that a baby could slip through a hole.

STORAGE POUCHES. Most framed carriers offer pockets or a pouch for carrying an extra diaper, a bottle, snacks, or other paraphernalia. Zippered pouches are better because things can't fall out. Plastic-lined versions can be used for damp items. Some heavy-duty carriers for serious hiking offer a variety of removable pouch accessories so you can choose what to add or take off. The downside of too many pouches: You have to heft whatever you pack in the carrier as well as baby.

How to choose

KEY DIFFERENCES. Some soft carriers are easier to use than others. Models that open on both sides are more convenient than those that open on only one side. In tests, most models did fine in terms of comfort. But parents noted some pressure points on the shoulders and neck with a couple of models. The size of the leg holes can be a problem in some baby carriers (see Ratings, page 200). With slings, you'll find models with thicker fabric, especially along the edge. Backpack-like framed carriers vary in comfort and ease of use.

RECOMMENDATIONS. Before buying a baby carrier, think about how much you'll use it. That will help you determine what to spend. A low-priced version may be fine for quick jaunts. If you plan longer treks with baby, consider a high-end model.

• **Read the directions.** Try to read them in the store to be sure they're clear. Putting the carrier on correctly can be essential to baby's safety. (Even with understandable directions, you might want help and tips from a veteran carrier wearer.) Follow manufacturers' weight and size limits.

• **Try it on.** You'll want to be able to see if you like wearing it, and

---

Shopping checklist

CARRIERS

○ Buy the right style for your baby's age and weight.

○ Try the carrier on in the store.

○ Look for thick padding.

○ Test the holding power of straps and fasteners.

○ Read safety and laundering instructions.

whether it will fit your baby comfortably. (A baby may dislike any carrier that makes her head feel confined.) If you're trying on a frame backpack, walk with it to make certain the frame doesn't hit the back of your head, that it's not too long for your height, and that the straps are close enough together that they won't slip off your shoulders.

CERTIFICATION. While no certification program exists for these products, a voluntary standard for soft carriers is being developed. One key point that will be addressed is the size of the leg holes. Some models of carriers have been recalled in recent years. Problems have included shoulder straps that could come loose and allow an infant to fall out and harnesses that could entangle a child, as well as leg holes big enough to let a child slip through.

Sitting pretty

For older babies, a high chair is a must. Infant activity seats, swings, and play yards can be a help during playtime.

The truth is, babies never just sit. Once in a seat, they'll wiggle, wave, coo, cry, nosh and nibble, and explore the environment however they can. So any "baby container" you choose must be safe and secure during all this activity.

A high chair is a necessity once baby can sit up—usually at about 6 months. In addition to standard high chairs, you'll find booster seats that you belt on to regular chairs, as well as chairs that hook on to the table. Infant activity seats and swings can help keep baby amused and soothed during fussy spells. Play yards provide an enclosed place to play or nap— at home or when traveling.

High chairs

Those simple wooden chairs of yesteryear with spindly legs have largely been supplanted by seats with adjustable heights and easy-to-open trays.

Once your child is sitting up on his own and eating baby food, you'll need a high chair. Since it must stand up to two or three years of spilling, pounding,

Contents

○ Buy a chair with a crotch post.

○ Make sure seat belts are well anchored.

○ Look for a tray that you can adjust or remove with one hand.

○ Test for resistance to tipping.

○ Look for a certification sticker.

and kicking, plus regular scrubbing, you'll want a model able to stand up to those challenges. You'll be opening and closing the tray often, so a tray that releases with one hand is an advantage.

What's available

The major brands of high chairs on the market are Chicco, Cosco, Evenflo, Graco, Kolcraft, and Peg Pérego.

A high chair usually consists of a frame of molded plastic or metal tubing and an attached seat with a seat belt and a footrest. There are still a few old-fashioned, wooden models, with a removable tray or arms that lift the tray over baby's head. You'll also find a few hybrid units, which can convert into other types of gear such as a play table and chair or a swing.

BASIC. High chairs at this end of the price range are simple, compact, and work quite well. Essentially plastic seats on steel-tubing legs, such models usually have no height or recline adjustments. The seat is thinly upholstered with a vinyl covering, and the pad is sometimes removable and washable. There may be rough, welted seams that can irritate the back of baby's legs. The tray is usually kept in place with pins that fit into holes in the tubing. Price range: $30 to $40.

MIDPRICED. These models are generally bulky and can eat up space in a small kitchen. Frames and seats are typically made of molded, rigid plastic. Cushioned, vinyl seat pads can be removed for washing. A few models have add-on quilted seat covers. Seats can be adjusted for height and sometimes recline in one or two positions so baby can use the high chair before he can sit up. Price range: $50 to $100.

HIGH-END. These generally compact models have thick, tubular frames topped by densely padded seats upholstered in vinyl. Some models come with add-on fabric covers removable for laundering. These chairs can be adjusted to many different heights and reclining positions with a simple squeeze-release mechanism. Some have folding, "A"-shaped frames to make them easy to store. Others sit on wheeled pedestals, like a tall office chair, which makes them easy to move around. Price range: $150 to $200.

Features to consider

CROTCH POST. A common problem with high chairs in the past was the possibility of baby slipping out under the tray and getting his head caught. To prevent that, high chairs now typically have a restraint that works when the tray is used. That restraint is usually a center post attached to the tray or to the seat—a "crotch post." It's not meant to replace the seat belt, though.

SEAT ADJUSTMENT. Seats can move up or down, and some recline. A height adjuster allows the seat to slide along the chair frame, locking into various positions. Height options range from nearly floor level to standard high-chair level, with the middle height low enough to allow the seat (with the tray removed) to be pushed under a dining-room table. A high chair with a reclining option may come in handy for a child who can't sit up yet. But more often than not a child that small will be fed in a parent's arms.

SEAT BELT. It should hold baby securely in place, with no leeway for standing up or climbing out. Some belts require your baby to sit on a strap that loops into the waist belt, which presents a cleaning challenge. Others are a three-point harness—two adjustable shoulder straps and a lock between the child's legs—or an adjustable five-point harness—two straps over the shoulders, two for the thighs, and a crotch strap.

TRAY. You'll want a lightweight tray that can be taken off with one hand or that swings to the side when not in use. Certain designs help contain spills: a tray that surrounds baby on all sides, a tray angle that channels liquids away from baby, and a tall rim all around the tray. Some chairs have two trays: a big tray with a deep rim for feeding and a smaller one for snacking or playing. Don't be lured by a claim that the tray is "dishwasher safe"—most trays are too large to fit in a dishwasher.

UPHOLSTERY. Many models have seat coverings—or entire seat panels —that come off for easier cleaning. Be sure fasteners won't cause upholstery to tear as you pull off the seat or coverings. Seat covers with patterns are better at concealing spills than solid ones.

LEGS. Some fold for storage. When shopping, make sure there is a secure locking system to prevent accidental folding. Such a system should automatically engage when the chair is opened.

WHEELS. While wheels may make it easier to move the high chair around, they can be a nuisance. They can allow the chair to move as you're trying to pull a tray off, or as you put baby in. Siblings may be tempted to take baby for a joyride when your back is turned. Wheels on some models appear to make the chair less stable. If you decide on a wheeled model, look for locks on the wheels, preferably on all four. Some models come with locking casters.

A high chair with an A-shaped frame can be folded for easy storage.

Messy

Put a plastic or metal high chair under the shower, and let hot water spray over it for a few minutes. Caked-on food wipes off easily.

CONVENIENCE FEATURES. Some chairs have nice but unnecessary features such as racks for hanging towels, wash cloths, or bibs, as well as cup holders and rear storage bins.

How to choose

KEY DIFFERENCES. High-end chairs, often sleek and streamlined, offer flexible positioning, extra-thick seat padding, and attractive upholstery. But many aren't certified, so you can't be sure they meet the current voluntary safety standard. Midpriced models offer the best value. They usually have an easy-to-remove tray, a sturdy seat belt, a tip-resistant frame, and a crotch post.

RECOMMENDATIONS. Buy the most stable model you can within the price category you choose. If you're looking for a compact model, look at the low or high end of the price spectrum. In the store, push the chair from side to side and front to back to see how well it holds its ground. Look for

Hook-ons: Use with caution

A fixture in restaurants and diners everywhere, hook-on chairs are space-saving alternatives, but they have some safety concerns. A hook-on high chair consists of a seat, backrest, metal frame, and pincer-like arms that attach to a table. The major brands are Chicco, Graco, and Inglesina. Friction and the weight of the child hold the unit in position. Most hook-ons have locking mechanisms, suction cups, or spring latches designed to enhance the chair's holding ability, as well as a restraining strap to secure the child. Most fold up for compact storage, which means you can stow a hook-on in your car's trunk and use it when eating out or traveling. Some have a large plastic tray and removable and washable upholstery similar to what you'll find on standard high chairs.

With a hook-on chair, there is a risk of the child dislodging the chair by pressing his feet against the table or on an ordinary chair and pushing back. Another problem is that many tables won't accommodate a hook-on. If you decide to use one, make sure it and the table are a good fit. Don't use a thin or glass tabletop—the high chair may lose its grip. A table with only a center post may tip over from the weight.

Located on the frame of a hook-on chair, a certification sticker shows it meets the minimum requirements of the American Society for Testing and Materials' voluntary standard and that its manufacturer participates in the pass/fail certification program administered by the Juvenile Products Manufacturers Association. Certified units are required to have a latching device that reduces the possibility of accidental folding.

an easy-to-clean, easy-to-use design. If you're buying a model with wheels, make sure they lock.

- **Look for rough edges.** Examine the underside of the tray for sharp edges that could scratch baby and for small holes or hinges that could capture little fingers.

- **Check for small parts.** Make sure caps or plugs that cover the ends of metal tubing are well secured. Parts small enough for a child to swallow or inhale are a choking hazard.

- **Assess seat cover.** Look for a chair with upholstery made to last. Test the quality of the material by pinching it between your fingers. It should feel thick, not flimsy. Make sure upholstery seams won't scratch baby's legs.

- **Regularly inspect the high chair.** After baby has been using the high chair for a while, check to make sure it's still in good shape. Check to see that the seat-belt buckles are secure, the folding-leg locks still lock into place, and small parts are firmly attached.

CERTIFICATION. Located on a high chair's tray or frame, a certification sticker shows that the model meets the minimum requirements of the American Society for Testing and Materials' voluntary standard and that its manufacturer participates in the pass/fail certification program administered by the Juvenile Products Manufacturers Association. Certified seats are required to have a passive restraint such as a crotch post; a locking device that prevents accidental folding; secure caps and plugs; sturdy, break-resistant trays; wide legs to increase stability; and no springs or dangerous scissoring actions that could entrap little fingers. Safety belts have to pass force tests. High chairs are covered by the federal safety standard for small parts.

Some models of high chairs have been recalled in recent years. Problems have included incidents of babies "submarining," or sliding, under the tray and chair legs that lack a secure folding mechanism.

Booster seats

These have replaced the stack of books that once raised a toddler to the level of the dinner table.

Typically made of molded plastic, booster seats are usually belted to the seat of a standard adult dining chair. Although some manufacturers claim their seats can come into use when baby reaches 6 months, we suggest

Some booster seats include a detachable tray.

○ Avoid models lacking
a seat belt and a
strap for the chair.

○ Measure your dining
chair to make sure
the seat will fit.

○ Look for a booster
with a choice of
heights.

postponing their use until your child is closer to age 1. Never leave a little one unattended at the table.

What's available

The major brands are Cosco, First Years, Fisher-Price, and Safety 1st. Booster seat designs vary somewhat. Some have a removable tray and a skid-resistant surface on the seat base. Some have a choice of two heights that allow the seats to grow with baby. Some disassemble for storage. One model—from First Years—can partially recline. A manufacturer may claim that the components of a booster seat are dishwasher safe—they'll probably take up the entire bottom rack. Price range: $10 to $25.

How to choose

KEY DIFFERENCES. A striking deficiency of some models is the absence of a seat belt, which is essential to holding children in boosters and preventing standing and falling, or a strap securing the booster to a chair. Only consider models that come with two sets of secure belts—a seat belt with a crotch strap to secure the baby in the booster, and strong webbed belts to hold the booster to the adult chair.

RECOMMENDATIONS. Before shopping, measure the chair to which you plan to attach the booster seat. The chair should have a seat area at least a few inches wider than the booster base. With some chairs, a booster seat tends to slip or fall off. Pedestal-base chairs, swivel chairs, rocking chairs, bar stools, benches, heavily padded chairs, and seats with cushions can't be safely used with a booster.

CERTIFICATION. No certification program exists for these products.

Infant activity seats

**These provide a comfy, semi-upright nest for baby,
with a commanding view of you and your baby's world.**

Most babies like to be where the action is. An infant activity seat gives a baby who can't sit up a place to hang out near you and the rest of the family during the first five or six months. Most models have a detachable, bent-wire play bar (sometimes covered with padding) that suspends plastic spin toys in front of baby that he can bat with his fists, and maybe interactive sounds and lights.

Some consist of a lightweight frame covered with a quilted, removable, washable backing designed to conform to your baby's shape. Others have a hard molded shell covered by thickly quilted upholstery.

Infant activity seats are meant for indoor use and should not be confused with or used as car seats. Manufacturers will suggest a seat weight limit, usually ranging from newborn up to 20 or 30 pounds. Putting a child who is over the weight limit into the seat can make it tip.

What's available

Many large manufacturers of baby products including Evenflo, Fisher-Price, Kolcraft, and Playskool sell infant activity seats.

LIGHTWEIGHT MODELS. Sometimes called "bouncers," these seats are somewhat springy, which may help keep baby relaxed and amused. The quilted backing is rounded to support the infant's still-fragile spine, while a semi-upright tilt affords a view of surroundings. This angle appears to be more comfortable for some babies after a big meal than the flat posture demanded by a crib. Supporting frames are made from metal wire, tubular metal, or heavy-gauge plastic, and most are curved underneath to allow the seat to rock. Some models have optional motorized vibration. Price range: $20 to $35.

HARD-SHELLED MODELS. These seats are a sturdier breed than the lightweights. Instead of a quilted material suspended from a frame, they are backed by a hard, molded shell with thickly quilted upholstery. Virtually all hard-shelled models have motorized vibration (sometimes with two speeds and a timer). Some simulate the sound of a heartbeat as heard from the womb or play computer-chip-generated classical music. But your baby may find such gadgetry more annoying than soothing. Price range: $70 to $155.

Features to consider

Skip the bells and whistles—and the lights, music, and jiggling—and concentrate on construction and features that will keep baby safe.

SEAT BELTS. Typically the belt is a single waist strap that threads through a wide fabric crotch fitting between baby's legs. Look for an assembly that is secure and fits around baby's waist. Belts that are simply strung from one side of the seat to the other may allow baby to slip or wriggle out.

PLAY BAR. Toys suspended from the play bar are usually small, colorful spinning toys. Some play bars have several positions and offer interactive noisemakers and lights.

No shocks

Take along a few screw-on electrical outlet covers as a babyproofing measure if you'll be staying at a hotel or in the homes of others who might not have them.

Shopping checklist

ACTIVITY SEATS

◯ Check stability of the seat.

◯ Look for a skid-resistant covering on the bottom of the base.

◯ Avoid seats with flimsy play bars or toys that appear likely to break off.

UPHOLSTERY. Seat padding can vary from basic to extra-thick. Because wet diapers are bound to come in contact with the fabric covering, upholstery should be removable and washable. There should be no loose threads or gaps in the seams.

EXTRAS. Some models have add-ons such as folding canopies that act as sunshades or mosquito netting. Both are useful protectors when the seat is used outdoors. So baby won't become overheated, use the seat only in the shade.

How to choose

KEY DIFFERENCES. Because an activity seat is only useful for a few months, an inexpensive lightweight one can serve as well as a top-end design, provided it's stable. Pay more and you'll get a hard-shelled seat with well-constructed toys, reclining and vibrating features, realistic (as opposed to tinny) music, and plush fabric. Seats also vary in legroom and depth. Be sure your baby has enough wiggle room and has adequate head and leg support.

RECOMMENDATIONS. For maximum steadiness, you'll want a base or rear support that's wider than the seat itself. Test the stability of a model in a store. When you press down on it from different positions, it shouldn't tip sideways. When rocked front to back, it should stay in place. The bottom of the base should have rubber pads or other nonskid surfaces.

If you're buying a seat with toys attached to a play bar, make sure they seem durable and unlikely to break off. If the frame is assembled with interconnecting parts, test to make sure they won't accidentally work loose. If the model uses a flip-back handle as a stabilizer, the handle should have a secure locking mechanism.

• **Use the seat safely.** The best place to put an infant activity seat is on the floor. Once baby really gets bouncing, the seat could slip off a high surface such as a table. If you do place the seat on a table, remember to keep it away from the edge.

If you carry the seat with baby inside, don't just rely on the handle; use both hands. The frame or handle could give way or baby could slip. Never leave a child in an infant activity seat unattended.

CERTIFICATION. Although no certification program exists for infant activity seats, they are covered by a federal safety standard for small parts. Some models of infant activity seats have been recalled in recent years. Problems have included seats with an unstable base, handles with faulty locking mechanisms, kickstands that may not hold the seat stationary, and toys or play parts that may break from the toy bar.

Baby swings

A swing may be useful, especially during the first three to six months, in helping to calm a crying baby. But they eat up floor space.

Designed for indoor use, baby swings are typically a seat suspended by a pair of arms attached to a frame with wide-standing, tubular-metal legs. They're handy for soothing a crying baby or occupying her while you make dinner or fold laundry. With a windup or battery-powered mechanism, swings are lightweight and can be easily moved from room to room, although they do take up a fair amount of space. Some parents of colicky babies swear by them, but before buying one, try out a friend's if possible. Your baby may not like the rocking motion.

What's available

The major brands are Cosco, Fisher-Price, Graco, and Kolcraft. To make a windup model swing, you wind a handle at the top or side of the frame, giving 15 to 30 minutes of movement. Automatic swings operate on a motor that uses four D batteries. Such models emit a low churning noise with each passage of the swing. You'll also see a few swing/high chair combinations. Such units tend to be cumbersome in both roles. Other models come with a cradle or bassinet attachment. Price range: windup, $40 to $65; automatic, $70 to $135.

Features to consider

Some models give you a choice of speeds, but more than four is overkill. A fast speed may annoy rather than relax a baby. A time-remaining indicator can help you keep tabs on the action. Multiple reclining positions can help you find the most soothing posture for your baby.

A built-in crotch post prevents baby from sliding out of the seat—an extra safety measure. There should also be a seat belt. The seat cover should be well padded and easily removable for washing. Frames without a top crossbar make it easier to put the baby in and take him out. Look for

○ Check for running
time.

○ Inspect swing
for tip resistance.

○ Look for a unit
with a crotch post.

○ Buy swing with wash-
able seat cushion.

a swing that has a wide stable stance and folds or dismantles for storage.

A cradle or bassinet attachment may have two swinging motions—side to side and front to back. (The former motion can press the infant against the side.) A few swings have a stand that holds an infant car seat.

Nice but not necessary: a front tray, with or without attached toys, and computer-chip-generated music, which may or may not be soothing to little ones and grownups.

How to choose

KEY DIFFERENCES. You'll have to decide between a windup and an automatic. A windup model may be perfectly adequate as long as it's stable and has a well-padded, reclining seat that affords easy access. Battery-operated models usually have a sleeker design plus more features, such as speed controls and toys attached to a front play tray.

RECOMMENDATIONS. Look for a sturdy, stable frame that won't tip. Examine the seat. It should be well padded, have a crotch post to prevent baby from sliding out, and offer a partially reclined position for snoozing. You'll also want a secure seat belt. If you buy a model with a cradle or bassinet attachment, make sure it's well mounted underneath, with no potential for breaking loose.

Limit the amount of time your baby swings, especially at a high or fast setting. More swinging time can make some babies dizzy. With battery-powered swings, start with the lowest setting—high settings may be too rough for your baby. Always follow the manufacturer's age and weight specifications.

CERTIFICATION. Although no certification program exists for these products, one is being developed. Swings are covered by the federal safety standard for small parts. Some models of baby swings have been recalled in recent years. Problems have included swing frames that aren't stable, frames or seats with sharp edges, harnesses that could entangle a child, seats that could collapse, and bassinets with floorboards that could break loose.

Play yards

These baby holders can be handy for home or travel. For safety's sake, buy a new model that meets the current voluntary safety standard.

Play yards provide a baby with an enclosed place for playing or napping. Most designs can be folded into the compact shape of a golf bag and slipped into a zippered carrying case for travel or storage. The frames are made of metal tubing, and the sides consist of mesh or woven nylon or some other moisture-resistant fabric. A rectangular shape allows the units to fit through doorways. (Play-pens, which play yards have largely supplanted, are square-shaped.)

A play yard's top rails are typically hinged at the center to allow for folding. Many play yards sold in the 1990s had rails that could collapse at the hinges, forming a steep "V"-shaped angle that put children at risk of entrapment and strangulation. Fourteen children were killed when play yards collapsed, according to the Consumer Product Safety Commission. To address the hazard, the industry's voluntary standard, updated in 1999, now requires that hinges automatically lock when rails are pulled upright. The rails must also undergo a strength test that mimics the force of an adult leaning on them. The CPSC has recalled models that pose a rail-collapse hazard, though many may still be in use. (The commission's web site, *www.cpsc.gov,* has recall details.) For safety's sake, you should use only play yards made in late 2000 or later and certified to the current standard. Don't buy (or sell) used play yards or accept (or give to others) hand-me-downs. They may predate the current safety standard and may have been recalled.

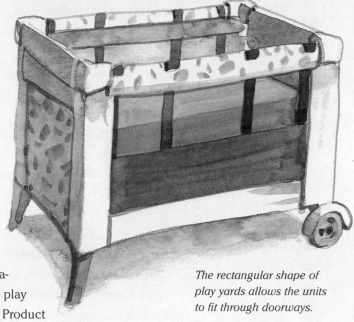

The rectangular shape of play yards allows the units to fit through doorways.

Most play yards carry the warning "Never leave your child unattended." That would appear to rule out using the play yard for overnight sleeping—yet odds are that's what many play yards are used for when traveling. Some manuals address this issue with this not-very-clear advice: "When used for sleeping, you must still provide the supervision necessary for the continued safety of your child."

If the play yard is used for sleeping, remember that the mattress pad is thin for a reason: to prevent a child from becoming wedged between the pad and the sides. Never add extra mattresses or padding, and don't use blankets or other types of soft bedding, which pose a suffocation hazard. Instead, layer baby for warmth with a T-shirt and a footed sleeper.

What's available

The major brands are Baby Trend, Century, Evenflo, Cosco, Graco, InStep, J. Mason, and Kolcraft. Most models have hinges and lock buttons in the center of the top rails. In setting up, you push down on the top of the folded unit until the legs are in position. You then pull the top rails up so they're locked. To fold up this design, you press the lock buttons and raise the top rails slightly. The handle in the center of the floorboard is then rotated and pulled up. An alternative design from J. Mason eliminates the top-rail hinge and uses screw-in legs. To set it up, you slide its legs through nylon sleeves on the play yard's corners and screw them into the top rail. Price range for play yards: $80 to $135.

Features to consider

WHEELS OR CASTERS. A pair of lockable rubber wheels or swivel casters on one end makes moving the travel play yard easier. With some designs, the unit can also be rolled when folded.

ATTACHABLE BASSINET. This provides a place for a newborn to nap. Look for a design that's easy to use. Stop using the bassinet when the baby is 3 months old, weighs 15 pounds, or can sit up, pull up, or roll over. Because an attachable bassinet can easily be dislodged, you should keep younger siblings away from it when it's being used.

ATTACHABLE CHANGING TABLE. When using this, you may find that you have to bend down uncomfortably far. Its safety harness should be used.

STORAGE. Storage compartments include zippered side pockets, hook-on fabric storage pouches, and clip-on parent organizer bags. They should be big enough to actually hold something and stay out of baby's reach.

CANOPY. Made of a combination of mesh and moisture-resistant and sometimes heat-resistant fabric, a canopy can help shield baby from the sun and mosquitoes. Because of the potential for heat buildup, a canopy should not be used in direct sun. During tests, CONSUMER REPORTS found that some canopies were hard to assemble.

CARRYING CASE. A sturdy carrying case with a shoulder strap can make toting the unit and storing it in the trunk of your car easier.

SIDE CURTAINS. Included with some play yards, they provide protection from the sun and wind.

PADDING. The floor pad is only about 1 inch deep and is usually made up of four panels that fold into a box for carrying the folded unit. It should be firm enough to protect baby during falls and stay in place so there is no danger of baby slipping or getting trapped between it and the floorboard.

TOYS. A few play yards have tactile toys sewn into an inside wall.

How to choose

KEY DIFFERENCES. Most models of play yards have passed the current safety standard. In CONSUMER REPORTS' tests, most of the units with hinges in the center of the top rails—the typical design—did fine in terms of safety, although rails bent to varying degrees during a test designed to mimic the force applied when an adult bends over a top rail to tend to a child. (A load was gradually applied at a 45-degree angle, reaching 100 pounds after 5 seconds and held for 10 seconds.) Rail-safety scores take into account how far the rails bent. With two models, the railing hinges broke. While the rails didn't fall into a steep "V," they sagged enough to raise concerns (a parent leaning on a rail as it breaks could fall forward and injure the child, for example). The one model judged excellent for rail safety was the J. Mason Safe Surround Play Yard. Unlike the others, it has a nonfolding top rail with no hinges, eliminating the possibility of collapse. But it folds into a relatively large bundle, and screwing its legs into its rails was judged difficult when the play yard was new.

RECOMMENDATIONS. We urge you to only consider a play yard made in late 2000 or later that meets the current safety standard. Look for the date of manufacture and the certification sticker on the packaging. With older models, there is a possibility that a top-rail hinge may collapse during use and trap the child. Those models have been recalled, but many may still be in use. If your child uses a play yard at a day-care facility or in a hotel, be sure it's a recent model.

Before each use examine padded sides and all areas where mesh and fabric are sewn together to see that there are no loose threads that could entangle fingers and toes. The floorboard should fit snugly against the springy mesh sides—gaps are an entrapment hazard.

Heed maximum height and weight limits—usually 35 inches and 30 pounds. Stop using a play yard when the child attempts to climb out.

CERTIFICATION. Located on the frame or packaging, a

certification sticker shows that the play yard meets the requirements of the American Society for Testing and Materials' voluntary standard and that its manufacturer participates in the pass/fail certification program administered by the Juvenile Products Manufacturers Association. Certified play yards with folding rails must have hinges that automatically lock the rails to prevent accidental folding. Play yards are covered by the federal safety standard for products with small parts.

In the 1990s, models that could accidentlly collapse and entrap a child in a "V" were recalled.

Diapering & toilet training

All told, your little one will probably use between 5,000 and 8,000 diapers. It's a good thing babies are so cute!

Cloth vs. disposable—the great diaper debate rages on. Before your baby arrives, you'll need to decide which type to use. Which is actually better? The answer is complicated and ultimately depends on personal preference.

On one hand, disposable diapers are undeniably convenient. The vast majority of babies wear them, and they're preferred by most day-care centers. But they commit you to spend more than $2,000 on diapers over the three years that is the typical length of time kids wear them.

On the other hand, cloth diapers are less expensive to use than disposables, especially if you do the laundering yourself. Babies who wear cloth diapers are less prone to diaper rash, probably because it's easier to tell when they're wet (and thus the diapers get changed more often). Cloth "diapering systems," with water-resistant outer coverings that close with snaps or Velcro, are almost as easy to use as disposable diapers. You still have to wash the cloth diaper insert, of course.

At first glance, disposable diapers, which pile up each year in landfills across the country, seem less "green" than cloth diapers. But cloth diapers

Contents

Fix it

Keep a roll of masking tape handy to mend torn tabs on disposables and to mend plastic pants.

have an environmental impact of their own in the form of the water and energy sources needed to launder them.

Whichever type you choose, diapers are a necessary evil until your child reaches age 3 or so. At that point, bring on the potty seat. With a fair amount of coaxing and patience on your part, the diapering days will finally come to an end.

Disposable diapers

All disposables are extremely absorbent. You'll see differences in fit and the ability to control leaks from brand to brand.

A disposable diaper has a gel between the paper lining and the outer shell that absorbs many times its weight in liquid. After a brief flirtation with separate versions for boys and girls (which were supposed to offer extra protection in key areas according to gender), the market has returned to unisex branding.

Diapers are often sized according to baby weight, beginning with preemie and newborn and progressing to sizes 1 through 6. Some store brands are simply marked small, medium, large, and extra large, with weight ranges listed on the packaging. The biggest diapers fit children 35 pounds and over.

As diapers get larger, you get fewer for the same price. A larger package might give you 68 diapers in size 1, but only 32 in size 6. As with many things, buying the largest packages can reduce per-diaper costs.

What's available

The major manufacturers are Kimberly-Clark, maker of Huggies, and Procter & Gamble, maker of Pampers and the generally less expensive Luvs. There are also store brands and generics—mostly sold in large grocery stores and discount retail chains.

Basic diapers have the same fasteners and absorbent core as a brand's premium lines but lack extras such as stretchy sides and waist and leg leak barriers. Most diapers have "fashion statements" such as colorful imprints of cartoon characters.

There are other types, too. You'll also see disposable training pants, intended for children who are working their way out of diapers. Swimming diapers have a water-resistant shell. Price range: 25 to 45 cents per diaper.

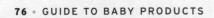

Features to consider

Some diaper features actually help your baby stay dry. Others cater to the usual need of marketers to create distinctive features to sell the product, often at a higher price.

FASTENERS. The type of fastener varies from brand to brand. Luvs and Pampers use reusable sticky tape. Unlike in the past, the tape can be repositioned without tearing the diaper's outer shell. Huggies use Velcro fasteners. These don't lose their sticking power when they come in contact with baby creams or powders, as do sticky tapes.

LEAK GUARDS. These elastic barriers improve fit around the waist and thighs and prevent leaks.

STRETCH SIDES. These help the diaper do a better job of fitting a baby's unique contours and, like leak guards, prevent leaks.

SHELLS. The shells of many diapers typically have a clothlike feel that promotes air flow and minimizes moisture, while those of a few less expensive diapers may still have the feel of plastic.

LINING. Most diapers have a lining of lotion that is supposed to protect baby's skin. But you'll still want to keep zinc oxide diaper cream on hand for the inevitable outbreaks of diaper rash.

How to choose

KEY DIFFERENCES. A good disposable diaper fits well with no gaps. It should be easy and quick to fasten, open, and refasten, and should stay closed without the fastener losing its grip or tearing the diaper. Premium diapers usually fit a bit better around the waist and legs than do less expensive ones. But leaks can still occur regardless of which brand or type you buy.

CONSUMER REPORTS' tests have shown that absorbency isn't an issue anymore. Even the lowest-capacity diaper could hold the equivalent of four or more urinations. But you'll need to change your tot more often than that, for comfort's sake and to ward off diaper rash.

Some diapers are touted for biodegradability, but there's no evidence that diapers break down in the landfill at differing rates.

RECOMMENDATIONS. Plan on your newborn using 100 diapers per week, but don't overstock on the newborn size. Babies with higher birth weights may not fit the smallest size. Start with a package of newborn and a package of size 1—about 48 diapers in all. Then buy in volume after you see which size your baby needs.

Shopping checklist

DISPOSABLE DIAPERS

○ **Try out different sizes and brands.**

○ **Use premium diapers if baby has problems with leaks.**

○ **Save by buying the biggest package available.**

Select the smallest diaper your child can comfortably wear—a larger diaper not only costs more, but also may not fit your baby well, allowing leaks. You may have to experiment a bit to find a diaper that fits your baby's quickly changing body. Sizes do vary from brand to brand. One brand's size 3 may fit children 12 to 24 pounds, while another's fits those 16 to 28 pounds. A brand's weight ranges usually overlap: Size 2 in one brand covers 12 to 18 pounds, size 3 16 to 28 pounds, and so forth.

Stores often put disposable diapers on sale as "loss leaders" to induce parents to shop at them. Watch for specials and stock up. You can sometimes get coupons by calling the customer-service lines of diaper manufacturers or visiting their web sites (though at the price of getting your name on marketing lists). Also check out coupon-giveaway web sites. See Reference section, page 179.

Cloth diapers

Today there are lots of options that make cloth a less cumbersome option than it was in the past.

No question, cloth diapers are much less convenient than disposables. You have to soak the soiled ones between laundry loads. And the demands of a new baby can make keeping up with the diaper onslaught a daunting proposition.

But there are ways to make the burden lighter. A diaper service—a nice baby-shower gift—can make cloth diapers easier to deal with (but the expense of one does away with the cost advantage cloth diapers have over disposables). Prefolded or preshaped diapers and "diapering systems" are easier to use than plain diapers.

What's available

Cloth diapers are made of different types of absorbent cotton fabrics: terry (like toweling, but softer); bird's-eye (similar to old-fashioned tea towels); gauze (thin and lightweight); and flannel (similar to the material used in flannel sheets and pajamas, but denser and thicker). Flannel is the softest against the skin and the most absorbent. A combination of terry and flannel is also quite absorbent.

DIAPER TYPES. There are three main types: Unfolded, prefolded, and preshaped. Unfolded diapers are rectangles of flat fabric that you fold to fit your baby's shape, holding them in place with diaper pins. This type allows you to concentrate layers where they work the best, but they take time to prepare. Prefolded diapers are also rectangular but have extra or absorbent layers in the center. Contrary to their name, they may require some folding when you put them on your baby. They too require pinning. With folded and prefolded, you'll also need to use waterproof pants. Preshaped diapers have a narrow crotch and wide wings that wrap around baby's waist. Some require diaper pins, but some have snaps to fasten them closed. With preshaped diapers, you have to buy different sizes as baby grows. Some have a moisture-resistant vinyl outer covering sewn onto the diaper, eliminating the need for water-proof pants. But the outer covering may not launder thoroughly (allowing detergent to remain and bacteria to grow) and may take longer to dry. Price range: diapers, $1 to $2 each, waterproof pants, $2 and up.

DIAPERING SYSTEMS. Diapering systems are the most expensive cloth option. This type is based on a moisture-resistant covering of nylon or polyester, into which you insert a folded diaper or a special washable liner.

The covering comes in a range of sizes to accommodate baby's growth. Velcro fasteners or several rows of snaps (for different fits) keep the outer covering closed. The most absorbent inner inserts use multiple layers of thick flannel resembling dense cotton velvet. With cute brand names such as Cotton Kids, Babykins, Kushies, and Snugglebottoms, diapering systems are available through specialty mail-order stores including Babyworks, The Baby Lane, Bareware, and Earthbaby. You can find diapering systems through many web sites.

DIAPER SERVICES. They're available mainly in sizeable metropolitan areas. For a monthly fee, diaper services deliver two to three dozen fresh diapers once or twice a week and take away soiled diapers. Diaper services wash at such high temperatures, the diapers are virtually sterilized. They'll also give you a diaper pail fitted with a plastic bag. Most companies designate a set of diapers to be used solely by your baby and guarantee no commingling. Price range: $50 to $70 per month.

How to choose

KEY DIFFERENCES. Of the different types of diaper material, flannel is the most absorbent. Diapering systems are superior to plain diapers in terms of absorbency, fit, and leak control and spare you the hassle of safety pins. But they are more expensive.

Shopping checklist
CLOTH DIAPERS

- Sample products before you order a lot.
- Choose flannel for best absorbency.
- Look for quick-drying, leak-resistant, adjustable outer pants.
- Buy two to three dozen, plus four to six pairs of waterproof pants.

RECOMMENDATIONS. If you choose cloth diapers, you will need two to three dozen to begin, plus four to six pairs of waterproof outer pants. Most companies selling diapering systems invite you to buy sample packs so you can determine which brand works best for you. It helps to compare diapering system prices. Don't forget to include postage and handling charges in your calculations.

DIAPER-WASHING BASICS. Wash diapers two dozen at a time. Presoak first, using your washer's highest water level and the hottest water. Launder with a hot wash and cold rinse.

You don't have to use special laundry detergent for babies. Any detergent labeled free of perfume or dyes will work fine. As long as you presoak, you don't need to use chlorine bleach, which cuts down diaper life. To remove stains, use chlorine-free bleach or washing soda. If your baby is prone to diaper rash, rinse diapers twice, adding three-fourths of a cup of white vinegar to the second rinse.

Don't use liquid fabric softener or dryer sheets. Your baby may have an allergic reaction to the fragrance. And fabric softener leaves a waxy buildup on diapers, making them water-repellent instead of absorbent.

Diaper pails

The type of diaper pail you'll need depends on whether you're using disposables or cloth diapers.

As their name suggests, disposable diapers are pretty easy to get rid of. They can be tightly wrapped, bagged, and thrown in the household trash. Or you can use a diaper pail designed especially for disposables. With cloth diapers, you'll want to soak them in a diaper pail before laundering.

Before tossing a disposable into the trash or a cloth diaper into the wash, it's best to flush fecal matter down the toilet, where it can be treated by a sewage system. You can sprinkle soiled cloth diapers with baking soda to help minimize odors.

What's available

FOR DISPOSABLE DIAPERS. The major brands are Diaper Genie, Diaper Nanny, Fisher-Price, and Safety1st. The Diaper Genie and its imitators use specially designed plastic sleeves to form an odor-blocking seal around each diaper. You drop the diaper into the sleeve, twist a knob, and close the lid. To empty the pail, you use a built-in device to cut the sleeve, pull out a long chain of encased diapers, and throw it away. The downside to all that convenience: the environmental ramifications of all that plastic waste that is created.

You'll have to keep a supply of liner refills on hand. Although such systems are fine for small diapers, larger diapers are harder to stuff in and fill up the unit more quickly. Even though these products are touted in ads as being able to cut down on odor, a pail can in time start to smell and require cleaning.

An alternative is bypassing these specialty pails altogether and going for a simpler model that works with ordinary kitchen trash bags.

FOR CLOTH DIAPERS. The best pails are strong enough to hold a considerable amount of water, but are also easy to carry, with a comfortable handle and a spout for pouring out soaking solution. You'll need a securely locking lid to prevent curious little ones from possibly falling in.

How to choose

KEY DIFFERENCES. Any disposable-diaper pail with a self-sealing mechanism will do the job. Diaper pails for cloth diapers vary in the sturdiness of the bucket. Look for a pouring lip and comfortable handles.

RECOMMENDATIONS. If you're using cloth diapers, you can't get by without a diaper pail. But there are cheaper alternatives for disposables, such as a kitchen trash can with a locking lid. Just put the soiled diaper in a plastic grocery bag, tie it shut, and toss it into the kitchen trash bag. It will hold a lot more diapers than a small diaper pail, and odors shouldn't be a problem, especially if you spray the inside of the trash can with disinfectant.

CERTIFICATION. No certification program exists for these products.

Changing tables

There are plenty of alternatives—from a blanket on the floor to a specially designed table. Your back will benefit if you buy a table.

You can diaper a baby anywhere you have room and the baby is safe from falling if she squirms—in the crib with one side lowered, on your own bed, or on a pad on the floor. But a changing table—a high wooden stand surrounded by rails—may be easier on your back. Whatever you decide, keep pads and diaper supplies in a couple of places in your home, especially if it has several levels.

Shopping checklist

CHANGING TABLES

○ Decide if you actually need one.

○ Choose a model with a secure safety belt.

○ Find a table with tall rails on three or four sides.

○ Look for tip-proof construction.

A changing table lets you tend to baby at a comfortable level.

What's available

Changing tables are sold alone or as part of a nursery suite, along with a crib, chest, and armoire. Sometimes a changing station is built on top of a chest or inside an armoire. Most models have wooden frames, but you may find some constructed of wicker. The table is usually surrounded by a restraining barrier made of rails or wood slabs on three or four sides. Protection on four sides is better. Most tables have open shelves that make it easy to reach diapers and clothing, but some have drawers instead. Make sure drawers are light enough that the table won't tip when they're pulled out. A safety belt—a single vinyl or nylon mesh strap with a wide buckle—is usually included. You'll want at least three changing pad covers.

Price range: $100 to $200 for models that coordinate with other furniture.

How to choose

KEY DIFFERENCES. A changing table with rails on all four sides and a safety belt is the safer choice. Models that coordinate with other pieces of nursery furniture may be appealing, but are more expensive.

RECOMMENDATIONS. Evaluate the furniture you plan to include in the nursery—you may decide that you don't need a changing table at all. If you do decide to purchase one, look for a model with rails on all four sides and a safety belt. Never leave a baby on a changing table unattended. And always use the seat belt, even if you think baby can't roll over.

CERTIFICATION. A certification program is being developed.

Diaper bags

A diaper bag may be your constant sidekick, so consider size, comfort, and durability, just as you would with any other frequently carried purse or tote.

When you and baby are on the go, you'll want a diaper bag for essential supplies. Any bag, of course, will work. Manufacturers offer specially designed bags in a wide variety of colors, fabrics, and designs, some much more practical and long-wearing than others. Many are quite stylish, and some easily double as a purse so you only have to carry one bag. Most have clear, or see-through, storage areas inside.

What's available

Major brands include Babies Alley, Eagle Creek, Kate Spade, Kenneth Cole, L.L. Bean, and Samsonite. Fabrics and patterns run the gamut from frolicking teddy bears and pastel backgrounds to sophisticated black, navy, and forest green. Designs include backpacks, tote-style bags, fanny packs, and bags that could pass for briefcases. Some diaper bags unfold like a garment bag and hang over door frames and crib railings or in bathroom stalls and closets, displaying their contents in neatly zippered pockets.

Price range: $20 for a low-end fabric or vinyl model to $100 or more for name-brand designer bags.

Features to consider

You'll want a serviceable size and weight and solid construction, with an easy-to-carry handle and convenient storage areas.

FABRIC. Bags made of quilted fabrics are often favored by gift givers, but heavy-duty, moisture-resistant fabric such as that used in luggage is more durable. Manufacturers continue to offer "baby colors"—pastels and light colored prints. But dark shades are less likely to show stains and wear. And a more adult look makes it more likely that the bag will be used for other purposes after baby graduates from diapers.

CONSTRUCTION. Assess workmanship details. Look for strong, adjustable straps (nylon webbing is a smart choice) and well-reinforced seams.

STORAGE. Easy-to-access compartments are a must. On the outside, elasticized pockets—sometimes insulated—hold bottles and baby food jars. Zippered compartments function as wallets. Clear vinyl or mesh pockets inside stow diapers, wipes, and other baby gear. (You may want to pack separate, sealable plastic bags for on-the-go diaper disposal.)

CHANGING PADS. All bags come with rectangular changing pads of various sizes that fit in the bag and can be wiped clean. Most fold to fit into a designated pocket. Some have a semirigid interior that helps maintain the pad's shape. Others have a Velcro strip that can attach to the bag. With some fanny-pack styles, the changing pad unfurls when you unzip a special compartment. Compartments that have closures are good, since babies love to overturn bags. Test all closures for ease of use. Zippers are the best bet— Velcro fasteners collect lint; snaps can pop loose.

EXTRAS. Nice features include latches for keys and pacifiers and a pocket for personal papers.

Ready

Keep a thermos of
warm water near the
changing table at night
for quick cleanups.
You'll avoid stumbling
around in the dark
and running the water
for what seems like
hours to get the
right temperature.

How to choose

KEY DIFFERENCES. Low-end models skimp on quality and durability, leaving you with a bag that may tear, fray, or get stained or sticky over time. High-end bags may be too big, or loaded with features you don't need. Among midpriced bags, you can find tough performers with sound construction and generous storage.

RECOMMENDATIONS. Carrying comfort is paramount. If you can, try the bag you're considering to see how well it fits your body. Wide or well-padded straps can make carrying the bag more comfortable. There should also be a loop for carrying by hand. The handles of a tote-style bag should be short enough that the bag doesn't drag on the ground when carried like a suitcase but long enough so it can be slung over the shoulder. Backpacks' shoulder straps should be adjustable for proper fit.

Potties and toilet-seat adapters

Potty training is complicated enough without a complicated potty. The simpler the device, the better.

Learning to use the toilet poses a significant challenge to a toddler. Small, baby-scaled seats that sit on the floor and ring-shaped adapters that reduce the diameter of an adult toilet seat make the job easier. Except for a few old-fashioned, folding wooden potties, most versions on the market are molded plastic. To encourage toilet training, take your toddler along when you shop for a potty or adapter seat and let him help choose it.

What's available

ONE-PIECE POTTIES. Sleek, simple, and easy to use, these smoothly finished pots that sit on the floor come in a variety of pastel colors. Or they're molded into colorful toy-like configurations, such as dinosaurs. The fronts have a raised rim to quell spraying. Most have a rear handle for easy emptying.

MULTICOMPONENT POTTIES. Also designed to sit on the floor, these low, barrel-shaped or cube-shaped units have a seat and a removable lightweight pot. With some models, the seat can be removed and used as an adapter with an adult toilet. Extras may include closing lids (not needed), a toilet-roll holder (also not needed), or an imbedded computer-chip tune that plays when your toddler does his business (may help reinforce success). A few potties turn over to make footstools once their usefulness as a potty is over, but this could cause problems for curious tots.

ADAPTER RINGS. These sit on top of the toilet seat to make it fit a child's small dimensions. If you've got an irregularly shaped toilet seat, this kind may not work well. Some adapters are rigid plastic with hooks underneath to engage with the seat when the adapter is pressed down. Others, padded with vinyl-covered foam, have a rim that rests inside the toilet ring. Some look like miniature adult toilet rings and raise and lower, too, using hinges fastened onto regular toilet seat screws.

PORTABLES. Flat (and flimsy) portable models are designed to fold for storage in a purse or diaper bag.

How to choose

KEY DIFFERENCES. Better models may have smooth, finished edges. Components need to snap together firmly without separating. Because backing up into the seat is awkward, it's important to select a design that won't slip on the floor and has a nonslippery surface. The pot should be easily accessible from the front or top (not the back) and slide out without a hitch to avoid spills.

RECOMMENDATIONS. Potties that sit on the floor perform best because they're portable and can be positioned anywhere for those critical first days of training. They also allay some children's fear of flushing, which can hamper the process. Choose the simplest potty you can find—it will be easier to rinse clean.

If you purchase a multicomponent potty, make sure the pot portion lifts out with no spill-causing jerks or hitches. An adapter ring should secure firmly to the adult seat without danger of the child and seat slipping.

TIPS ON TOILET TRAINING. The age for mastering toilet training has gotten progressively older. Forty years ago, the age might have been age 1 or thereabouts. More recently, child psychologists have pointed out that toilet training works better and faster when a child is developmentally able to follow simple directions and link a couple of tasks in sequence. Usually this occurs at age 2 or later. With the advent of disposable diapers, babies are delaying learning to use a toilet to age 2, 3, and beyond. No one knows how exactly disposables have prolonged the diapering stage, but it's thought that greater diaper absorbency makes children less aware they're wet, and that, in turn, has weakened the child's association between urinating and needing to use the potty. During toilet training, cotton or cotton/polyester underwear may be better than disposable training pants, which may make it difficult for a child to perceive wetness.

Teaching a child to use the toilet is pretty complicated. Your toddler has to sense when she's about to go. She needs the motor skills to get herself to the bathroom, to pull down her pants, and to back into the potty, or mount the adult toilet, and do so before her immature "holding muscles" let go. For most children, the procedure doesn't come naturally. It may require commitment from parents to home in on this learned behavior until it's mastered. Needless to say, reward—whether praise or treats—works a whole lot better in shaping a tot's behavior than threats and punishment.

If you find your child is resistent to toilet training, consider letting older children model what's expected. Also consider using children's picture books on the subject. Toilet training typically takes several weeks. Don't be surprised if even after a few successful trips to the potty your toddler has accidents a while longer.

Bathing & dressing

A gentle touch, unscented toiletries, and soft clothing are easiest on baby's sensitive skin.

Stores are filled with fancy frills, adult-like duds, and designer baby toiletries. But if babies could talk, they would probably tell us they'd rather go naked, or at least wear soft clothes that are easy to put on and take off. Their delicate skin needs tender care, not lace, scents, or additives. When buying toiletries and clothes, simplicity is best.

A couple of weeks after your baby is born, it will be time for the first bath. A tub built especially for a baby may help keep squirming to a minimum. On the other hand, you may decide that you don't need one. A kitchen sink lined with a towel or a baby-sized foam bath cushion may work just fine.

Bathtubs

A tub with a baby-friendly design can make a slippery, splashy job easier—for both you and your infant.

A baby bathtub provides an appropriately compact place for bathing. Better models are made of firm molded plastic that won't bend under the weight of

Contents

Shopping checklist

BATHTUBS

◯ Consider a mini-tub especially designed for infants.

◯ Look for slip-resistant surfaces.

◯ Buy a tub with a drain for easy emptying.

◯ Consider a smooth overhanging rim for easier carrying.

the water when you pick them up. Often baby bathtubs have an angled shape and slip-resistant foam lining that allow a baby who can't sit up to recline in a semi-upright position. Usually a baby bathtub can be placed in a sink, in a household bathtub, on the counter, or on the kitchen table. Once a baby is able to sit up, you can dispense with a special tub and use a regular one.

There is one baby-bathing product that should be avoided. A bath seat, or bath ring, is a plastic baby seat made with suction cups on the bottom that attach the unit to a regular bathtub. Bath seats are supposed to make it easier to handle a baby during bathing, but dozens of infants have drowned using them. In many cases, the parent's back was turned momentarily. In 2001, the Consumer Product Safety Commission found that bath seats give parents "a false sense of security" and unanimously voted to begin developing a mandatory safety standard. The CPSC voted against banning bath seats in 1994.

Needless to say, a baby or toddler should never be left alone in a tub. Also be careful about scalding water. When using a regular tub, always turn the hot water off first and watch out for hot metal spigots.

What's available

Major baby-product brands including Evenflo, Graco, and Safety 1st make baby bathtubs. You'll see simple tubs that are flat on the bottom (usually the least expensive option), tubs with angled backs for bathing small babies, hybrid tubs that can be used by infants or toddlers, and travel tubs that can fold up like a suitcase. Price range: $12 to $30.

Features to consider

A slip-resistant foam lining can help keep baby from sliding around. A rounded crotch projection can keep baby in a safe position. A drain with an attached plug can make the tub easier to empty. A smooth, overhanging rim around all sides facilitates carrying. Some tubs have adjustable seats. Some models have suction cups that attach the unit to a regular bathtub.

A pitcher for rinsing and storage nooks for soap and shampoo are often included but obviously aren't essential. Translucent plastic models in the trendy baby colors of bright blue, purple, and turquoise can brighten up bath time.

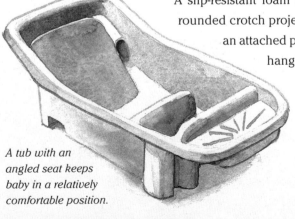

A tub with an angled seat keeps baby in a relatively comfortable position.

How to choose

KEY DIFFERENCES. Just about any tub will be awkward to use, mainly because bathing a squirmy baby—who may dislike temperature changes and being put in water—is awkward in itself. The better baby tubs are sturdy, with slip-resistant surfaces molded into the plastic, and features that make them easy to handle. Spending more on a tub may get you heavier material (which will make the tub less likely to bow when carrying water) and a smoother finish along the seams.

RECOMMENDATIONS. If you have a sink in which your baby can sit or semi-recline with the help of a folded towel or foam bath cushion, that may be all you need. A bath cushion—a large sponge with a baby-shaped indentation —is usually available anywhere you can buy baby gear and costs about $5.

CERTIFICATION. No certification program exists for baby bathtubs.

Dress up

When putting a shirt on your child, put a small treat such as a raisin or piece of dry cereal into your child's hand so he or she will make a fist to push through a sleeve.

Baby toiletries

A simple approach works best. Sensitive baby skin doesn't need lotions, powders, or fragrances that have been adapted from adult products.

Traditional baby toiletries include wipes, diaper-rash cream, liquid soap, and shampoo. Lately, formulations using chamomile, lavender, and other aromatic plant essences or fragrances have hit the market. As appealing as they may be to adults, they're really not appropriate for babies, whose skin may react badly to all the extra ingredients.

Some manufacturers have hopped on the antibacterial bandwagon, adding antibacterial towelettes or wipes "gentle enough for baby's skin," as well as antibacterial soap. But some studies suggest that these products may actually encourage growth of resistant bacteria.

Toiletry supplies for your baby

- One package (a half dozen) baby washcloths.
- Two to four soft cotton towels.
- Baby shampoo—but no need to shampoo for the first six weeks.
- A pair of blunt-tip scissors or baby-sized fingernail clippers.

- Nasal aspirator (a bulb to clear mucus from a baby's nose).
- Fragrance-free cleansing bar or liquid soap designed especially for babies. But use no soap, only plain warm water, for the first four weeks.
- Baby sunscreen.

Baby's medical kit

- Antiseptic for umbilical cord care (ask your doctor for specific recommendations).

- Zinc oxide-based diaper cream.

- Petroleum jelly.

- Infant's Tylenol or another brand of infant's acetaminophen (never administer without a doctor's approval and dose instructions; never give aspirin).

- Pedialite—an easily absorbed liquid that helps prevent dehydration during bouts of diarrhea or vomiting.

- Compressed cotton pads (cotton balls can fray).

- Cotton swabs (for baby's "nooks and crannies" but never inside the ears).

- Infant thermometer—rectal, axial (armpit), or ear type; digital (more accurate and safer) or mercury (less expensive).

What's available

SOAP. Don't use it early on. It can irritate skin—especially in the delicate genital area—and interfere with the skin's natural protective lubricants. Just use mildly warm water until baby is about 4 weeks old. Then you can switch to a cleansing bar (gentler than soap-based products), such as unscented Basis, Dove, or Neutrogena, or liquid baby soap. If baby's skin seems dry, an unscented lotion such as Eucerin or Lubriderm may help.

POWDER. Talcum powder is no longer thought of as an acceptable baby product. The particles are readily inhaled, and a relatively small quantity can cause a form of pneumonia. Some companies have switched to cornstarch as a powder base, marketing it as a "natural" ingredient. But baby bottoms really don't need any powder at all. Just dry baby thoroughly.

DIAPER CREAMS. Ointments containing zinc oxide such as Balmex and Desitin are excellent barrier creams, protecting from irritating stools. Petroleum jelly may be effective at soothing dry skin.

BABY WIPES. For the first few months, clean the diaper area with warm water. Reserve wipes for when you're away from home. For older babies, wipes can be used regularly, but avoid the scented or antibacterial versions.

SHAMPOOING. In the early months, a baby's delicate hair doesn't need shampooing; doing so can lead to scalp dryness and itchiness. At 6 weeks, lathering up once or twice a week with baby shampoo is fine. Be careful about getting lather near the eyes—even shampoos touted as "tearless" can be irritating.

How to choose

Shampoo, liquid soap, diaper-rash cream, and plain wipes are all you need. Complicated products and extra ingredients can irritate an infant's skin, causing rashes and other allergic reactions.

CERTIFICATION. No certification program exists for these products.

Infant clothes

Soft, simple, washable clothes keep baby comfortable—and minimize dressing hassles and upkeep for you.

It will take every ounce of willpower not to load up your shopping cart with teeny tiny jeans, velvet dresses, and trendy togs. But you *know* that all babies want is to be comfortable. The basic necessities—even if they're hand-me-downs—will keep your little cutie content.

Footed sleepers keep baby comfy day and night.

What's available

The mainstays (beyond the ever-present diaper) are side-snap T-shirts, Onesies (one-piece shirts that snap closed over the diaper at the crotch), a gown with an elasticized bottom, and footed sleepers, which are useful day and night.

You'll find every imaginable pattern, color, and animal or cartoon-character print. Even basic clothing is divided into "boy" or "girl" versions, with "girl" styles the bigger sellers.

Cotton, which is soft and absorbent, continues to be the most common fiber, although many garments are made of cotton/polyester blends, which dry quickly and resist wrinkles. You'll also find thick, soft knits and fleece made of microfiber.

Climate and season have a bearing on what you'll buy. When it's warm, you'll want lots of short-sleeve T-shirts. Cold weather demands leggings, sweaters, hats, mittens, and booties to keep baby warm when you go out.

Sizes are usually based on age, although they typically fit babies younger than indicated: preemie, 0 to 3 months, 3 to 6 months, 6 to 9 months, 9 to 12 months, 12 months, 18 months, 24 months. One manufacturer's 6 to 9 months may be different than another's. Read the weight and length charts found on the back of most garment packages. You can also consult a size chart, which many baby-clothing stores keep on hand.

Features to consider

Ease of dressing plus softness and safety should be your primary concerns. Since most babies dislike having anything pulled over their head, look for garments easy to take off and put on. Choose front-opening or side-snap tops. Until a child is toilet trained, easy access to the diaper area is essential, so opt for snap-open legs or loosely elasticized waists. Velcro closures are particularly quick and convenient. (When laundering, close them so they don't fill up with lint and threads and lose their holding power.)

COMFORT. Inside seams on all clothing should be smooth, not rough, and lie flat rather than sticking out. Don't buy clothes with tight elasticized bands on arms, legs, neck, or waist. (Elastic must be very loose or it can irritate skin and restrict circulation.) Bypass anything that could be scratchy—unpainted metal zippers, appliqués, or snaps with a rough or an uneven backing. If an appliqué is made of heat-welded plastic, check for sharp edges on the back.

FABRIC. As with adult clothing, labels on baby apparel must state fiber content. All-cotton knits may look large when new, but will shrink as much as 10 percent and become thicker with repeated washing. Polyester/cotton blends are less expensive than pure cotton and more resistant to wrinkles and shrinkage. Avoid thin, semitransparent items, or any garments that show signs of poor finishing, such as unclipped thread.

FOOTWEAR. Wait until your child is a confident walker before buying shoes. Instead, choose socks or booties that aren't too tight around the toes.

How to choose

KEY DIFFERENCES. Low- and midpriced garments deliver soft but sturdy fabrics, competent workmanship, and plenty of baby style. They're also usually machine washable. Upscale baby clothes cost more (sometimes amazingly more) than standard garments, without a proportionate increase in quality and durability. If you buy such clothes, know you're

Cleanup

Color code washcloths if you use them for cleanup; one color for the bath, one for diapering.

Laundering infant and toddler clothes

Everything that touches baby's skin, including clothes, cloth diapers, towels, and washcloths, should be laundered with a fragrance-free, dye-free detergent. Despite marketing claims to the contrary, you don't need to buy a special laundry detergent for babies. Any liquid or powder laundry detergent labeled free of perfume and dyes will be fine.

Spot cleaner can be used for stains, but you should rinse well. Avoid using liquid fabric softener or dryer sheets with infant and toddler clothing. They can add potentially irritating fragrance and can interfere with fabric absorbency. Liquid fabric softener may also increase the flammability of all-cotton fleece, terry cloth, or velour.

Avoid dry cleaning. Residue from chemicals may be irritating.

doing it for style. In addition, high-fashion clothes may require hand laundering, even dry cleaning. Remember that your baby will quickly outgrow anything you buy.

RECOMMENDATIONS. Stock up on basics before baby arrives: six to eight T-shirts that snap on the side for newborns, six to eight Onesies, three pairs of booties or small socks, and three or four items to sleep in such as footed sleepers or nightgowns elasticized at the bottom (also called sacks). Sleepers and sacks are preferable to covering a baby with blankets.

For outdoor winter wear, buy two small knit sweaters and a knitted cap or a hat with an elasticized chin strap to keep baby from batting it off. You'll also want either a zip-up bunting with legs; a sack with sleeves, legs, and a hood; or a hooded jacket. The outer garment should be warm but not so bulky that it could interfere with safety belts on a car seat or stroller. In the summer, buy a small brimmed hat with an elasticized chin strap for protection from the sun.

• **Be size-wise.** Purchase very little in newborn size. Your baby will outgrow these tiny garments quickly—sometimes in less than a month. It's more practical to stock up on clothing in the 3-to-6-months or 6-to-9-months size. But don't use sleepwear that's too big for your baby. The pockets of air created makes it more flammable (see Certification, page 94). If your baby is born early or is very small, you can find preemie sizes of basic shirts in large discount chains, from catalogs, and on the web.

• **Be price-wise.** Watch for sales and specials on brands you like, especially at the end of each season. Large chains have promotions regularly, sometimes even weekly. Buy in your baby's current size, and also stock up on larger ones. Web sites often have good deals, too. Clicking on "clearance," "overstocks," or "sale" can help you snag some real bargains.

• **Consider used.** Put the word out among parents you know. You may get quite serviceable clothes delivered by the boxload to your front door. Check out a baby consignment store for good deals on clothes for special occasions such as fancy dresses, since they're only used once or twice. Inspect hand-me-downs carefully for unraveling thread, loose snaps, or scratchy appliqués and elastic bands.

• **Safety.** Tiny buttons, hooks, pompons, bows, and appliqués in clothing can be choking hazards. Routinely check clothes and fasteners for such loose items. Avoid loosely knitted items—sweaters, booties, or hats—that can trap a baby's tiny fingers or toes. Cut all loose threads before your baby

Shopping checklist

INFANT CLOTHING

○ Stick with washable fabrics.

○ Look for front-opening tops.

○ Buy garments with easy access to diapers.

○ Look for smooth, nonscratchy seams and finishing.

○ Use weight-length charts to determine size.

wears a garment. Before you put on socks or booties, turn them inside out to look for small threads that could capture small toes.

CERTIFICATION. The Consumer Product Safety Commission allows manufacturers to make sleepwear without added flame retardants for sizes under 9 months. The only condition is that the sleepwear be tight-fitting to avoid trapping the amount of air needed for fabric to burn as well as to reduce the chances of contact with a flame. Similarly, our recommendation is for you to use sleepwear that fits snugly.

Dry feet

Use your portable
hair dryer to dry
winter boots quickly.

Toddler clothes

In addition to being comfortable, toddler clothes should be able to stand up to climbing, stumbling, exploring, and spilling.

Just like baby clothes, toddler duds need to be soft and comfortable. But durability is also essential for these young crawlers and walkers. The "miniature adult" look is quite popular. Choices include all-cotton and cotton/polyester tops in bright prints with color-coordinated leggings for girls; mock turtlenecks and pants for boys; and richly colored corduroy and knit overalls and slipover shirts for both girls and boys. Bold primary shades and mild pastels abound, along with cheerful patterns and cartoon characters.

What's available

The most practical tops are colorful T-shirts with snap openings either on one shoulder or down the front. Overalls cover shirt gaps. Pants with an elastic waistband (so they can be pulled up or down without your help) can be handy. Sizes are based on height and weight: 2T for 35 to 36 inches and 26 to 29 pounds; 3T for 37 to 39 inches and 30 to 34 pounds; and 4T for 40 to 42 inches and 35 to 38 pounds.

Features to consider

Look for the same practical comfort features you sought in infant clothes—ease of dressing, soft fabrics, nonscratchy seams, loose elastic, and washability. Durability is important, too. Look for reinforced seams and extra stitching at stress points such as the edges of pockets, the crotch, and waistband. On the other hand, toddlers outgrow clothes faster than they outwear them. Because they tend to get into messes, being able to wash a garment many times without fading or unraveling is critical.

Hot-weather clothing should be lightweight and absorbent—all-cotton or mostly cotton knits and fabrics. For cold weather, avoid overbundling your child and layer thin garments for warmth instead.

Shirts with wide necks make self-dressing easier, as do pants with loose elastic waistbands that a tot can pull down in a hurry for bathroom emergencies. Snaps and zippers can be tricky for little hands to operate. Large buttons and Velcro closures work better than small, frustrating buttons.

FABRIC. Labels on toddler clothing, as well as on adult apparel, must state fiber content. Many people prefer all-cotton knits for their soft feel and absorbency. You may find that these knits seem large when removed from the package, but they'll shrink as much as 10 percent with repeated laundering. Cotton/polyester blends are less expensive than all-cotton clothing, more wrinkle resistant, and less likely to shrink. But they do tend to hold on to oily stains.

FOOTWEAR. Socks or booties with skidproof soles are a good indoor option for fledgling walkers. When shoes are needed (for toddling outside), look for styles with soft sides and soles, such as flexible, moccasin-like designs. Sneakers are fine, but not models with artificial arches or with crepe soles that could catch on carpeting and cause falls. So-called orthopedic shoes with stiff soles and artificial arches are of no benefit to a normal baby's feet and may even hamper balance. Babies don't even have arches for the first two years. Buy boots a size larger than your tot's shoes, so they're easy to slip on and off.

OUTERWEAR. Snowsuits or other winter outerwear should be water-resistant and have a built-in hood (but no drawstring, which is a strangulation hazard). A knit hat can provide added protection from the elements. Mittens need a nonslip surface on the palm so a tot can pick up objects easily.

UNDERWEAR. When your child is ready for toilet training, simple cotton or cotton/polyester underwear may work better than disposable training pants. The latter may make it more difficult for a child to perceive wetness, which could delay toilet training (see "Potties and toilet-seat adapters," page 84). Thick, absorbent cotton training pants tend to shrink, bunch, and lose stretchiness with laundering. Cotton/polyester tends to hold up better.

How to choose

KEY DIFFERENCES. Low- and midpriced clothing works fine for fast-growing toddlers. Spending more may get you high fashion,

○ Buy durable,
  washable fabrics.
○ Look for sturdy
  construction.
○ Choose clothes that
  are easy to put on.
○ Check flammability
  information on labels.

but expensive clothing is likely to be impractical for everyday life—and no toddler wants to stop exploring to save clothing wear and tear.

RECOMMENDATIONS. Since most toddlers like to pick out what they wear in the morning, consider purchasing patterned tops and solid-colored bottoms, or vice versa, so all your child's outfit selections will roughly go together.

Avoid buying overly large outfits in the hope that your child can wear them until he outgrows them. They will only make toddlers look baggy and possibly cause them to trip. Instead, settle on a few, simple, well-fitting outfits that all go together and rotate them.

Inspect any potential garment for sturdy fabrics, and additional knee reinforcement for pants.

• **Safety.** At the recommendation of the Consumer Product Safety Commission, most major clothing manufacturers have agreed to remove, sew down, or shorten the strings for hooded clothes, including those for toddlers. We recommend that parents cut strings on children's clothing—snip off hood strings or dangling waist strings on coats, and cut any strings that fasten a pair of mittens or gloves together. Better yet, buy clothing without strings. They can become entangled on play equipment, posing an injury risk.

Since "hand to mouth" is almost a reflex action for toddlers, their clothes should be free of small, decorative features, such as bows and buttons, which can pose choking hazards.

CERTIFICATION. Under rules set by the CPSC, sleepwear for children older than 9 months must be either flame-resistant or snug-fitting. Loose-fitting clothing such as T-shirts should not be used as children's sleepwear. Look for information on flame resistance on the labels.

Feeding time

For the first six months, breast milk or formula is all a baby needs. After that, it's a whole new world of tastes and textures.

As parents of a newborn, you'll have a million things to do—but planning meals won't be one of them. Until your child is about 6 months old, breast milk or formula will take care of breakfast, lunch, dinner, and middle-of-the-night feedings. You'll need to have bottles and nipples on hand whether you nurse or bottle-feed. Breastfeeding moms should consider nursing bras and breast pumps. If you're bottle-feeding, you should hold off on buying formula until after your baby is born. Sensitive babies can only tolerate a special type of formula. The hospital will load you up with samples appropriate for your baby when you go home. You can try them out to help determine which brand you prefer. Consult with your pediatrician if you have any questions or concerns.

Between 4 and 6 months, your baby will start to seem interested in "real food." You can then, under your pediatrician's guidance, begin moving toward solids—mainstream brands of baby food, organic lines, or mashes you make yourself. But breast milk or formula will continue to be a diet staple until your baby reaches age 1.

Contents

Breastfeeding

Breastfeeding confers immense health benefits on your baby. Human milk provides a unique mixture of components necessary for baby's digestion, brain development, and growth. Breastfed babies have been found to have fewer instances of ear infections, diarrhea, respiratory illnesses, allergies, and urinary-tract infections than formula-fed infants. They also have been found to have fewer doctor and hospital visits than formula-fed babies. Benefits to mothers include faster recovery of the uterus to prepregnancy size and less postpartum bleeding.

It's up to you to determine how long you want to breastfeed. The American Academy of Pediatrics recommends that women who can breastfeed do so exclusively for about the first six months and that breastfeeding, complemented by the gradual introduction of iron-enriched solid foods, should continue at least until age 1. Some mothers wean their babies when they return to work a few months after birth. (If you decide to wean your baby before age 1, you'll need to use formula.) Others back on the job use a breast pump or a combination of breastfeeding and formula. Even if you do decide to use formula exclusively, consider breastfeeding for at least a few days, so your baby can get the benefits of the nutrient-rich, immunity-enhancing colostrum that mothers produce before their milk comes in.

Not everyone decides to breastfeed. Some women are simply uncomfortable with the concept. In rare instances, mothers can't make enough milk to provide adequate nutrition for their babies. Often an inability to build up an adequate supply of milk occurs when mothers try to schedule nursing as opposed to nursing "on demand"; when nursing is supplemented with formula; or when an ineffective breast pump is used instead of nursing. Women who have a serious medical condition should consult their doctors before breastfeeding.

Breastfeeding doesn't always come as second nature. New mothers can feel frustrated when things don't click immediately. The first week or two can be a learning experience for a newborn, too. The problem may be related to how the baby is positioned at the breast, or how often or how long the baby is allowed to nurse. Don't go it alone. There are lots of sources of help—from other mothers to hospital lactation consultants. The International Lactation Consultant Association *(www.ilca.org)* and La Leche League *(www. lalecheleague.org)* are other sources of expertise.

Grown up

When young children no longer want to drink from a baby cup or "sippy cup," give them commuter cups to use. They hold more and spill less. And they make a child feel grown-up.

Nursing bras

Time to put away those lacy demi-cup bras. During breastfeeding, comfort, convenience, and easy care will be your top concerns.

Nursing bras aren't a necessity. But they can certainly make the process easier, with cups that lower or open from the top when a small, plastic clasp is squeezed or a metal hook is slid out of its loop. Accessories such as nursing pads for sopping up leaks and bra extenders for accommodating fluctuating breast and rib-cage sizes are sold separately. Some mothers simply prefer to use a regular stretchy bra, which saves having to fool with tiny clasps when there's an impatient baby at hand.

What's available

Just as with regular bras, there are a variety of designs for nursing bras: underwire models; soft, cotton-knit sport styles; and traditional versions with circular-stitched cups. Since your breast size will change over time, look for a stretchable bra with fasteners that will allow you to adjust the size. Allow room for pads, or shields. The latches that open the cup for nursing should be simple to operate with one hand. Some mothers find a center-front-latched bra easier than dealing with separate cup-opening devices. Price range: $12 to $20.

NURSING PADS. These come in washable form, either fabric and foam or cotton, or as disposable paper pads. The latter are convenient but more expensive in the long run. You can make your own out of cotton handkerchiefs, terry-cloth squares, cotton diapers, or folded cotton T-shirt fabric. Avoid toilet paper or facial tissues, which can hold in moisture, irritate skin, and disintegrate when wet. You can find nursing pads at drugstores, baby stores, and from a variety of web sites.

BRA EXTENDERS. It can be difficult to predict bra fit during the last month of pregnancy and the early weeks after birth. A bra extender, which attaches to the back band of a bra, helps to adapt bras to fit during size changes. They're available at lingerie stores or online and cost $2 or so.

How to choose

KEY DIFFERENCES. The best nursing bras are stretchy, absorbent, and don't bind the breasts in any way that could interfere with milk flow.

They're machine washable, with no special laundering or care requirements.

Watch out for designs that make the bra hard to use, such as awkward clasps. Some nursing bras have cups or underwires that can bind and interfere with the function of milk ducts, which, in turn, can cause pain and possible inflammation. Large-breasted women may have to search hard to find a nursing bra that provides adequate support.

RECOMMENDATIONS. Shop for three to four nursing bras in the later months of pregnancy as your breasts and rib cage enlarge. The typical increase during pregnancy is one bra size and cup size, with a return to prepregnancy size within 10 to 12 weeks after delivery. Plan to purchase three to four nursing bras when breastfeeding becomes well established and breast size stabilizes.

You can buy nursing bras at department stores, but you might want to go to a maternity shop to purchase your first one. A professional fitting will ensure a comfortable fit and let you know the correct size for later on.

Special nursing clothes have strategically placed slits that facilitate feeding. But a front-opening blouse or a stretchy T-shirt and cardigan sweater can be just as convenient and discreet.

Breast pumps

A breast pump allows you to breastfeed if you return to work —and gives others a chance to feed the baby.

A breast pump allows you to store milk for later use. You'll want a pump that's appropriate to your situation. Mothers returning to work need to have much more breast milk on hand than those who stay home with their babies or are supplementing breast milk with formula. Some employers provide breast pumps for their employees to use in special nursing rooms.

An ideal pump comes as close to a baby's sucking action as possible. A baby's natural sucking rhythm is 40 to 60 cycles per minute (one pull per second or a little less). Large, hospital-grade and midweight plug-in pumps operate at 30 to 60 cycles per minute. Other pumps are usually less efficient. Pumps also vary by the type of suction they apply. Intermittent action better imitates a baby than a constant vacuum.

Using a breast pump will definitely take some practice. You'll need to learn how to position it correctly and adjust the suctioning to get the best results. Pumps will also require assembling and disassembling for cleaning.

Thirsty

Use the lightweight plastic bottles that bicyclers use as spill-proof containers for kids.

What's available

Breast pumps come in four basic types: large, hospital-grade models; midweight, plug-in models; small, battery-operated units; and manual models. The major brands are Ameda, Avent, and Medela.

HOSPITAL-GRADE. These piston-operated powerhouses are about the size of a car battery and weigh as much as 11 pounds. Originally manufactured for use in hospitals, these have sensitive controls that allow you to regulate suction rhythm, intensity, and pressure. Accessories permit dual pumping so you can empty both breasts at once. Some people may find these pumps heavy and noisy—they produce a rhythmical swishing sound. These are quite expensive to buy, but you can rent them from hospitals, medical-supply stores, lactation consultants, and many drugstores. Price range: $500 to $1,700 to buy; $18 to $20 to rent weekly, $50 to $65 to rent monthly.

PLUG-IN. Usually no bigger than a shoebox, these are less efficient than the hospital-grade models they try to imitate, but they still work pretty well. Most offer intermittent action, though some use a constant vacuum. Some models include dual pumps. Price range: $160 to $270.

BATTERY-OPERATED. These can be useful if you're away from your baby now and then—for a night out or a couple of hours during the day. Using C batteries, these lightweight, compact devices can fit discreetly in a purse or briefcase. They're relatively quiet and can be used just about anywhere. Some can plug into household current. But the suction is slow and tedious, achieving only 5 cycles per minute. You'll probably have to manage the cycling of suction by tapping your finger over an air vent. The constant vacuum can cause nipple discomfort. Price range: $30 to $60.

MANUAL. These small pumps are OK for occasional use. A couple of models might even be efficient enough to be used every day without too much discomfort or time invested. You produce the suction yourself by squeezing a bulb or lever or by manipulating a syringe-style cylinder. Such pumps are usually less expensive than electric models, don't need an electrical source, and operate silently. But any small pump could tire your hand and arm. And manual pumps are often markedly slower than other pumps.

A hospital-grade breast pump is pricey, but you can rent one.

There are many different designs of manual pumps. Cylinder, or piston-style, pumps usually allow you to control pressure to minimize discomfort. Some manual models let you operate them with one hand. They're easier to use than those requiring one hand to hold, one to pump.

Avoid the simple bicycle-horn-style bulbs found in drugstores. They simply apply a thin rim of pressure around the areola and can cause bruising and tissue damage. You can express milk with your hands more effectively.

Price range: $30 to $45.

Features to consider

A breast pump should not allow milk to come in contact with the gasket that separates the pump from the collection unit. (Any parts of the pump that do touch your breasts or the milk containers should be washed in the dishwasher, or with hot, soapy water, and drained dry before each use.) Some pumps offer different suction and cycling settings as well as the ability to pump both breasts at the same time.

Add-ons include battery capability, a professional-looking carrying case with insulated storage compartments, and an adapter that attaches to a car's cigarette lighter. (Yes, mothers can pump while in a car, but we don't recommend that they do so while driving.)

Other useful features include a comfortable breast shield, or funnel, that can be rotated for easier arm positioning. Look for easy-to-clean surfaces, and the ability to attach to regular-sized baby bottles and nipples.

How to choose

KEY DIFFERENCES. Between types, there is a huge difference in the volume of milk pumped in a given time. Large, hospital-grade units and midweight plug-ins are efficient enough for daily use. Battery-operated and manual models are usually more appropriate for occasional use.

RECOMMENDATIONS. If you plan to use a breast pump regularly, rent a hospital-grade pump or buy a midweight plug-in model. You may consider renting a hospital-grade pump for the first two or three months and then buying a less expensive model. Talk to others about what has worked well for them, since you can't return a breast pump after you buy it. Once your baby reaches 4 to 6 months and starts moving toward solids, he can go longer without having to be fed breast milk or formula.

• **Getting help.** For information on pump rentals in your area and referrals to lactation consultants, contact the International Lactation Consultant Association or La Leche League. The hospital where you delivered your baby may have a lactation consultant on staff.

Since using a breast pump can be tricky, most manufacturers now supply informational brochures with their units. You can also call manufacturers' customer-service lines (listed in the Reference section, page 203).

CERTIFICATION. No certification program exists for these products.

Baby formula

Powder or concentrate? Added iron? Your doctor can help you select the best formula for your baby.

While there are clear advantages to breastfeeding, not all mothers can do it. Others choose not to. For them and mothers who decide to supplement breastfeeding, there is baby formula. Usually derived from cow's milk, it provides most but not all of the crucial components of breast milk.

What's available

Formula can be served up in one of three versions: powder, concentrated liquid, and ready-to-feed liquid. The major brands are Carnation Good Start, Enfamil, Isomil, and Similac. Many are generous with free samples, which the hospital will give you when you go home. You'll find store brands at mass merchandisers such as Kmart and Wal-Mart.

When stored as directed, powders are the least expensive option and, when unopened, last the longest. Next in terms of cost are concentrated liquids. Both powders and concentrated liquids require care in measuring the added water. Too little water can produce a mix that, over time, can damage the baby's kidneys. Too much can result in malnutrition or overdilution of the baby's bodily fluids. Ready-to-feed liquid formulas are the most convenient and fastest, but they're also the most expensive. Although the major brands of formula are roughly equal, it's generally recommended that you stick with one brand.

Annual cost of using formula exclusively: $1,500 to $4,000, depending on your baby's nutritional requirements.

How to choose

Your pediatrician is the best source of advice on what to feed your baby. But your baby's needs will drive the choice too. Most formulas contain added iron, while others, such as soy formulas, are for babies allergic to cow's milk. Lactose-free formulas are available for babies who have problems digesting milk sugar. There are also hypoallergenic formulas for problems such as allergies to protein in cow's milk or soy formulas.

Talk to your pediatrician before using any type of bottled water for formula. Bottled water intended for infants must meet standards for tap water established by the Environmental Protection Agency. It may have fluoride added, but too much fluoride can be toxic. The bottles warn against using if your baby is already getting fluoride some other way. Just as with tap water, it's recommended that you boil bottled water for one minute before mixing it with formula. When buying formula, check for the expiration date required by the Food and Drug Administration.

Some mothers decide to supplement breastfeeding with formula. If you decide to go this route, consult your pediatrician on how to proceed. So your milk supply won't run out, breastfeed at a regular time each day, say, for baby's breakfast and at bedtime.

Baby bottles

Styles and colors abound, but your priority should be to find bottles that are easy for baby to hold and easy for you to clean.

Even a breastfed baby will likely need bottles—for pumped breast milk, for a supplementary bottle of formula, and maybe an occasional serving of water or juice. After a baby turns 1 and is weaned from formula or breast-milk, whole cow's milk—usually delivered by bottle—will be a diet staple.

What's available

Your main choices will be standard bottles, angle-neck bottles, and disposable bottles. Bottles are made of clear or semitransparent, colored plastic or glass. You buy nipples separately. You may also see novelty shapes such as animals or footballs. The main makers of baby bottles are Ansa, Evenflo, Gerber, and Playtex.

STANDARD BOTTLES. The classic shape with straight sides, these bottles are easy to fill and hold, can be used repeatedly, and allow you to gauge formula amounts accurately. They also offer many more nipple options compared with disposables. Most breast pumps and all baby-bottle warmers are designed solely for use with standard bottles. There are two sizes: 4 or 5 ounces for infants and 8 or 9 ounces for older babies. Some bottles have compartments that allow you to postpone mixing powdered formula and water until serving time, when you rotate a portion of the top of the bottle. Price range: $1 to $5.

ANGLE-NECK BOTTLES. These bottles are bent at the neck, making them easier for the parent to hold at the correct position. Their shape causes formula to collect at the bottle's nipple end, so baby is less likely to swallow air. Some have straws inside for getting formula from the base of the bottle, which is supposed to reduce air intake. But the straws can be hard to clean. Angle-neck bottles can be awkward to fill—you must hold them sideways or use a special funnel to pour liquid in. Price range: $3 to $4.

DISPOSABLES. With these, a rigid outer holder, called a nurser, holds a disposable plastic pouch, or liner. The liner is inserted into the nurser, with its top edge stretched over the nurser's rim. You pour in formula and hold the liner in place by fastening the nipple, which has to be cleaned after use. Price range: $10 to $12 for a starter set with 4- and 8-ounce holders and liners; 3 to 4 cents each for flat, vinyl liners; 5 to 6 cents for tubular stay-open liners.

How to choose

KEY DIFFERENCES. Disposables spare you the chore of cleaning bottles, but end up costing more than standard or angle-neck bottles. Novelty shapes are relatively hard to clean and can harbor bacteria. Semitransparent colored bottles can be stained by juices. Glass bottles can break.

Bottle warmers: A handy extra

If you're heating formula, an electric bottle warmer can be useful for night feedings when getting to your kitchen is a hassle. Most units run on household current and require you to fill a chamber with water to produce steam. Others use a car's cigarette lighter to produce heat. Bottle warmers work with standard or angle-neck bottles, but usually not disposable bottle systems. Look for a model that has an automatic shut-off to prevent overheating.

RECOMMENDATIONS. Choose the type and material that's most comfortable for you and your baby. You may have to experiment a little. Prices vary markedly. Baby boutiques, supermarkets, and most drugstores charge most, while major discount chains usually offer savings.

• **Storing filled bottles.** Baby formula or breast milk should be refrigerated when it's stored in bottles. Insulated compartments inside diaper bags and breast-pump carrying cases or cooler packs in regular, zippered carrying cases are useful ways of keeping bottles cold while you're away from home. Discard leftover formula after each feeding.

• **Heating bottles.** Formula is fine right out of the refrigerator, but many babies prefer it warmed up. The best way to warm formula is to hold the bottle under a stream of warm water from the faucet. Using a microwave oven to heat bottles can cause uneven hot spots that you may not be able to detect. Shaking the bottle vigorously can help distribute the heat. Never put disposable bottles in the microwave—the plastic liner could explode after it's been removed from the oven, possibly scalding both you and your baby.

Nipples

These vary in shape and materials, with disposable systems using a type different from what standard and angle-neck bottles use.

Nipples are sold separately from bottles. Made of latex or silicone, they come in several shapes: the traditional bell shape, an "orthodontic" design, and a flattened shape just for disposable bottles. Whichever type of nipple you choose, inspect it regularly. For safety's sake, the nipple should be replaced at the first sign of tearing or cracking. Nipples are usually sold in packs of three or six, with the price per nipple ranging from 33 cents for standard bottles to more than $1 for fancier models.

What's available

The major nipple brands are Avent, Evenflo, Fisher-Price, Gerber, and Playtex. Some brands offer slow-, medium-, and fast-flow nipples, which have different sizes of holes. There are special nipples for preemies or newborns. You'll find two materials and three shapes:

LATEX. Amber-colored latex nipples, the most familiar type, are available in both standard and orthodontic shapes, and for both standard (and angle-neck) and disposable bottles. Available in a variety of hole sizes, latex nipples can also be boiled with a toothpick in the hole, which enlarges the opening for better flow.

Latex nipples are sometimes preferred over silicone nipples for newborns because of their flexibility. But they can have the taste and the smell of rubber and tend to swell and crack after two or three months of regular use. (They also tend to whiten when wet, which is harmless.) Saliva, heat, and sunlight can cause them to become sticky and clogged. To clean, use hot soapy water and a bottle brush. They shouldn't be put in the dishwasher.

In rare instances, latex nipples may spark allergic responses in latex-sensitive babies. At risk may be babies who have undergone a lot of surgery or have spina bifida.

SILICONE. Clear, odorless, taste-free, and heat-resistant, silicone is also dishwasher-safe. Being less porous than latex, silicone nipples may be better at resisting bacteria. Because they have a tendency to split and tear, you shouldn't use a bottle brush or nipple brush. The holes in a silicone nipple cannot be enlarged.

STANDARD-SHAPED. This is the traditional bell shape, available with a variety of hole sizes: smaller for newborns and standard for older babies.

Pacifiers: For when baby gets cranky

A pacifier can be useful in soothing a fussy baby. It consists of a latex or silicone nipple mounted on a plastic shield. Two ventilation holes in the shield can admit air if a baby gets the shield caught in the mouth or throat. Some pacifiers have knobs on the back; others have rings. Replace a pacifier every few months.

Available separately are carrying cases as well as short, clip-on ribbons that attach the pacifier to clothing and prevent it from always ending up on the floor.

Use of a pacifier may reduce harmless thumb and finger sucking. (Some experts have theorized that babies have a built-in need for sucking that yields no milk.) But some babies simply don't like pacifiers and will repeatedly spit them out. You'll know your baby's preference after a few tries. Use of a pacifier has been associated with an increased risk of middle ear infections.

The Consumer Product Safety Commission requires that pacifiers be able to pass a "pull test" after boiling and cooling to insure that they won't come apart. All pacifier packages must carry a warning label advising against the use of string to hang a pacifier around a child's neck—a strangulation hazard.

Mouth Wash

Use your hand,
dipped in water,
to wash the face
of a reluctant child.
Most children don't
seem to fight as
much as if you use
a cloth, and you'll
do just as good a job.

ORTHODONTIC. According to manufacturers, these resemble a mother's nipple when it is elongated in the baby's mouth. As the theory goes, this can minimize tongue-thrusting and future bite problems. But these claims have not been substantiated. An hourglass shape makes these nipples harder to clean and may contribute to quicker deterioration. When this nipple weakens, the narrow center may collapse. To get around this problem, some companies have created nipples that are gently rounded with some curvature in the center.

NURSER NIPPLES. Disposable bottles typically use a more flattened nipple that is supposed to resemble a breast. Newer versions feature a softer, more rounded bulb than in the past. You can buy a special brush for latex nurser nipples.

How to choose

KEY DIFFERENCES. Finding the right flow may be a matter of trial and error. A nipple should offer some resistance, but if a nipple is too resistant, your baby has to struggle to get milk. Generally, younger babies prefer a slower flow. Nipples with holes in the rim let you control flow by tightening or loosening the lid. (You need to read the directions on the package.) "Dripless" nipples produce such strong resistance, they may all but block milk flow.

RECOMMENDATIONS. Buy a variety of nipples and experiment until you find shapes and materials that your baby seems to like.

Baby food

At 4 to 6 months of age, babies are ready to start mouthing and chewing solid food. It's a messy but important milestone.

The first solid food that a baby eats is usually a thin gruel consisting of a tablespoon or two of dry infant rice cereal mixed with breast milk or formula. If the baby doesn't demonstrate a food intolerance, you can gradually make the cereal thicker and try oatmeal, barley, wheat, and combinations such as rice and bananas or mixed cereal. At 6 months typically, you can begin to add mashed fruits, vegetables, and meats that you buy in jars or make yourself. Later you can also try bite-sized foods such as Cheerios and pieces of breads, cheeses, and meats cut up for easy chewing. Your pediatrician will be your best source of advice.

What's available

The major brands of baby food are Beech-Nut, Gerber, and Heinz. Earth's Best is an organic line owned by Heinz.

CEREAL. Commercial infant cereal, which comes dry or in jars, is fortified to supplement the nutrients in breast milk or formula. Some cereal has fruit added.

FRUIT, VEGETABLES, MEATS. Mashed fruits—bananas, pears, apples, apricots, peaches—usually have vitamin C added. Vegetables commonly found in baby jars include peas, carrots, squash, and sweet potatoes. Certain vegetables aren't suitable for babies: Spinach and beets contain nitrates in amounts that are too much for a baby, and vegetables such as broccoli and Brussels sprouts may give a baby gas. When it's time to introduce meat, you can try commercial brands of puréed beef, chicken, ham, lamb, turkey, and veal. Products made with meat juices may be labeled "with broth." Meat products with added starches will carry the words "with gravy." A fruit or vegetable is sometimes combined with meat to improve taste or minimize the need to open two jars.

ORGANIC FOOD. Suppliers of organic baby food say their products avoid the use of synthetic pesticides or fertilizers. Animals used for meat products are fed organically grown feed without additives. The products are also supposed to be free of added sugars and starches. An independent organization provides certification.

JUICES. Infant juices are available, although a less expensive option is to give baby adult juice diluted with water. (Citrus juice can upset little stomachs and should be avoided until a child's second birthday.) In addition to fruit-juice basics such as apple and white grape, there are many fruit-juice combinations, some of which contain yogurt and fruit-vegetable blends. Some have added calcium or vitamin C. Go easy, though. Too much juice can cause diarrhea. And when babies drink juice, they may take in less breast milk or formula, which contains the nutrients they really need. Your pediatrician may deem extra liquids necessary in very hot weather.

Commercial brands usually divide baby food into three stages: beginner (stage 1), intermediate (stage 2), and toddler (stage 3).

BEGINNER. Made for babies starting on solids, it's usually a preparation of a single ingredient such as bananas, apples, or carrots, finely puréed for easy swallowing.

INTERMEDIATE. Intended for more experienced eaters, it has a texture that is smooth, but not as fine as beginner foods. You'll also find combinations of ingredients, to add interest: apples and plums, for instance.

TODDLER. For children 9 months and older, this stage offers larger-sized portions to keep up with baby's growing appetite.

How to choose

KEY DIFFERENCES. Baby-food labels are required to indicate ingredients and nutritional values. But beyond that, information is limited to such facts as, say, the percentage of the daily value (DV) that a vitamin or mineral in the baby food provides, and the terms "unsweetened" or "unsalted."

Beginner foods offer the purest ingredients. Sweet potatoes are sweet potatoes and peas are peas, without the addition of sauces or flavoring.

RECOMMENDATIONS. When buying commercial baby food, read the ingredients, nutritional values, and expiration dates listed on the label. All baby-food jars have a depressed area, or "button," in the center of the lid. Reject any jars with the button popped out—an indication that the product has been opened or the seal broken.

• **Making your own.** Homemade baby food is usually simple to prepare. It's often cheaper than commercial offerings and can retain some nutrients destroyed by the high temperatures of commercial processing. It's also a good way to get baby used to your style of home cooking.

You'll need only a fork to mash such foods as bananas or canned pears. A baby-food grinder (found in baby stores), food processor, or blender lets you process more fibrous foods. Boil, bake, or steam first, then purée well. Add cooking water, breast milk, or formula to smooth the texture, but omit butter, oil, sugar, or salt. Don't use honey as sweetening for babies under 1 year old. It can encourage the growth of bacteria related to botulism.

• **Other alternatives.** The canned fruit and vegetable aisles of your supermarket may contain easy, economical alternatives to commercial baby food. Canned pumpkin, for example, is well puréed, as are many types of applesauce (buy without added sugar). You can purée anything further at home. Baby-food cookbooks have suggestions and recipes. Also ask your pediatrician for advice.

CERTIFICATION. The U.S. Department of Agriculture oversees meat, including recalls of foods that include meat, while the Food and Drug Administration oversees other foods.

Chapter 9

Playtime gear

**By far, your baby's favorite 'toy' is you.
Playthings that are engaging and age-appropriate
can add to the fun.**

Toy manufacturers go all out to entice parents and grandparents with new creations that promise to delight children and even turn them into budding prodigies. But you know how kids are. They often prefer to play with the boxes rather than the toys that came in them, and they have been known to walk right past an expensive "smart" toy to snuggle with good old teddy. You'll also find that your baby's favorite means of entertainment—and learning—is interacting with you and other caregivers.

Sharing space with toys in the nursery and all around the house are bigger playthings such as doorway jumpers and "stationary entertainers," also known as "exersaucers," which are replacing walkers as a way for a baby who can't yet walk to play in an upright position. Gates keep baby enclosed in a relatively safe space while playing.

Of course, there's no denying that some toys will delight and entertain your child tremendously. The trick is figuring out which ones. Shopping for playthings is a treat for parents, as you try out new gizmos and perhaps pick up new versions of your own childhood favorites.

Contents

Toys

Playthings that appeal to a little one's eyes, ears, and sense of touch will be the most intriguing. Safety and durability are key concerns.

When you shop for toys, your baby's level of development will help you determine what's appropriate. Rattles and teething rings are for the youngest babies, whose grasping skills are primitive. Mobiles that suspend toys and objects over the crib are for those too young to sit up. Once babies have gained some hand control, sorting toys can help them learn about shapes and dimensions. Stacking toys, blocks, and activity boxes help them practice hand-eye coordination.

Many toys have brilliant color schemes, with vivid primary colors as well as high-contrast black and white. Because babies are drawn to the pattern of the human face, many toys sport eyes and noses. Unbreakable mirrors are often embedded in toys so babies can coo over their own images.

Babies experience much of their world through sucking, so expect that most toys will go straight to the mouth. As babies' hand skills develop, toys will be touched, clutched, and pounded. Household objects such as car keys, TV remote controls, and spoons can be more interesting than "real" toys.

Toddlers love ritualistic play—repeating the same activities over and over, including stacking and restacking small play figures or blocks. Push and pull toys are also favorites. Surprises, such as unexpected sounds or motions, are appealing as long as they aren't *too* surprising. Toddlers also love to play in the bath, so there are a whole host of bathtub animals, sprayers, cups, and other toys for soapy fun.

What's available

Safety and a good fit with your child's current skills are two essentials. In "Playtime options," page 115, you'll see toys that demonstrate positive, baby-captivating features as well as safe construction and realistic demands on baby's capabilities. The box on the opposite page outlines the kinds of toys available and appropriate for each age range.

Look for the manufacturer's recommended age range on the front of the toy package—such as "6 months to 1 year"—and take it seriously. More than a friendly hint, such a guideline can alert you to a possible choking hazard, the presence of small parts, or the need for skills and judgment that your child might not yet have.

Match toys to baby's play stage

Babies move through a series of distinct developmental stages as they mature. The best (and safest) toys match a child's level of interest and evolving body skills. Here's a look at children's maturing play skills and age-appropriate toys.

BIRTH TO 3 MONTHS

Baby enjoys looking at the world around him—lights, shapes, patterns, and colors. He moves his arms and legs, opens and closes his hands, swipes at objects, and tries to reach for them. Hearing is fully developed.

Suggested toys: Those with high-contrast patterns such as simple faces; musical crib mobiles with objects or patterns that face baby; toys with mirrors for reflecting light; rattles that make interesting noises; and hanging toys to bat. For safe mouthing, there should be no sharp edges or small parts that can detach.

4 TO 8 MONTHS

Baby can now reach for and grasp objects, move them from one hand to the other, and play with her feet. She will search for the source of sounds.

Suggested toys: Floor gyms; textured soft toys that can be safely mouthed; soft balls with sounds inside; musical toys and rattles; chewable vinyl or cloth baby books; and toys with flaps or lids that can be opened and closed.

9 TO 23 MONTHS

Baby plays by shaking, banging, throwing, and dropping toys; searching for hidden objects; taking objects out of containers; and poking into holes with his fingers.

Suggested toys: Stacking and building gadgets with rounded edges; bath and squeeze toys; soft dolls and puppets; lightweight balls; baby books; musical toys and toy telephones; and push-pull playthings such as toy cars and trucks.

BY 2 YEARS

A toddler can build block towers (and enjoys knocking them down). She also likes playing with large balls, can turn pages of a book, and can sort things. She is interested in toys that can be taken apart and put back together, and likes to play make-believe with toy animals and dolls.

Suggested toys: Cardboard books; blocks; nesting toys and simple sorting toys; buckets and shovels; dolls; balls; child-sized trucks, cars, and trains; bath toys; swings; toy telephones; and children's keyboards.

BY 3 YEARS

At this stage, a child can climb, kick balls, pedal a tricycle, and turn handles. He enjoys drawing with crayons and building with blocks. Other fun things he can do include playing make-believe with toy figures and animals, sorting objects by shape and color, and solving simple puzzles.

Suggested toys: Building blocks; puzzles with knobs; art supplies such as clay, crayons, and paper; props for make-believe; dolls and stuffed animals; and outdoor play equipment.

Continued on page 122

How to choose

KEY DIFFERENCES. It's all about fun—and safety. Some toys—building blocks, for example—encourage infants and toddlers to experience new textures and new uses for their hands, mouths, and feet. Others elicit a relatively passive response. Battery-operated toys containing musical chips are widely sold, but the novelty for baby and you is likely to wear off quickly.

Poorly constructed inexpensive toys—the kind sometimes sold in drugstores, service stations, airports, and dollar-buys-all stores—are no bargain. Flimsy plastic toys often have small parts that can break off easily, or sharp edges that can be dangerous.

RECOMMENDATIONS. When choosing, consider the classics such as stackable "doughnuts," shaper sorters, and interlocking plastic "beads"— there's a reason they've been around so long. Ask other parents for suggestions. Browse stores, catalogs, and web sites for ideas. Used toys, especially solid, molded-plastic items, are a great buy. Thrift stores, consignment shops, and yard and garage sales often have toys in excellent condition.

Carefully check every toy yourself before giving it to your child to see that it's well made and safe. Keep toys out of the crib, and if you use a mobile, remove it from the crib as soon as your baby tries to pull up.

Follow manufacturers' age recommendations to hold baby's interest, as well as to ensure safety. You may think that a more "advanced" toy will present a welcome challenge. But in reality, a plaything that surpasses a

Toy safety: Know the basics

All toys sold in this country have to meet federal safety standards. Teethers and squeeze toys must be large enough not to pose choking hazards. The same goes for rattles, which also must be designed so they can't separate into small pieces.

Labels on crib gyms and mobiles warn parents to remove them when baby can push up on his hands and knees (about 6 months). Every toy must have a low level of lead in any paint and smooth surfaces rather than sharp points and edges. No small parts that could fall out and become a choking risk (including small balls and marbles) are allowed on playthings for children under age 3.

Other items on the safety checklist: no pinching parts; no small wires that could poke through; no strings, cords, or necklaces that could capture a baby's neck.

Playtime options

This sampling gives you an idea of toys that are fun and safe. Age recommendations are those of the manufacturers. Retail prices vary widely, so the price listed here may not match what you'll encounter.

▲ **Tiny Love Symphony-In-Motion Mobile** *(Model 00496, $45, birth to 5 months)*

A complex, battery-operated mobile that plays Bach, Beethoven, and Mozart and makes quirky movements with bright toys, spirals, and balls. Runs on 3 AA batteries (not included).

International Playthings Earl E. Bird *(Model E00102, $13, birth and up)* ▶

A cheerful fabric bird with teething rings, crinkles, squeaks, knobs, and textures.

▲ **Lamaze First Mirror by Learning Curve** *(Model 97105, $20, birth and up)*

This removable, nonbreakable mirror fastens onto a colorful, fabric-covered foam wedge that's the right height for crawling babies.

Tiny Love 1-2-3 Discovery Lane
(Model 00470, $49, 3 to 18 months)
This play mat unfolds from a tent shape to a curving crawl path with a mirror, crinkling squeeze toys, a water mat with play fish inside, and other shapes and sounds.

International Playthings Fire Engine *(Model 02018, $19, 18 months and up)* ▶
This toy opens up to reveal a driving set with a small steering wheel. When closed, it's a pushable fire truck with a siren.

▲ **Chicco Crank Spin N' Sort**
(Model 66101, $15, 1 to 4 years)
Six shaped blocks fit into individual holes in a bucket with a handle. When shapes are in their proper holes, knobs on each side rotate to release the blocks into a container with a trap door.

◀ Fisher-Price Activity Table *(Model 71138, $23, 9 months and up)*

One side of this play-activity table is for building with stackable blocks, while the other offers multiple activities including a drop-through chute, squeaking buttons, and more.

Fisher-Price Activity Walker *(Model 71040, $23, 6 months and up)* ▶

This walk-and-play toy on wheels has a knobbed handlebar, colorful flip tables, a telephone dial, beads, and a mirror.

◀ Discovery Toys Stack and Learn Sensory Tower *(Model 1514, $15, 12 months and up)*

Five rings of different colors, rattling sounds, and textures stack onto a self-standing, rounded rod.

▲ **Tiny Love Gymini Deluxe Noah's Ark**
(Model 00801, $49, birth to 10 months)

Soft, foldable arches and play mat with a suspended turtle mirror, whale rattle, musical sea horse, rainbow with bell rattle, and other activities for baby to watch and bat.

▼ **Kids II Shake N Spin** *(Model 829-12, $3, birth and up)*

A fist-sized colorful teether and rattle combines textures, rattles, and clicks.

◄ **Infantino Primary Colors Decorative Sky Wall Mobile (Model 159068, $20, 3 months and up)**

A colorful fabric mobile and mirror with fabric smiley faces hangs over baby's diaper table.

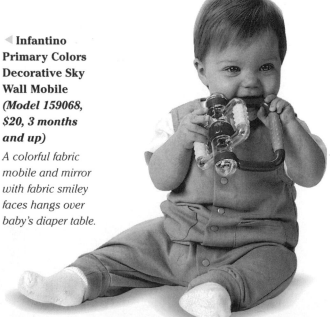

▲ **Step 2 Kangaroo Climber** *(Model 7904, $110, 18 months to 4 years)*

An activity gym for indoors or outdoors with a crawl-through tunnel, Dutch door, and slide. Dismantles for storage.

◄ **International Play-things Squeak E. Mouse (Model E00503, $30, 18 months and up)**

A doll to teach dressing skills using its shirt, shorts, shoes, zippered and buttoned vest, and small backpack.

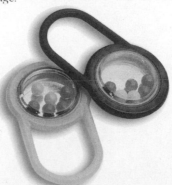

◄ **First Years Shake & See Rattle (Model 2151, $2, birth and up)**

Multicolored balls circle inside a mirrored rattle with a soft, chewy handle.

Lamaze Lion and Ellie Footfinders by Learning Curve *(Model 97229, 3 months to 12 months, $8)* ▶

A lion and an elephant on the tips of play booties that rattle.

▼ **Fisher-Price First Words Phone** *(Model 71654, $13, ages 6 months and up)*

A pretend cordless phone with music, a computerized voice, lights, volume control and on/off button (3 AA batteries not included).

▲ **Brio Ted & Tess Carousel** *(Model 31021, $115, 6 months and up)*

A red, green, and yellow spinner that rotates small smiling bears inside when the top handle is pressed.

▶ North American Bear So-o-o Big Bear Mobile *(Model 1770, $54, birth to 5 months)*

Small bears in striped jammies look down and spin while a music box plays "Row, Row, Row Your Boat."

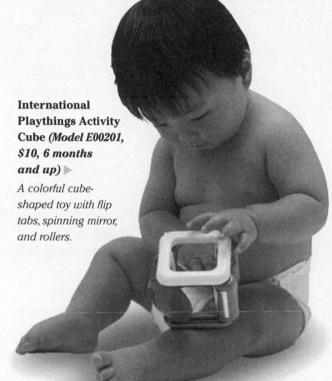

International Playthings Activity Cube *(Model E00201, $10, 6 months and up)* ▶

A colorful cube-shaped toy with flip tabs, spinning mirror, and rollers.

▼ Lamaze Discovery Farm by Learning Curve *(Model 97704, $13, birth to 9 months)*

A soft book for baby with play animals inside that make noises.

Continued from page 114

child's current stage of development will be more of a source of frustration than pleasure (one reason why a baby may turn away from what's offered to clutch a familiar favorite).

• **Size.** Babies love putting things in their mouths. They can't help themselves. But small objects can pose choking hazards. You can test an item for safe size by slipping it through the tube of a toilet-paper roll (about 1¾ inches in diameter). If the toy passes through, it's too small for baby to play with.

• **Durability.** All baby toys should be unbreakable. Stuffed animals or any toys made of fabric should be washable and bite-proof. Pull on fur to be sure it won't shed, and see that fabrics are heavy enough to keep stuffing inside. Look for anything else that could be bitten or chewed off: hard, sewn-on parts, such as eyes, buttons, or wheels, and soft, small pieces, such as strings, ribbons, and stuffed animals' ears. Dyes should be colorfast.

CERTIFICATION. The Consumer Product Safety Commission regulates toys sold in the U.S. They must have acceptably low levels of lead in paint. If they're glass or metal, they must have smooth surfaces. Toys meant for children under 3 may not have small parts that could pose a choking, ingestion, or inhalation hazard. In recent years, the CPSC has recalled some models of rattles, mobiles, and toys that are parts of other products such as walkers. A certified toy meets the minimum requirements of the American Society for Testing and Materials' voluntary standard, and its manufacturer participates in the pass/fail certification program administered by the Toy Industry Association.

Walkers

A walker gives a baby a set of wheels—maybe before he's ready to cope with the consequences of fast-paced mobility.

A walker is a molded plastic frame with a baby seat suspended in the center and wheels attached to the base. It's designed to allow baby to get around by pushing with her feet. The typical age range for using this device is 6 to 15 months, when the child can sit up unassisted, but before she can walk well on her own.

Walkers are problematic for various reasons. Despite the word "walker," the device doesn't help a baby acquire walking skills. It calls for a set of

Feedback

Take a picture of your child playing with or wearing a gift received from a relative or friend, and send it as a thank-you note to the gift giver.

leg and back movements that is entirely different from what is needed for crawling or balancing on two feet. When a baby stays in the upright position demanded by a walker's seat rather than crawling around, the strengthening of thigh and back muscles that are critical for walking may be delayed. But more important, wheeled walkers pose a significant risk of injury because they let a baby be mobile in ways beyond her coping. A walker can fall down stairways or steps between levels; turn over when wheels get snagged; roll against stoves and heaters; and, outdoors, fall over curbs and into swimming pools. Safety gates can be helpful, but they aren't a guarantee of safety. Many accidents involving walkers occur despite the presence of safety gates—either because the gates were closed incorrectly or they didn't hold up to the impact of the walker.

For all of these reasons, even though a voluntary safety standard was created for walkers in 1997, the American Academy of Pediatrics continues to urge banning their manufacture and sale. To comply with the safety standard, a walker must either be too wide to fit through a standard doorway, or have features, such as a friction strip made of rubberized material on the bottom, that stop the walker if its wheels drop away at the edge of a step.

What's available

The major brands are Baby Trend, Cosco, Graco, Kolcraft, and Safety 1st. Also called "mobile entertainers," walkers come in different shapes—circular, rectangular, square, and even styled like a small car. There are typically four to eight wheels on the base. Walkers usually don't have seat belts, even though it's possible for a baby to fall or climb out of them. Price range: $30 to $70.

Features to consider

A friction strip touches the floor when the wheels fall away on stairs or uneven pavement, making it difficult for a baby to push the walker forward. Gravity may still prevail at the top of the stairs, though. Most walkers that meet the voluntary safety standard have a friction strip.

A parking stand generally allows wheels to be lifted off the floor to limit baby's scooting. Seat height can be raised or lowered, using either a locking mechanism located under the front tray, slots in the base of the walker, or adjusters on the inside of the seat. Some models offer a bouncing feature. Seats may be removable for laundering. Most walkers have rimmed trays, often with toys attached, some of which are equipped with lights and/or

○ Note that stationary entertainers are safer.

○ Look for a walker with a friction strip underneath.

○ Inspect any toys suspended from a walker.

Talk

Get your child a
toy phone to talk
on while you're
on the real one.

electronic sounds. Toys are sometimes suspended from a removable, "U"-shaped frame. Many models, especially larger ones, fold for storage.

How to choose

KEY DIFFERENCES. Most of the manufacturers that have decided to meet the voluntary standard have opted for the friction strip on the base, but it's not a failsafe design. Note that even a certified model may still pose a risk.

RECOMMENDATIONS. Consider safer alternatives, such as stationary entertainers (see below). They offer equal or greater play value than a walker, and much greater safety. If you decide to buy a walker, consider the layout of your home. If you're concerned about containing your baby in a room with standard doorways, try to find a model with an extra-wide base. Even if your walker has a friction strip, consider using it only in a room with no access to stairs leading down.

A walker should be used on a flat surface that is free of objects such as dangling cords that could cause it to tip over. It should not be used near any source of heat, such as a stove, or near water, such as a swimming pool. Both feet of the child in the walker should touch the floor or ground. Never leave a child in a walker unattended or out of sight. Examine attached toys for size (they should be too large to fit through the tube of a toilet-paper roll, about 1¾ inches in diameter) and look for small parts that can break off or screws that can loosen.

CERTIFICATION. Located somewhere on a walker's frame or packaging, a certification sticker shows that the walker meets the minimum requirements of the American Society for Testing and Materials' voluntary standard and that its manufacturer participates in the pass/fail certification program administered by the Juvenile Products Manufacturers Association. There may also be a label that says something to the effect of "Meets new ASTM safety standard for steps and stairs" or "Meets new ASTM standard for walkers." Walkers are also subject to federal standards regulating small parts.

Stationary entertainers

Because they lack wheels, these play stations are safer alternatives to walkers. They can help keep baby amused when you need your hands free.

Also known as "exersaucers" or "exercisers," these all-in-one, molded-plastic play stations resemble walkers—but without the wheels. That makes them a safer choice. Most stationary entertainers have a circular frame with a rotating, high-backed seat recessed in the center, and a surrounding flat tray at the top with a variety of fastened-on toys. Babies can use them as soon as they can sit up independently (at about 6 months) and will outgrow them when they become fairly confident walkers (between 12 and 15 months). The heaviest use will likely be between 8 and 10 months. Some of the drawbacks of walkers remain, though. Like them, entertainers force your baby to maintain an erect posture that does nothing to help him learn to crawl or walk.

Some stationary entertainers can convert to other types of baby gear as baby grows into the toddler years. With a few adjustments, one model becomes a child's table. Another design can be transformed from a stationary entertainer into a floor play set for toddlers, with a small track for cars and a set of farm toys.

What's available

The major brands are Cosco, Fisher Price, Graco, Kolcraft, and Safety 1st. Models come with a solid flat base, a rocking base, or freestanding legs. Units are typically 26 inches in diameter and 26 inches tall and may fold for storage. Some entertainers are barebones, with only a few toys, while others are more elaborate, with maybe six or more play items vying for baby's attention. Although piling on the toys seems like a good idea, simpler models may offer baby more visibility, more tray space for handheld toys or feeding, easier cleaning, and less confusion. As with walkers, there usually isn't a seat belt even though it's possible for a baby to fall or climb out of the units. In addition to plain entertainers, there are hybrid units that can convert to doorway jumpers. Price range: $40 to $85.

Features to consider

Most entertainers have seats that swivel 360 degrees, legs that contain springs allowing the unit to bounce when baby moves, and push-down tabs that anchor the seat in a stationary position when you're feeding baby. Seat heights are adjustable to three or four levels. More expensive models have thicker seat padding and come loaded with toys. Seat pads are often removable for cleaning.

All entertainers feature a play tray with attached interactive toys, such as a spinning ball, mirrors, clackers, and rings. You'll also find models that come with soft toys and electronic toys that produce sounds and lights. Some models have a detachable keyboard/soundmaker.

How to choose

KEY DIFFERENCES. The better stationary entertainers have a thick, sturdy frame; no sharp edges or hardware underneath or on top; comfortable, soft fabric edging on the sides and legs of the seat cushions; sturdy fasteners for the seat; and well-designed, well-secured toys for little hands. The seat should swivel smoothly without any hitches, and there should be no gaps in the rim between the edge of swivel mechanism and the tray that could conceivably capture small fingers. Spending more money will get you a stationary entertainer with many toys and battery-operated sounds.

RECOMMENDATIONS. Stationary entertainers with a solid, flat base are the most stable. Avoid models that can't be anchored in a stationary position. Models with freestanding legs can inch across the floor, or "walk," if the child inside bounces around enough. A rocking base can shift as baby rocks (some rocking models have a push-down tab that stops the motion).

Examine attached toys for size (they should be too large to fit through the center of a toilet-paper roll, about 1¾ inches in diameter) and for small parts that can break off.

Although most babies enjoy being in an entertainer, some don't. If you can, borrow a unit from a friend to let your child try it out before you buy.

Stationary entertainers shouldn't be used for more than 30 minutes at a time to avoid taxing baby's weak back and leg muscles. A baby should never use a stationary entertainer without supervision.

CERTIFICATION. Although no certification program exists for stationary entertainers, they are subject to the federal regulation of small parts. A voluntary standard is being developed. Some models of entertainers have been recalled in recent years. Problems have included sharp edges on seats and toys that can expose sharp hardware.

Doorway jumpers

These bouncy baby seats are suspended from a door frame and are only usable if you have solid, well-secured molding around your doorways.

Jumpers are designed to be hung by a clamp from the top of a door frame that matches a manufacturer's size specifications. Springs or bungee-style cords suspend the seat from the clamp so prewalking babies can jiggle themselves up and down when they press down on the floor. The doorway clamp resembles an ice hook and has nonslip tips. Doorway jumpers are geared for babies from 5 months to walking age (12 to 15 months).

Like stationary entertainers and walkers, jumpers require baby to stay in an upright position, which does nothing to strengthen thigh and back muscles critical to crawling or walking. And while some infants enjoy jumpers, some actually get "seasick" from the motion. Jumper dangers arise when straps or clamps break, allowing the apparatus to fall. Babies may also bump into the sides of the door frame, either because vigorous jumping causes them to bob around, or because a sibling tries to swing the baby.

What's available

The major brands are Cosco, Evenflo, Fisher-Price, Graco, and Jolly Jumper. In addition to plain doorway jumpers, there are hybrid units that can convert to stationary entertainers. Jumpers usually lack seat belts, but there is little likelihood of the child falling or climbing out. Price range: $25 to $35.

Features to consider

Jumpers have straps that adjust to a child's "jumping height." Most have a removable, washable seat. Some feature support bars in the front and back of the seat, while others have solid, molded frames that encircle the baby. Those with frames usually have some type of bumpers to help protect woodwork. There might be a small tray to hold toys or snacks.

How to choose

KEY DIFFERENCES. You'll find differences in quality of the construction of the springs, suspension cords, supports, and seat. Not all door frames are constructed in a way that can adequately support a doorway jumper.

RECOMMENDATIONS. If you decide to use a jumper, buy one with specifications that match your door frame. Inspect the jumper every time you put baby inside to be sure the straps are securely fastened and the clamp will hold. Limit jumping time to 15 minutes at a stretch, so baby doesn't become nauseated. Pushing a jumper as if it were a swing can cause the baby to strike the side of the doorway.

CERTIFICATION. Although no certification program exists for jumpers, they are subject to the federal regulation of small parts.

Shopping checklist

JUMPERS

◯ Buy a unit with sturdy straps, clamps, and hardware.

◯ Make sure the door frame fits the jumper's specifications.

◯ Match unit's age and weight range with your baby.

Baby gates

A gate can keep a baby in a relatively safe area or out of a dangerous one. But install it carefully, and be aware of its limitations.

Gates that fit into doorways are often used to protect curious, exploration-oriented toddlers. They're designed to restrain children ages 2 or younger. Because gates can be pushed down or dislodged, you should consider one only as a supplemental safety measure.

What's available

The major brands are Evenflo, First Years, Fisher-Price, and Safety 1st. Gates are attached to doorways in two ways: pressure-mounted and hardware-mounted. Some gates are made with wood slats, similar to old-fashioned accordion-style models, but with top and bottom rails. Some are constructed with a frame and bars made of enamel-coated tubular steel. Gates of plastic or wire mesh may be framed with end tubes and top rails of either wood or coated metal. A few gates are made with transparent plastic center panels.

PRESSURE-MOUNTED GATES. These gates usually have two sliding panels that adjust to make the gate fit the doorway. A pressure bar or some other locking mechanism wedges the gate into place against the wall. Originally, pressure gates were designed for doorways measuring between 28 and 32 inches. Most houses and apartments have wider door openings, so manufacturers now offer elongated models—some as wide as 48 or even 60 inches. Some models have optional extensions that you have to purchase separately.

Pressure-mounted gates are useful in areas where falling is not a major concern, such as in a doorway separating two areas, or at the bottom of a stairway to discourage a child from venturing upstairs.

Although easy to install, this type is also fairly easy to dislodge. Even the most stable pressure-mounted gate will work loose over time. Manufacturers now recommend that a pressure-mounted gate should not be used at the top of steps or a stairway.

Price range: $20 to $90.

HARDWARE-MOUNTED GATES. If properly secured to the door jamb with the supplied plates and screws, these

A pressure-mounted gate is easy to install but also fairly easy to dislodge.

are the more secure choice for a baby. You must drill holes into the woodwork to install them, but you can fill in the holes with putty when you no longer use the gate. Many of these gates can be easily removed from the mounting hardware for times when you want the doorway free. And they may be installed so they will swing open only one way—such as away from the stairs—for maximum safety. Price range: $25 to $110.

SPECIALTY GATES. These are made to adjust to uneven baseboards, or have extra hardware to attach to things such as wrought-iron railings or wooden newel posts.

Features to consider

Gate safety depends on solid construction, reliable hardware, and the absence of entrapment hazards.

CONSTRUCTION. The finish should be even and the construction sturdy. Surfaces should be smooth, splinter-free, and fashioned with rounded rather than sharply squared edges. Vertical slats or bars should be no more than 2⅜ inches apart. Gates should not have openings or protrusions at the top edge that might snag clothing or necklaces.

HEIGHT. To prevent an adventurous child from climbing over, a gate must stand a minimum of three-quarters of the child's height. Most gates measure 22 inches or more from the floor. When a child is taller than 36 inches or weighs more than 30 pounds (typically about 2 years), a gate is no longer adequate.

LATCHES. A certified gate is required to have a latching mechanism that requires two actions to release. Often a dual-action latch can be opened with one adult hand. There are different types of latches. A gate with a squeezing mechanism opens by compressing parts of the gate, but such a latch can be uncomfortable to use, so test it in the store. Other options include a pressure-release handle and one that lifts up. Some models use a foot pedal—but it requires strong pressure to release. A battery-operated model opens electronically, with a wall-mounted switch.

How to choose

KEY DIFFERENCES. Hardware-mounted gates are safer than pressure-mounted, but no gate can be guaranteed to keep a child in or out. Metal is more durable than wood. Some metal gates have a support bar that crosses the floor beneath the gate, which could cause tripping when the gate is closed.

○ Use the hardware-mounted type to block the top of a stairway.

○ Use the pressure-mounted type for same-level areas or the bottom of a stairway.

○ Look for a gate with a top rail and without "V"s or protrusions.

○ Choose fine mesh over mesh with wide openings.

○ Try to find an easy-to-operate dual-action latching mechanism.

RECOMMENDATIONS. For shielding stairs and steps, choose a hardware-mounted gate that can swing away from the stairway. Pressure-mounted gates are suitable for separating rooms on the same level.

Any gate should have a flat top rim and smooth hardware. If you choose a model with mesh panels, look for a fine weave—wide-holed mesh may provide a foothold for climbing.

Take width measurements of the doorway opening along with you when you shop. Follow mounting instructions carefully. Frequently check hardware where it attaches to the gate and wall. Loose hardware not only makes a gate less effective, but can be a choking risk. Keep large toys, such as stuffed animals or riding toys, away from the gate so they can't be used as step stools.

• **Gates to avoid.** Old-fashioned, accordion-style wooden gates that open to form diamond-shaped spaces with wide "V"s at the top are an entrapment hazard. Such gates have not been manufactured for more than 15 years, but you may still encounter one at a garage sale. If you have this type of gate, replace it with a new model.

• **Gate alternatives.** You might consider installing an actual door, a screen door, or a half-door with a latch out of your child's reach and a strong self-closing mechanism. As a safeguard for small fingers, look for a pneumatic or hydraulic door-closer that comes with a pressure adjustment to prevent slamming.

CERTIFICATION. Located somewhere on the frame or packaging, a certification sticker shows that the gate meets the minimum requirements of the American Society for Testing and Materials' voluntary standard and that its manufacturer participates in the pass/fail certification program administered by the Juvenile Products Manufacturers Association. The standard addresses issues including the size of typical doorway openings, gate height, and strength of top rails and framing components. A certified gate must have a dual-action latching mechanism and a permanent label warning that the gate is designed only for children 6 months to 2 years, that consumers should follow manufacturers' instructions, and that using a gate won't necessarily prevent all accidents.

Some gates have been recalled in recent years. Problems have included plastic parts that break, posing choking hazards.

Recording baby's first year

New technology and old reliables help you mark the milestones and chronicle everyday joys.

Each new day of year one can bring an exciting baby event, from first smile to first tooth to first step. You'll want to get ready now to capture each memory.

Most people have a baby book tucked away somewhere that their parents lovingly filled with snips of hair, lists of visitors to the hospital, and the minutiae from the first trips to the doctor. These days, even with all the high-tech ways now available to mark baby's progress, there's still something very satisfying about taping mementos into a baby book and filling in the blanks. Most baby books have spaces for snapshots, and some feature a dental chart so you can mark the date of each new tooth, or an attached envelope where you can tuck a lock of baby's hair.

If you're so busy with baby's milestones that you have little time to write about them, you may want to use a first-year calendar, which you can fill in with stickers designed to mark each event. Such a calendar is also an

Contents

excellent way to involve an older sibling in keeping track of baby's progress. You can buy baby books and first-year calendars at greeting-card, stationery, and baby stores.

In addition to these familiar old favorites, today's parents have resources and options from the World Wide Web that previous generations never dreamed of. For instance, some parenting web sites allow you to create your own customized birth announcements. You supply a digital photo (or let the site convert your standard film to a digital format), fill in the announcement form, and provide an e-mail list. Family and friends who receive the e-mail can ooh and ahh. Going a step further, some hospitals offer to announce your newborn's arrival with a free webcast, using technology called streaming media. During a live, real-time broadcast via the web, family and friends can see the new addition in your hospital room (see "A webcast featuring your baby," page 143).

Many parents post photos on a personal web site. Web portals such as Yahoo! or Lycos and other services have information on how to set one up. Of course, you can also e-mail photos to Internet-connected family and friends. New film-developing options mean you don't even need a digital camera—just ask for digital storage when you drop off your film.

Home movies—those grainy, jumpy productions of yesteryear—have been replaced by home videos that you can edit and embellish with music using your PC and play back on your VCR, or even turn into QuickTime shorts for sending online.

CONSUMER REPORTS regularly tests the equipment you need to record baby's first years. We've found that today's gear—cameras, digital cameras, and camcorders—generally provide very good results. Although your child will grow fast, you can create a lasting record you'll always cherish.

Film cameras

**Today's point-and-shoot cameras are convenient,
easy to use, and produce very pleasing photographs.**

Film cameras are mature products that have attained a fairly high level of quality. Nearly all can produce snapshots of tots that are sharp and properly focused and have little distortion or other drawbacks. In addition, with film cameras, it's possible to get some of the benefits of digital cameras. When you drop off a roll for processing, simply ask for the photos to be stored digitally, on a floppy disk or a photo CD. Other options include scanning negatives or prints using a scanner and computer.

What's available

Major camera brands include Canon, Fuji, Kodak, Minolta, Nikon, Olympus, and Pentax. Most make point-and-shoot cameras in both 35mm and APS (Advanced Photo System) formats. Many also make SLR (single-lens reflex) 35mm cameras, larger cameras that use interchangeable lenses and let you see exactly what the lens sees.

All three types of camera handle focusing, exposure, and shutter-speed settings automatically. Flashes are built into practically all point-and-shoot models and some SLR models. The lowest-priced film cameras are fixed-focus, like an old-fashioned box camera. Many of these are "disposable" models, for which you send in the entire camera to a lab to get the film developed.

COMPACT 35MM CAMERAS. Small, light, and inexpensive, these cameras are capable of producing exceptional photos. Since you don't have to worry about focus or lighting, you can just grab the camera and snap the shot—handy when baby suddenly performs a feat you simply must get on film.

Because you don't see exactly what the camera sees when you look through the viewfinder, you may have some trouble framing the shot so it contains exactly what you want, with no cut-off heads or noses. But point-and-shoot cameras are perfectly adequate for snapshots. And if you request digital storage when you have the film processed, you can then crop and edit the shots with computer software.

Price range: $6 to $12 for a single-use camera; $20 and up for fixed-focus models; $60 and up for automatic, nonzoom cameras; $80 and up for a model with a zoom lens.

APS CAMERAS. Advanced Photo System cameras closely resemble 35mm point-and-shoot models, but with one important difference: They use a unique film cartridge that holds the film at all times, from loading to shooting to processing. The film frames are slightly smaller than 35 mm, but the cameras make the most of each frame. You can get an APS camera to make a normal snapshot ("S" in APS parlance), a slightly wider view ("H"), or a panorama ("P"). You can change from one view to another with each new frame. And whenever you order reprints, you can order

Special

Ask your older child to take care of something special for you while you're in the hospital— perhaps a scarf or a piece of jewelry.

different views—a panoramic version of a standard shot, for example.

Each APS film cartridge has a unique number on it. The negatives are returned in the same cartridge, along with an index print.

Most APS cameras have autofocus and a zoom lens. There are very few single-use APS models.

Price: A few dollars more than comparable 35mm models.

35MM SLR CAMERAS. Bulkier than point-and-shoot models, SLR cameras not only offer the option of interchangeable lenses, but also let you see what the camera sees. With an SLR, you can compose a shot precisely.

The generally high-quality optics deliver the best image quality. If your SLR has both autofocus and a built-in flash, it can be as quick to use as a point-and-shoot camera.

Price range: $200 and up for the camera body; $100 and up for a moderate-range zoom lens.

Features to consider

A zoom lens, available on many models, will magnify your subject two to four times. A 3x lens zooms from about 35 mm (for a fairly wide angle) to about 105 mm (for a moderate telephoto). Generally, the higher the zoom ratio (4x as opposed to 2x) and the larger the maximum aperture, the higher the cost of a zoom lens.

Aperture, indicated by the f-number, governs how wide the camera will open the lens when you take a photo. (The smaller the f-number, the larger the opening.) A wider aperture allows more light to reach the film, so it can increase your odds of taking good pictures indoors without a flash, using a given speed of film and shutter speed. A wider aperture also raises the price of the camera.

Shutter speed determines how long the aperture stays open during a single shot. A fast shutter speed (1/1000 to 1/8000 of a second or so) lets you photograph a moving subject, such as a toddler on the go.

Programmed auto exposure, common on all but the cheapest models, allows the camera to regulate both the shutter speed and the aperture to achieve a properly exposed photo, in either bright or low light. An exposure-compensation feature lets you compensate for any brightness differences between the background and the subject to prevent underexposure when the background is bright—that sunny day in the park, for example—or overexposure when it's unusually dark. SLRs and more advanced compact models may also offer several preset exposure modes that suit various situations.

Autofocus lets you obtain crisp images without having to manually focus. Low-end cameras typically cover preset ranges, permitting quick shots but dispensing with the more precise focusing of higher-priced models. Multiarea autofocus reduces the risk of focusing on the background of a scene by accident. Focus lock lets you freeze the focus onto whatever appears at the center of the viewfinder. This means you can keep the focus on baby, while you move around to change the angle of the shot. Compact film cameras typically use an infrared beam to focus. In-the-viewfinder signals in many models will let you know when your subject is too close to be in focus or when you've gone out of flash range.

Built-in flashes cover various distances, from 4 or 5 feet to 10 feet or more. The smartest ones track with the zoom lens to broaden or narrow the beam. A fill-flash setting lets you fill in harsh shadows in sunlit portraits.

"Red eye" occurs when a flash reflects off your subject's retinas. Since you'll want to capture those baby blues or big browns, you might look for red-eye reduction, which typically uses a light before the main flash to constrict the subject's pupils. A flash located farther from the lens reduces red eye. (You can easily retouch a print to eliminate red eye, using a black fine-point marker or a special red-eye correction pen. If you opt for digital storage, you may be able to remove red eye as you edit the photos on your computer.)

Motorized film handling automatically advances the film, then rewinds it when you reach the end of the roll. With a 35mm camera, you drop in the film, pull out the leader, and close the camera; with APS, you merely drop in the cartridge. Mid-roll change, a feature found in some APS cameras, lets you reload partially-exposed rolls of film—useful if you often switch between different film speeds.

A self-timer delays the shutter so you can be in the picture yourself. Certain models offer a wireless remote shutter release. Another common add-on is date-stamping, which imprints photos with the date they were taken.

How to choose

KEY DIFFERENCES. Point-and-shoot cameras, whether they take 35mm or APS film, have attained a fairly high level of quality. Of course, the cameras don't perform identically. SLR cameras show you exactly what will appear

Lullaby

Tape-record the sound of a running dishwasher, a running shower, or water filling the tub, and play it back to lull a child to sleep.

on film. Even the best point-and-shoot cameras show only about 90 percent of the area that actually appears. Despite the smaller size of their negatives, APS cameras often produce prints as clear as those from 35mm cameras, particularly if they aren't enlarged greatly.

Don't expect too much from the built-in flash that's standard on point-and-shoot cameras. External-flash units (such as the detachable ones available for some compacts and SLRs) provide more light for your subject than do the built-in flashes.

RECOMMENDATIONS. Spending more gets you more features and often better optics. Nevertheless, you can expect a fairly high level of quality from 35mm point-and-shoot models—even from a very low-priced camera. For maximum versatility and image quality, however, SLR models still remain the best (if bulkiest and most expensive) choice.

• **Try before you buy.** A camera that's easy to grip is a plus. Be sure that you can see the viewfinder's image clearly. If you wear glasses, you might want a camera with a diopter adjustment to help you see the viewfinder's image clearly without them.

• **Storing prints.** Prints can get scattered, or you may accumulate so many that you lose track of what you have. Photo albums are one way to organize them. You'll find looseleaf album refills that accommodate negatives as well as different sizes of prints. A scrapbook allows you to paste down pictures and supply your own handwritten captions. You can also buy boxes designed to store prints or even use ordinary shoeboxes.

Digital cameras

With digital images, you're more involved in the creation of the print than you are with images captured on film.

Digital cameras, which employ reusable memory cards instead of film, give you far more creative control than do film cameras. With a digital camera, you can transfer shots to your computer, then crop, adjust color and contrast, and add textures and other special effects. Final results can be made into prints, cards, even T-shirts, or sent via e-mail, all using the software that comes with the camera. Since the technology requires some fiddling, digital may appeal more to relatively serious amateurs than to casual snapshooters. But as digital image-handling becomes simpler—and camera prices keep dropping—the advantages may more easily win you over.

Digital cameras share many features with digital camcorders, such as an electronic image sensor, LCD viewer, and zoom functions. They also share some features with film cameras, such as lens and flash options. Some camcorders can be used to take still pictures, but the typical camcorder's resolution is no match for that of a film camera or a good digital still camera.

What's available

The leading brands are Sony, Kodak, Olympus, and Nikon, with other brands from consumer-electronics, computer-imaging, and traditional camera and film companies.

Digital cameras are typically categorized by how many pixels, or picture elements, the image sensor contains. A one-megapixel camera has 1 million such elements. In general, the more pixels, the sharper the image.

Cheap, sub-megapixel cameras have 640 by 480 pixels (307,200 in all). A one-megapixel model makes sharp 5x7-inch prints and very good 8x10s. Two- and three-megapixel models can make excellent 8x10s and pleasing

Printing photos on an inkjet

Most inkjets can turn out high-quality color photos. Here are some tips on getting the best results from your inkjet:

• Use the next-to-best setting. Producing an 8x10-inch photo at a printer's best setting can take about 10 minutes (faster inkjets can cut that time in half). The next-to-best setting greatly speeds printing, often with little impact on quality.

• Use the Print Preview feature, found in most image-handling programs, to avoid false starts. If you want to try out your print during the editing process, use standard bond instead of pricey photo paper. Or print in a smaller size.

• Handle with care. Inkjet ink can smear if touched before it dries. Color inks in general are less water-resistant than black, especially on photo paper. Some ink is vulnerable to light, meaning exhibited photos may show fading and color shifts.

• Shop for cartridges. Comparison-shopping sites such as *www.shopper.com* and *www.computershopper.com* can yield savings of 25 percent or more (not including shipping). With prices in hand, try brick-and-mortar office-supply chains or warehouse clubs. Don't overbuy —an ink cartridge's shelf life is about 18 months unopened, 6 months once installed. Be wary of off-brand refills or refilling cartridges yourself with ink-and-syringe kits. Printer warranties often exclude coverage for damage attributable to third-party refills.

11x14s (a size larger than most inkjet printers can handle). There are also four- and five-megapixel models, but they are probably more than most home users need.

Price range: sub-megapixel, below $100; one-megapixel, $150 to $500; two-megapixel, $250 to $700; three-megapixel, $500 to $1,000.

Features to consider

Digital cameras use aperture and shutter speed to take pictures even though they don't use film. Aperture indicates how wide the lens opens (the smaller the f-number, the larger the aperture). The shutter speed indicates how long the aperture remains open when you snap a picture.

Most digital cameras are highly automated, with features such as automatic exposure control (which manages the shutter speed or aperture—or both settings—according to available light) and autofocus.

Instead of film, digital cameras typically record their shots onto flash memory cards, such as CompactFlash or SmartMedia, which come in capacities of 8, 16, or more megabytes. Once quite expensive, flash-memory cars have tumbled in price—32-megabyte cards can be had for less than $50. A few models store shots on regular diskettes, while more expensive Sony models use a proprietary media known as Memory Stick. Some newer cameras use 3-inch CD-R discs.

To save images, you transfer them to a computer, typically by connecting the camera to the computer's USB or serial port or inserting the memory card into a special reader. Some printers can take memory cards and make prints without putting the images on computers first. Image-handling software such as Adobe PhotoDeluxe, MGI PhotoSuite, Microsoft Picture It, and Ulead PhotoImpact lets you size, touch up, and crop digital images using your computer. Most digital cameras work with Windows or Macintosh machines.

The file format commonly used is the highly compressed JPEG. (It's also used on the Internet for photos.) Some cameras can save photos in TIFF format, but this uncompressed setting yields enormous files.

Digital cameras typically have both an optical viewfinder and a color LCD viewer. LCD viewers are essentially 100 percent accurate in showing what you get—better than most of the optical viewfinders, but they gobble up battery power. You can also view shots you've already taken on the LCD. Many digital cameras provide a video output, so you can view your pictures on a TV screen.

On call

Put an extension phone in your baby's room, or carry a cordless phone with you when you need to change a diaper.

Certain cameras let you record an audio clip with a picture. These clips devour storage space. Some allow you to record limited video, but the frame rate is slow and the resolution poor.

A zoom lens provides flexibility in framing shots and closes the apparent distance between you and baby—ideal if you want to quickly switch to a close shot. A 3x zoom is comparable to a 35-to-105-mm lens on a film camera; a 2x zoom, to a 35-to-70-mm lens. Optical zooms are superior to digital zooms. Digital models double or triple the zoom range, but only by magnifying the center of the frame without actually increasing picture detail, resulting in a somewhat coarser view.

Sensors in digital cameras are typically about as sensitive as ISO 100 film, though some let you increase that setting. (At ISO 100, you'll likely need to use a flash indoors and in low outdoor light unless you use a tripod.) A camera's flash range tells you how far from the camera the flash will provide proper exposure: If baby scoots out of range, you'll know to close the distance. But digital cameras tolerate some underexposure before the image suffers noticeably.

Camera and camcorder batteries

Flash point-and-shoot cameras, digital cameras, and camcorders all consume giant gulps of power. That can pose a problem when your child is taking her first steps and you're running low on juice. Most point-and-shoot film cameras use a lithium battery or AA or AAA alkaline batteries. Digital cameras often come with rechargeable batteries—lithium-ion, nickel-metal-hydride (NiMH), or, rarely now, nickel-cadmium nickel-metal-hydride (NiCD)—but many also take AA alkaline cells. Rechargeable lithium-ion, NiMH, or, rarely, NiCD batteries are used in camcorders. Nonrechargeable lithium batteries should not be confused with rechargeable lithium-ions.

In a CONSUMER REPORTS test mimicking the high power drain of a film or digital camera with a flash, the best NiMH battery significantly outperformed the best alkaline cell. NiMH cells have a relatively high initial cost—about $30 to $50 for a system comprising a charger and four AA batteries—but their reusability makes them less expensive long-term than standard alkalines. NiMH cells are also an environmentally safe choice. Unlike the NiCD cells they're supplanting, they can be disposed of with ordinary refuse.

The newer lithium-ion rechargeables also work well and can be disposed of with ordinary refuse, but they don't come in AA or AAA configurations.

Red-eye reduction shines a light toward your subject just before the main flash. (A camera whose flash unit is farther from the lens discourages red eye. Computer editing may also correct it.) With automatic flash mode, the camera fires the flash whenever the light entering the camera registers as insufficient.

How to choose

KEY DIFFERENCES. In CONSUMER REPORTS' most recent tests, image colors looked fine. Digital cameras did much better with fluorescent lighting than regular processing labs have done with film. (Fluorescent lighting can give photos a greenish cast.) Tests also showed that a higher pixel count alone doesn't necessarily produce better picture quality. In those tests, some 2-megapixel cameras outperformed some 3-megapixel ones.

The image-handling software provided with a digital camera is generally easy to use. The results are usually pleasing—or readily altered further if you're not satisfied. The software does have its limits, though. It can't fix an out-of-focus image or brighten a too-dark one.

RECOMMENDATIONS. A 2-megapixel model offers good quality at a relatively moderate price. Look for a camera with a 3x optical zoom lens and good image-handling software. Avoid cameras that use a floppy disk for storage. Only a small number of images fit on a disk.

Online processors are happy to store your photos digitally and let you caption shots, arrange them into albums, send e-mail "postcards," and so on. In fact, online storage can be a good backup even if you store the images on your computer or transfer them to a CD.

• **Try before you buy.** Quite a few cameras offer a shallow grip or no grip. Some LCD viewers are awkwardly situated so they could easily be soiled with nose or thumb prints. If you wear glasses, you might look for a camera viewfinder with a diopter adjustment so you can remove your glasses while using the camera.

Camcorders

Finer picture quality and easier editing have improved the performance of these "movie makers," especially the digital models.

From the moment their "star" is born, many parents want to capture events on video. (Some even put the birth on tape.) Yawns, cries, and coos in the hospital are followed by the homecoming, and each milestone thereafter.

Digital camcorders generally offer very good to excellent picture quality, along with very good sound capability, compactness, and ease of handling. Making copies of a digital recording shouldn't result in a loss of picture or sound quality. Analog camcorders generally have good picture and sound quality and are less expensive. Some analog units are about as compact and easy to handle as digital models, while others are a bit bigger and bulkier.

With the right hardware and software, it's relatively easy to connect a digital camcorder to a computer for video editing. Your computer will need lots of hard-drive space and speed—a second of video from a digital camcorder occupies 3 to 4 megabytes—but even computers costing less than $1,000 are capacious and fast these days. You'll also need a 4-pin-to-6-pin FireWire cable and matching input at the computer end, known as a FireWire, an IEEE-1394, or an iLink port. If your computer lacks such a port, you can buy an adapter card and FireWire cable.

Editing video shot on an analog camcorder may be slightly more cumbersome. Instead of a using a FireWire port, you'll need to have a video-capture card installed in the computer. The card will have an analog video input. Or you can use an outboard video capture device, which typically uses a USB connection to the PC.

What's available

Sony dominates the camcorder market, with several models in a number of formats. Other top brands include JVC, Panasonic, RCA, and Sharp. Digital models come in two formats: MiniDV or Digital 8. Some weigh less than 2 pounds and are designed to be comfortable to hold.

MINIDV. Don't let the size deceive you. Although some models can be slipped into a large pocket, MiniDV camcorders can record very high-quality images. MiniDV models use a unique tape cassette. The typical recording time is 60 minutes at SP speed. Expect to pay $8 for a 60-minute tape. You'll need to use the camcorder for playback—it converts its recording to an analog signal, so it can be played directly into a TV or VCR. If the TV or VCR has an S-video input jack, you'll get the best possible picture. Price range: $600 to $2,000.

DIGITAL 8. Also known as D8, this format gives you digital quality on Hi8 or 8mm cassettes. Hi8 tapes are cheaper than MiniDV cassettes, and an 8mm

Hot

Run the cold water last so that if the baby touches the faucet it won't be hot and burn little hands.

tape is about half the price of a Hi8. The format records with a faster tape speed, so a "120-minute" cassette lasts only 60 minutes at SP. This format can also play your old Hi8 or 8mm tapes. Price range: $600 to $1,200.

You'll find analog camcorders in four compact formats—VHS-C, Super VHS-C, 8mm, and Hi8. They weigh around 2 pounds, and like digital models, are designed to be held in the hand easily. Picture quality is very good, though generally a notch below that of the top-performing Mini DVs.

VHS-C. This format uses an adapter to play in any VHS VCR. Cassettes most commonly hold 30 minutes on SP. JVC and Panasonic are the major brands of this format. Price range: $300 to $700.

SUPER VHS-C. S-VHS-C is the high-band variation on VHS-C and uses special S-VHS-C tapes. (A slightly different format, S-VHS/ET-C can use standard VHS-C tapes.) One tape yields 40 minutes at SP. Only JVC offers models in this format. Price range: $500 to $700.

8MM. For this analog format, you need the camcorder for playback. Cassettes hold a lot—the most common size, 120-minute, yields 2 hours at SP and costs about $3.50. Canon, Sharp, and Sony make 8mm models. Price range: $250 to $700.

HI8. This premium, "high-band" variant of 8mm promises a sharper picture. For full benefits, you need to use Hi8 tape and watch on a TV set that has an S-video input. Price range: $300 to $500.

Features to consider

A flip-out LCD viewer is becoming commonplace on all but the lowest-priced camcorders. You'll find it useful for reviewing footage you've shot and easier to use than the eyepiece viewfinder for certain shooting poses. Some LCD viewers are hard to use in sunlight, a drawback on models that have an LCD viewer only and no eyepiece.

Screens vary from 2½ to 4 inches measured diagonally, with a larger screen offered as a step-up feature on higher-priced models. Using an LCD viewer shortens recording time by draining batteries faster than the eyepiece viewfinder does.

An image stabilizer automatically reduces most of the shakes from a scene you're capturing. Most stabilizers are electronic; a few are optical. Either type can be effective, though mounting the camcorder on a tripod is the surest way to get steady images. If you're not using a tripod—and you may not, because even if baby remains cooperatively still, you will

Grabby

Don't use tablecloths until your child in the high chair is past the grabbing stage.

probably want to change the position from which you are shooting—try holding the camcorder with your hands and propping your elbows against the sides of your chest.

A full auto switch essentially lets you point and shoot. The camcorder automatically adjusts the color balance, shutter speed, focus, and aperture (also called the "iris," or f-stop, with camcorders).

Autofocus adjusts for maximum sharpness; manual focus override may be needed for problem situations, such as low light. (You may have to tap buttons repeatedly to get the focus just right.) With many camcorders, you can also control exposure, shutter speed, and white balance. Macro focus keeps the picture clear when you shoot small subjects at close range—such as that smiling face.

The zoom is typically a finger control—press one way to zoom in, the other way to widen the view. (The rate at which the zoom changes will depend on how hard you press the switch.) Typical optical zoom ratios

A webcast featuring your baby

Using a technology called "streaming media" —live-action audio/video on the Internet— BabyPressConference.com puts baby and new parents on the Internet, right from the maternity unit. Dozens of hospitals across the country that have licensed the necessary equipment participate.

Each baby broadcast is limited to viewers selected by the parents. BabyPressConference e-mails them a password and instructions for downloading the necessary software (you'll need MediaPlayer on your computer to view the video). During the webcast, guests can type in and send questions, which parents can answer "on the air."

The success of the webcast may depend on the speed of the viewer's Internet connection. The amount of RAM and the PC's video card may also have an impact. While the live version of the webcast can't as of this writing be viewed on a Macintosh, Mac users can view the archived webcast online for two weeks after the live event. The service is free, and parents have the option of purchasing a CD-ROM of the webcast. In addition, through retail links, the invited guests may shop for baby gifts online.

BabyPressConference also offers a free Family Page, customized for parents-to-be and open only to invited guests. Features include a due-date countdown, chat room, photos such as an ultra- sound image, and shopping links.

For more information and to see which hospitals offer the webcasts, log on to *www.babypressconference.com.*

range from 10:1 to 26:1. The zoom relies on optical lenses, just like a film camera (hence the term "optical zoom"). Many camcorders offer a digital zoom to extend the range to 400:1 or more, but at a lower picture quality.

Regardless of format, analog or digital, every camcorder displays tape speeds the same way as a VCR. Every model, for example, includes an SP (standard-play) speed. A few 8mm and Hi8 models have a slower LP speed, which doubles recording time. All VHS-C and S-VHS camcorders have an even slower EP (extended-play) speed, which triples recording time. With analog camcorders, however, slower speeds worsen picture quality.

Quick review lets you view the last few seconds of a scene without having to press a lot of buttons.

For special lighting situations, preset auto-exposure settings can be helpful. A "snow & sand" setting, for example, adjusts shutter speed or aperture to accommodate the high reflectivity of snow and sand.

A light provides some illumination for close-ups when the image would otherwise be too dark. Backlight compensation increases the exposure slightly when your subject is lit from behind and silhouetted. An infrared-sensitive recording mode (also known as "night vision," "zero lux," or "IR-filter") allows shooting in very dim or dark situations, using infrared emitters. You may use it for nighttime crib shots, although color representation won't be accurate in this mode.

Audio/video inputs let you record material from another camcorder or from a VCR, useful for copying part of another video onto to your own. (A digital camcorder must have such an input jack if you want to record analog material digitally.)

Unlike the built-in microphone, an external microphone that is plugged into a microphone jack won't pick up noises from the camcorder itself, and typically improves audio performance.

Features that may aid or enhance editing include a built-in title generator (which superimposes printed titles and captions); a time and date stamp, and a time code, which is a frame reference of exactly where you are on a tape, recorded by hour, second, and frame.

A remote control is helpful when you're using the camcorder as a playback device or when using a tripod while you're positioned off to the side —or getting into the picture yourself. Programmed recording starts the camcorder recording at a preset time.

How to choose

KEY DIFFERENCES. Digital camcorders have set a new standard in CONSUMER REPORTS' picture-quality tests. Pictures are sharp, free of streaks and other visual "noise," and have accurate color. Audio quality is not quite as impressive, at least using the built-in microphone. Still, digitals record pleasing sound that's devoid of audio flutter (a wavering in pitch that can make sounds seem thin and watery), if not exactly CD-like, as some models claim.

The best analog model we've tested is on a par with the lowest-scoring digital. In the most recent tests, the lowest-scoring analog model delivered soft images that contained a lot of video noise and jitter, and reproduced colors less accurately than any digital model. And while sound for 8mm and Hi8 camcorders is inherently free of audio flutter, all the VHS-C camcorders suffered from some degree of that audio-signal problem.

RECOMMENDATIONS. If you don't want to spend a lot, an analog camcorder is a good value—now about $300, compared with $750 just few years ago. Analog models may also appeal to you if you have little interest in video editing. If you want to upgrade, consider a digital model. Prices are as low as $600 and are continuing to fall.

• **Try before you buy.** Before buying, make sure a camcorder fits comfortably in your hand and has controls that are easy to reach.

Reference

Contents

Contents

Product guide

BABY MONITORS

Using cordless phone technology, all baby monitors operate on the 49-MHz or 900-MHz analog frequency. You put the transmitter in the baby's room and take the small and portable receiver, which has a flexible antenna, with you, whether in another room or even outside. Basic monitors simply transmit sound one-way. Pricier models also serve as two-way walkie-talkies/intercoms. Some versions allow you to clip the transmitter onto a toddler's clothing. Most units run on household current and disposable or rechargeable batteries. The 900-MHz frequency may give a unit expanded range. Multiple channels may help avoid interference from neighboring devices. Most come in white with colorful accents, but you'll also see colors such as teal. Most monitors are audio, but there are a few video monitors, some using their own video screens, others the screen of a TV.
• **Related article** page 29

LINE/MODEL	PRICE	DETAILS
EVENFLO *Mass-market brand is a relative newcomer to the baby-monitor market.*		
Constant Care 1000 Sound Lights Monitor	$20	One-way, 49-MHz, claimed 400-foot range. Two channels. Runs on household current or battery. Pay more for 900-MHz, transmission; low-battery indicator, headphone jack.
Constant Care 3000 Two-Way Communicator	$50	Monitor/intercom. 49-MHz. Two channels. Runs on household current or rechargeable battery. Low-battery indicator, out-of-range indicator lights and tone, folding antennae.
THE FIRST YEARS *Mass-market brand that specializes in accessories for the nursery.*		
Safe & Sound	$28	One-way, 49-MHz. Two channels. Depressing button on transmitter makes receiver emit sound for easy finding. Runs on household current or rechargeable battery. Low-battery indicator.
Crisp & Clear	$40	One-way, 900-MHz transmission. Two channels. Runs on household current or rechargeable batteries (included).
FISHER-PRICE *Originator of category has broad range of models, including design that can be used with a toddler.*		
Super-Sensitive	$25	One-way, 49-MHz. Two channels. Runs on household current or 9-volt battery. Volume control.
Sound 'n Lights Monitor Two models	$35-$40	One-way, 49-MHz. Two channels. Runs on household current or 9-volt battery. Out-of-range and low-battery indicators. Pay more for model with two receivers.
Sounds So Clear	$40	One-way, 900-MHz. Two channels. Volume control. Runs on household current or 9-volt battery. Low-battery indicator.
Infant-to-Toddler	$50	One-way, 900-MHz. Two channels. Transmitter can detach from its base and clip to toddler's clothing. Runs on household current or 3 AAA batteries and one 9-volt battery.

LINE/MODEL	PRICE	DETAILS
GRACO *Mass-market brand has selection of audio baby monitors.*		
UltraClear and Sound Sleep	$30-$45	Basic line in white or choice of translucent colors. One-way, 49-MHz. Two channels. Volume control, belt clip. Runs on household current or 9-volt battery. Pay more for models with two receivers.
Listen 'n Talk and Family Listen 'n Talk	$50-$70	High-end line in choice of colors. Two-way, 900-MHz. Two channels. Volume control. Runs on household current or 9-volt battery. Pay more for two receivers.
SAFETY 1ST *Brand of child-safety and other juvenile products has broad selection of audio and video monitors.*		
Crystal Clear	$20	One-way, 49-MHz. Two channels. Runs on household current or 9-volt battery. Low-battery indicator, light indicators, two AC adapters.
Clear Connection with Sound Lights Nursery Monitor and Two Receiver Gift Set	$20-$30	One-way, 49-MHz. Two channels. Runs on household current or 9-volt battery. Low-battery indicator, three sound level lights. Pay more for two receivers.
Super Clear Rechargeable and Sensitive Sound	$25-$35	One-way 49-MHz. Two channels. Runs on household current or 9-volt battery, receiver has rechargeable battery. Sound level lights, low-battery indicator. Pay more for 900-MHz transmission and up to 1,000-foot range.
Grow with Me Intercom	$50	Monitor/Intercom. Two-way, 900-MHz. Four channels. Transmitter can detach from its base and clip to toddler's clothing. Runs on combination of household current, rechargeable battery, and AAA battery. Low-battery indicator.
Child View Monitor & Television	$150	Black-and-white video monitor. 2.4-GHz. Three channels. Wall- or table-mounted camera displays on receiver's 5-inch screen. Three AC adapters. Sound-level lights.
In-Sight Hand-Held Monitor & Television	$200	Color video monitor. 900-MHz. Three channels. Wall- or table-mounted camera displays on 2-inch active-matrix screen or attaches to conventional TV. VCR mode. Runs on four AA batteries. Low-battery indicator. Belt clip.

CAR SEATS

Car seats come in several configurations: rear-facing infant seats, convertible seats, toddler/boosters, and booster seats. (For preemies, you'll need a special "car bed," which allows the baby to fully recline.) A rear-facing infant-only seat, as it says, only faces the rear of a car and is for use with babies from 5 to 20 pounds (a few claim higher weight limits for larger babies). **Convertible seats** can be used in rear-facing mode for infants, then turned around for use with children who weigh between 20 and 40 pounds. Another option is a **toddler/booster seat** with a built-in harness. You can use this type of seat with the harness for children between 20 and 40 pounds, then remove the harness and use the car's own safety belts for children between 40 and 80 pounds. Regular **booster seats** have no harness, but simply raise the child so he can safely use the adult belts.

Most seats are comprised of a molded plastic shell fitted with a padded fabric-and-foam cover, which can usually be removed for washing. Some rear-facing infant seats can detach from a base that stays in the car, allowing parents to "let sleeping babies lie" as they move them out of the car. Many infant seats can also snap into a special stroller frame (see Travel Systems, page 176).

Depending upon the model, a system of webbed straps and latches secures the child into the seat. Look for a seat with a five-point harness system. The seats themselves are secured into a vehicle by the vehicle's own safety belts or through a new federally mandated anchor/tether system called LATCH wherein a top-tether strap is attached to an anchor behind the seat. Booster seats are designed to raise a child to a level where he can safely use the adult lap-and-shoulder belts.

• **Related article** page 31   • **Ratings** page 192.

LINE/MODEL	PRICE	DETAILS
INFANT CAR SEATS		
BRITAX *High-end British brand offers the only infant car seat with a top-tether strap.*		
Handle with Care	$150	Infant-only seat with choice of fabrics. Fits babies 5 to 20 pounds. Five-point harness, rear tether strap, adjustable base that doubles as rocker, head support, canopy, handle with two locking positions.
CENTURY *This leader in car seat sales has a broad selection of infant car seats.*		
Assura, SmartFit, Celestia, Avanta	$45-$85	Broad line of infant-only seats with choice of fabrics. Basic units fit babies 5 to 20 pounds, have three-point restraint, level indicator, canopy, four-position handle. Pay more for unit that fits babies up to 22 pounds, five-point restraint, car base or adjustable car base.
COSCO *Mass-market brand has sole infant-only car seat that can take a child up 35 pounds.*		
Arriva, Designer 22	$30-$70	Broad line of infant seats with choice of fabrics. Basic units fit babies 5 to 22 pounds. Three-point restraint. Pay more for canopy, car base.
Designer 35, Opus 35	$70-$110	Infant seats with a choice of fabrics, fit babies 5 to 35 pounds. All have adjustable headrests and four-position buckles. Pay more for two bases and a rotating centerpiece in the handlebar for easier carrying.
Ultra Dream Ride	$50	Infant seat/car bed with blue checkered fabric. Fits babies 5 to 20 pounds. Can be used in air bag position. Three-point harness.
EDDIE BAUER $110 **INFANT CAR SEAT/CARRIER, EDDIE BAUER 35 LX**		Two upscale seats with designer looks. The first fits babies 5 to 22 pounds, the second, 5 to 35 pounds. Five-point harness, base, turnabout handle, removable protective boot cover, canopy. Pay more for foam overgrip handle, no-thread belt path, 4-position base and adjustable headrest.

LINE/MODEL	PRICE	DETAILS
EVENFLO *Mass-market brand offers broad selection of infant car seats.*		
First Choice	$40	Basic infant seat with light-blue figured fabric. Fits babies 5 to 20 pounds. Three-point harness, canopy.
On My Way Position Right V, Position Right V Comfort Touch, Discovery, Adjust Right, Adjust Right V	$50-$75	Line of infant-only car seats with choice of fabrics. Fits babies 5 to 20 pounds. Three point harness, car base, canopy. Pay more for five-point harness, adjustable car base.
FISHER-PRICE *Mass-market brand offers one infant-only model.*		
Stay in View	$70	Seat with blue-and-green checkered fabric. Fits babies up to 20 pounds. Three-point restraint, high-back car base with mirror that enables viewing of baby from front seat, carrying strap, canopy.
GRACO *Mass-market brand offers a line of infant car seats and a car bed.*		
SnugRide SnugRide DX5	$60-$180	Midpriced line of infant seats with choice of fabric. Fits babies up to 20 pounds. Three-point restraint, head support, adjustable car base, adjustable handle, rotating canopy. Pay more for five-point restraint, rotating canopy with visor and window.
PEG PÉREGO *Known for its strollers, this Italian brand has branched out with one model of infant car seat.*		
Primo Viaggio	$120	High-end infant seat with choice of fabrics. Fits babies up to 20 pounds. Five-point harness, car base, canopy.

CONVERTIBLE CAR SEATS

LINE/MODEL	PRICE	DETAILS
BRITAX *High-end British brand offers a couple of convertible seats.*		
Roundabout, Advantage	$210-$250	High-end convertible seat with choice of fabrics. Rear-facing for babies 5 to 30 pounds, forward-facing for toddlers 20 to 40 pounds. Five-point harness, top-tether strap. Pay more for Advantage's more-adjustable harness.
CENTURY *Mass-market brand offers a broad selection of convertible car seats.*		
Accel, Bravo, Encore, SmartMove, and STE	$60-$135	Broad grouping of similar convertible seats with choice of fabrics. Rear-facing for babies 5 to 22 or 30 pounds, forward-facing for toddlers 20 to 40 pounds. Five-point restraint. Pay more for extra padding and additional reclining options.
COSCO *Mass-market brand offers broad selection of convertible car seats, including two that extend to toddlers.*		
Touriva, Olympian, and Deluxe Regal Ride	$45-$130	Broad grouping of convertible seats with choice of fabrics. Rear-facing for babies 5 to 35 pounds, forward-facing for toddlers 22 to 40 pounds. Five-point harness, top-tether strap. Pay more for extra padding.

Continued

LINE/MODEL	PRICE	DETAILS
COSCO *Continued*		
Triad	$100	Midpriced convertible car seat with blue fabric. Rear-facing for babies 5 to 35 pounds, forward-facing for toddlers 22 to 40 pounds. Attachments for lower LATCH anchors (also works with lap or lap/shoulder belt), five-point harness.
Alpha Omega	$130	Midpriced convertible car seat/booster with choice of fabrics. Rear-facing for babies 5 to 35 pounds, forward-facing with harness for children 22 to 40 pounds, forward-facing with car's lap/shoulder belt for children 30 to 80 pounds. Five-point harness, removable pillow for toddlers, removable car base, no rethreading required.
Eddie Bauer 5-Point	$90	Upscale convertible car seat with designer look. Rear-facing for babies up to 35 pounds, forward-facing with harness for toddlers 22 to 40 pounds. Top-tether strap, five-point harness, removable infant insert, removable toddler pillow.
Eddie Bauer Three Car Seats in One	$160	Upscale convertible car seat/booster with designer look. Rear-facing for babies up to 35 pounds, forward-facing with harness for toddlers 22 to 40 pounds, forward-facing with car's seat belt for children 30 to 80 pounds. Removable five-point harness, removable infant insert, removable pillow for toddlers, removable car base.
EVENFLO *Mass-market brand offers broad selection of convertible car seats.*		
Secure Advantage V, Conquest V, Horizon V, Odyssey V, Medallion V	$50-$130	Broad grouping of similar convertible car seats with choice of fabrics. Rear-facing for babies 5 to 30 pounds, forward-facing with harness for toddlers 20 to 40 pounds. Five-point harness. Pay more for three position reclining seat, removable infant insert, extra cushioning.
Triumph	$130-$140	Convertible car seat; rear-facing for babies 5 to 30 pounds, forward-facing with harness for toddlers 20 to 40 pounds. Five-point harness. All mechanisms with front adjustability.
FISHER-PRICE *Mass-market brand offers two convertible car seats.*		
Safe Embrace, Safe Embrace II	$100-$140	Midpriced convertible car seat with blue fabric. Rear-facing for babies 6 to 30 pounds, forward-facing with harness for toddlers 22 to 40 pounds. Five-point harness. Safe Embrace has top tether. Pricier Safe Embrace II attaches to lower LATCH anchors.
SAFELINE KIDS *Brand offers combination stroller/convertible car seat.*		
Sit 'n Stroll	$190	An all-in-one stroller/convertible car seat with a five-point harness. Rear-facing for babies 5 to 22 pounds, forward-facing 20 to 40 pounds. T-shaped push handle and rubber wheels retract into the seat's shell in carseat mode. Sunshade.

LINE/MODEL	PRICE	DETAILS

TODDLER SEATS AND TODDLER/BOOSTER SEATS

BRITAX *High-end British brand has several seats for toddlers, including one for children with special needs.*

LINE/MODEL	PRICE	DETAILS
Freeway Plus and King	$180-$190	Toddler seat with choice of fabrics. With harness for toddlers 20 to 40 pounds. Top-tether strap, five-point harness.
Expressway/Isofit	$180	Toddler seat in burgundy checkered or puppies fabric. With harness for children 20 to 40 pounds. Attachments to lower LATCH anchors, works with lap and shoulder belt, top-tether strap, five-point harness.
Traveller Plus	$450	Toddler/booster seat in blue fabric. With harness for children 22 to 105 pounds. Five-point harness has double tether; also works with lap belt or lap and shoulder belts. Appropriate for children with special needs. Extra padding, adjustable headrest.

CENTURY *The biggest-selling brand of child-safety seats has a line of toddler/booster seats.*

LINE/MODEL	PRICE	DETAILS
Breverra, Ascend, Classic, Metro, and Transit	$50-$80	Midpriced line of boosters with choice of fabrics. With harness for children 30 to 40 pounds, with car's seat belt for children 30 to 80 pounds. Removable three-point harness, removable seat pad. Pay more for armrests.
NextStep DX, MX, SE	$80-$110	Midpriced line of toddler/booster seats in choice of fabrics. With harness for toddlers 20 to 40 pounds, with seatbelt positioner for children 30 to 80 pounds. Removable five-point harness, fold-down armrests. Pay more for extra padding.

COSCO *Mass-market brand has broad line of toddler/booster seats.*

LINE/MODEL	PRICE	DETAILS
High Back, Adventurer II High Back, Commuter, Ventura, Vision	$40-$70	Basic line of toddler/booster seats in choice of fabrics. With harness for toddlers 22 to 40 pounds, with seatbelt positioning for children 30 to 80 pounds. Removable five-point harness. Pay more for armrests, cup holder, adjustable pillow.
Alpha Omega	$130	See entry under convertible models.
Eddie Bauer High Back	$90	Upscale convertible seat with designer look. With harness for toddlers 22 to 40 pounds, with car's seatbelt for children 30 to 80 pounds. Top-tether strap, removable five-point restraint, mesh side pockets.
Eddie Bauer Three Car Seats in One	$160	See entry under convertible models.

EVENFLO *Mass-market line offers two toddler/booster seats.*

LINE/MODEL	PRICE	DETAILS
Express and Express Comfort Touch	$50-$60	Toddler/booster seats in choice of fabrics. With harness for toddlers 20 to 40 pounds, with car's seatbelt for children 30 to 80 pounds. Removable five-point harness. Pay more for extra padding.

Continued

LINE/MODEL	PRICE	DETAILS
EVENFLO *Continued*		
Apollo	$100	Toddler/booster seats in choice of fabrics. With harness for toddlers 20 to 40 pounds, with car's seatbelt for children 30 to 80 pounds. Removable five-point harness, extra padding, cup holder. All mechanisms with front adjustabililty.
FISHER-PRICE *Mass-market line offers one toddler/booster seat.*		
Grow with Me	$100	Toddler/booster seat in beige fabric. With harness for toddlers 20 to 40 pounds, with car's seatbelt for children 30 to 80 pounds. Removable five-point restraint, removable wing cushions.
GRACO *Mass-market brand has a couple of toddler/booster seats.*		
Cherished CarGo, CarGo Express, Treasured CarGo, Grand CarGo	$45-$60	Toddler/booster seat in beige fabric. With harness for toddlers 20 to 40 pounds, with car's seatbelt for children 30 to 80 pounds. Removable five-point restraint. Pay more for pillow, cup holder, storage pocket, and up-front harness adjust.

BOOSTER SEATS

LINE/MODEL	PRICE	DETAILS
BRITAX *High-end British brand offers two high-backed booster seats.*		
Star Riser Comfy	$120	Belt-positioning booster seat for use with lap and shoulder belts; with blue fabric. Detachable back, expandable seat.
Roadster	$110	Belt-positioning booster seat for use with lap and shoulder belts; with leopard-skin patterned fabric. For children 40 to 80 pounds. Adjustable height and width.
EVENFLO *Mass-market brand has a backless booster.*		
Right Fit	$25	Backless booster with green fabric. For children 40 to 80 pounds. Adjustable shoulder-belt positioner, removable and washable seat pad.
Sightseer	$30-$40	High-back booster for children 30 to 80 pounds. Pay more for extra padding.
FISHER-PRICE *Mass-market brand has high-back booster.*		
Safe Embrace	$60	High-back booster with blue-and-red plaid fabric. Uses car's seatbelt for children 30 to 80 pounds. Adjustable shoulder-belt positioner.

CARRIERS, FRAMED

Frame carriers are basically backpacks with baby seats. They easily go where strollers can't, such as on a hiking trail or through a crowd. They're intended for children who can sit up without support—usually at least 6 months old. Some carriers have adjustable hip belts to accommodate adults of different heights. Frame carriers can be used until the young passenger reaches the unit's weight limit (between 40 and 60 pounds) or until she becomes too heavy for comfortable toting (usually about one-quarter of your body weight). Some models designed for serious hikers include a "hydration system," a long straw attached to a water bottle in a compartment on the pack. Important safety features include a three- or five-point harness for the child, and leg holes narrow enough so the child won't slip through but wide enough not to constrict the baby's thighs. Also look for straps that comfortably distribute the load. A sternum strap or waist belt makes the carrier more comfortable and stable for you.

• **Related article** page 56

LINE/MODEL	PRICE	DETAILS
EVENFLO *This mass-market brand recently acquired the Gerry and Snugli brands.*		
Trooper	$50	Aluminum frame pack for child up to 40 pounds with three-point adjustable hip belt, shoulder harness, adjustable sternum strap, and waist belt. A large, removable storage compartment, three-point restraint for child. Weighs 4 pounds.
TrailTech, Trail Blazer	$70-$100	Molded plastic frame pack for child up to 45 pounds. Has five-point adjustable hip belt, sternum strap, adjustable seat height, contoured shoulder staps, three-point harness for child, retractable kickstand, and removable storage pack. Pay more for additional padding and removable canopy. Both weight 7¼ pounds.
KELTY K.I.D.S. *This brand, famous for packs, has been making frame carriers for about a decade.*		
Town, Country	$100-$125	Aluminum frame pack for child up to 45 pounds. Mesh back panel, zip-off tote pack, child shoulder harness, nighttime reflective tape, retractable kickstand. Pay more for headrest and a sternum strap. Town weighs 4½ pounds, Country 5 pounds.
Trek, Elite, Explorer	$155-$240	Same features as Country but adds a lumbar pad and a back pad for extra support on long hikes. Pay more for a sun/rain hood. The Explorer adds hydration system and changing bag. Trek weighs close to 6 pounds, Elite weighs over 6 pounds fully equipped, Explorer weighs more than 9 pounds.
Expedition	$275	Same as Explorer but adds a higher grade of fabric, more storage compartments, and stirrups for young passenger. Weighs more than 9 pounds.
R.E.I. *This maker of packs and other outdoor equipment offers frame carriers.*		
Tagalong, Piggyback	$100-$140	Aluminum frame for child up to 60 pounds: padding at waist, shoulder, and back, padded seating area, foldout kickstand, front pocket, shoulder and waist belts for child. Pay more for a rear pack, rearview mirror for parent to view child. Both models accommodate a rain bonnet (sold separately for $18). Tagalong weighs 4 pounds, Piggyback weighs 5 pounds.

CARRIERS, SOFT, AND SLINGS

There are two main types of fabric carriers: soft carriers that attach to the parent using a system of straps and buckles, and slings, which are essentially large pieces of fabric that fasten above one shoulder with a double-ring closure. Both types of soft carriers let parents tote a baby next to their chest; some allow baby to ride on hip or back. Babies are often soothed by the rhythmic motion of being carried this way, and parents enjoy having both arms and hands free.

Most carriers can be adjusted to accommodate discreet breastfeeding as well. It's a good idea to try out a few different models before settling on one. Some models can be adjusted to fit tall adults.

● **Related article** page 56   ● **Ratings** page 200

LINE/MODEL	PRICE	DETAILS
BABY BJORN *High-end Swedish brand is known as a soft-carrier innovator.*		
Baby Carrier	$90-$200	Soft carrier for babies 8 to 33 pounds. Choice of six colors. Wide shoulder straps. Baby can face in or out. When baby faces out, head support is folded down. Pay more for leather.
CROWN CRAFTS *Brand of assorted soft good baby products.*		
BabySling	$35	An over-the-shoulder sling for babies up to 30 pounds. Washable cotton with padded edging, and dual-ring adjustments. Available in four colors.
EVENFLO *This brand acquired Snugli, one of the original soft-carrier brands. Evenflo now has the largest number of front-carrier models.*		
Double Take, Simple Comfort	$15-$20	Basic line of soft carriers for babies 7 to 26 pounds. Baby can face in or out. Second seat position for larger baby. Padded seat and backrest. adjustable seat width. Pricier Double Comfort model has dual side entry and additional padding.
Out & About Early Care	$30	Unique, one-shoulder design for newborns that allows a cradle carrying position with extended back and neck support for proper positioning and nursing. Weight range: 7 to 21 pounds. Baby can face in or out. Can be used as a sling, or for nursing. Has a zipper pocket mesh lining with air venting foam padding.
Easy Comfort Plus Front & Back, Porte Bé Bé Premier	$40-$60	Front or back carrier for babies 7 to 26 pounds. Baby can face either in or out, or can ride on a parent's back at around 6 months. Has contoured shoulder straps with additional chest support for parent. Also has a padded adjustable waist belt. Side entry/exit, adjustable height, and removable pillow for baby's head. Pay more for adult lumbar support, padded hip belt, and inner foam padding.
FISHER-PRICE *A brand of available at mass-merchandise and toy stores such as Toys "R" Us.*		
Deluxe Perfect Support	$40	Front carrier for babies up to 26 pounds. Baby can face in or out. Carrier comes with a separate sling attachment. Has a padded headrest for the baby, and an adjustable harness with hip padding. Also includes a bib and weather shield.

LINE/MODEL	PRICE	DETAILS
GRACO *Mass-marketed American brand. New to the category.*		
Baby Classics 3-in-1 Soft Carrier	$50	Front or back carrier for babies 8 to 21 pounds. Baby can face in or out. Thickly cushioned head support, multiposition straps for parent, and padded lumbar waist belt. Also includes a weatherguard hood, a bib, and a zipper pouch for keys .
INFANTINO *Imported brand of assorted baby goods. Available at Kmart and Wal-Mart.*		
Bebe Style	$35	Front carrier for babies 8 to 26 pounds. Faces in or out. Available in four different fabric combinations. Detachable head support, elasticized back storage compartment.
Classic Baby Sling	$30	Sling for babies 8 to 30 pounds. Elasticized, cushioned sides. Can be used as side carrier for older babies.
Cozy Rider	$25	Front carrier for babies 8 to 20 pounds. Faces in or out. Available in three different fabric combinations. Detachable, wrap-around head support adjusts with hook-and-loop closures. Plastic clip helps hold shoulder straps in place.
Kipling Heartbeat Carrier	$70	Front carrier for babies 8 to 23 pounds. Faces in or out. Firm back supporter for baby. Padded head support and leg openings. Rear storage pocket and key or toy holder.
On-the-Go!	$30	Front carrier for babies 8 to 23 pounds. Faces in or out. Available in four different fabric combinations. Reinforced, removable head support with adjustable straps, three-position seat, drawstring pocket in rear.
6-in-1	$40	Front or back carrier for babies up to 35 pounds. Baby can face in or out, and can go on back. Many settings for different baby sizes. Includes free instructional video.
KELTY *K.I.D.S. Backpack brand offering a high-end front carrier.*		
Koala, Kangaroo	$55-$70	Front carrier for babies from 8 to 25 pounds. Baby can face out or in. Has semi-firm interior shell for added support. Offers adjustable height (fits from 4'11" to 6'8" adults), water bottle compartment on hip belt, and key pocket. Koala includes hood, bib, and storage sack.
KIDCO *Brand of assorted baby products.*		
Womb with a View	$70	For babies 8 to 26 pounds. Baby can face in or out. Includes two bibs. Removable leg strap for smaller infants.
OVER THE SHOULDER BABY HOLDER *One of the original sling brands.*		
Over the Shoulder Baby Holder	$40	Fabric sling available in three sizes and multiple fabrics. Birth to four years. Allows newborn to recline and discreetly nurse. Supports tots and children 6 months and older in hip-straddling position.
PRINCE LIONHEART *Brand of assorted baby products for feeding, diapering, and organizing.*		
KOALA CARRIER	$85	Front and back carrier for babies from birth to 2 years. Cushioned shoulder straps, sash-style waist strap. Inner seat and zippered outer pouch/head support.

LINE/MODEL	PRICE	DETAILS
PRINCE LIONHEART Continued		
Koala Sling	$45	Fabric sling for babies up to 30 pounds. Available three patterns. Has an adjustable shoulder strap and offers discreet nursing position.
THEODORE BEAN *A fashion-oriented brand of diaper bags and carriers.*		
Carrier, Collection	$75-$190	For babies 8 to 40 pounds. Available in vinyl, micro-mesh, and leather. Baby faces in or out. Has a pod insert for use with small babies. Includes a snap-on sun shade and bottle holder. Pay more for Italian leather in a variety of prints.
TOT TENDERS *A small brand specializing in carriers for multiple babies.*		
Six-Position Baby Carrier	$45	For babies newborn to approximately 35 pounds. Allows baby to face in or out. Fully adjustable, washable, pacifier holder.
Gemini Twin Carrier	$60	Front double carrier faces parent, carrying babies one or two at a time. For babies weighing up to 14 pounds each when carried together, or can be used as a single carrier up to 25 pounds.
Maxi-Mom Single Carrier, Maxi-Mom Twin Carrier, Maxi-Mom Triple Carrier	$45-$100	Newborn to approximately 30 pounds per carrier. Seven positions for a single baby, 12 for twins, 18 for triplets. Babies can face in or out, on chest or back, or each parent can carry a baby. Fully adjustable. Head support, padded leg holes.
WEEGO *A new brand specializing in carriers.*		
Three Ways	$90	Front or back carrier for babies from 5 to 35 pounds. Padded, zipper-backed carrier with head and back support. Baby faces in or out, and can go on back. Has an inner and an outer pouch, three bibs, and can be used for nursing. Comes in 4 colors.
Weego Preemie Soft Baby Carrier	$100	Modified Weego Soft Baby Carrier for 3-pound preemies to 35-pound toddlers with all the same features. Comes in blue and white seersucker.

HIGH CHAIRS

For the most part, high chairs are now made of molded plastic—easy to wash, easy to move around. Seat cushions are typically easy to remove and wash. All come with a seat belt and most with a crotch post or T-bar restraint, which helps keep the baby from sliding out. Useful features include a seat whose height adjusts and a tray you can release with one hand. Casters let you slide the chair easily. A chair that reclines can accommodate a baby who can't yet sit up, but a baby that small is usually held by a parent during feeding. A few models can convert into other types of gear such as a play table and chair or a swing.

• **Related article** page 61

LINE/MODEL	PRICE	DETAILS
CHICCO *Italian brand with one high-end model.*		
Mamma	$150	Foldable metal A-frame with choice of fabric designs for cushion. Crotch post, five-point restraint. Six height positions, three-position reclining seat, two-position tray, locking casters, footrest, cup holder.
COSCO *Mass-marketed brand sells budget-priced high chairs.*		
Li'l Diner	$40-45	Basic line with tubular metal legs and blue-and-yellow checkered cushion. Crotch post, three-point restraint. Molded footrest, four-position tray with one-hand release. Pay more for four-position tray with compartments for cups, jars, and utensils.
Options 5	$50	Multiuse chair of molded-plastic A-frame and vinyl cushion. Crotch post, three-point restraint. Seven height positions, reclining seat, removable footrest, four-position tray with one-hand release, compartments for cups, jars, and utensils, towel bar. Can be lifted from frame for use as infant activity seat.
EVENFLO *Mass-marketed brand sells moderately priced high chairs.*		
Steps to Grow	$90	Multiuse chair of molded plastic with vinyl cushion. Crotch post, two height positions, one-hand tray release. Three-point harness. Converts into play chair and table.
Easy Comfort	$100-$110	Foldable, tubular-metal A-frame, with vinyl or fabric cushion. Three-point harness. Eight height positions, four reclining positions, lockable casters. One-hand tray release.
FISHER-PRICE *Mass-marketed brand has one combination model.*		
Swing 'n Meals	$100	Automatic swing and high-chair combination has foldable A frame, crotch post. As a swing, the seat reclines. As a high chair, it adjusts up and down. Footrest, in high chair mode. There's a small, removable tray for the swing, larger one for the high chair. Uses three D batteries.
GRACO *Mass-market brand offers several lines of high chairs.*		
Easy Chair	$30	Basic line has tubular metal legs. Crotch post, two-point restraint. Removable vinyl seat pad.

Continued

LINE/MODEL	PRICE	DETAILS
GRACO *Continued*		
Easy Seat	$40	Basic line has tubular metal legs and wide molded plastic feet. Crotch post, two-point restraint. Five height positions, removable vinyl seat pad, compartmentalized tray with one-hand release.
Neat Seat	$50-$75	Line has tubular metal legs and wide molded plastic feet with cushions in a choice of fabrics. Crotch post, two-point harness. Five height positions, removable vinyl seat pad, compartmentalized tray with one-hand release, three reclining positions. Pay more for locking casters, five-point restraint, washable cloth seat pad with secondary vinyl seat pad.
DoubleTray	$80-$90	Line has tubular metal frame with kickstand-style rear legs and cushions in a choice of fabrics. Crotch post, five-point restraint. Two trays (small snacking, larger, multiposition tray with one-hand release), six height positions, three reclining positions, removable cloth pad and vinyl seat pad. Folds for storage. Most models come with attachable toys. Pay more for reversible cloth seat pad.
KOLCRAFT *Mass-marketed brand with two models.*		
Perfect Height and Perfect Recliner	$50-$70	Line has tubular metal legs and tray with one-hand release. Crotch post, three-point restraint. Six height positions. Pay more for three reclining positions, tray toys, removable cloth slipcover.
PEG PÉREGO *High-end Italian brand is credited with originating height-adjustable high chair.*		
Prima Pappa	$160-$180	High-end line with foldable, metal A-frame and cushions in a choice of fabrics. Crotch post, five-point restraint. Seven height positions, four reclining positions, locking casters, two-position tray with one-hand release, removable vinyl seat pad. Pay more for imitation leather-seat pad.
Prima Pappa Roller	$190-$200	High-end line with nonfoldable metal H-frame and cushions in a choice of fabrics. Crotch post, five-point restraint. Seven height positions, four reclining positions, locking casters, two-position tray with one-hand adjustment, removable imitation leather seat pad, rear mesh storage bin, adjustable push handle.

MULTISEAT STROLLERS

Multistrollers are worth considering if you have twins, triplets, or closely spaced siblings. They come in two configurations—side-by-side and tandem (one seat behind the other)—and have many of the same features available on regular strollers.

Features that make a stroller cost more include an alu-minum (instead of steel) frame, fully reclining seats, a reversible handle, or generous padding. Jogging strollers, with bicycle-style wheels and brakes, let parents cover rougher terrain than a mall or a sidewalk. The larger the wheels, the easier it is to push the unit and run.

• **Related article** page 48

LINE/MODEL	PRICE	DETAILS
APRICA *High-end Japanese brand produces one multipassenger model.*		
Embrace	$500	Tandem carriage/stroller with navy aluminum frame and blue fabric, fully reclining seats, reversible and height-adjustable handle, four sets of inde-pendently swiveling wheels, two bonnet-style hoods, stands when folded.
BABY JOGGER *Brand that invented jogging stroller has two multipassenger models.*		
Twinner II	$450-$490	Three-wheel side-by-side sports stroller with choice of fabrics. Seats two children weighing total of up to 100 pounds. Aluminum frame, 100-pound capacity, bicycle-style hand brake. Five-point harness, canopy, and basket. Choice of 16- or 20-in. alloy wheels.
Triple	$570	Four-wheel side-by-side sports stroller with choice of fabrics. Seats three children weighing total of up to 100 pounds. Has two 16-in. front wheels, two 20-in. rear wheels, dual, bicycle-style brakes, five-point harnesses.
BABY TREND *Mass-market brand makes a tandem frame for car seats.*		
Expedition Double	$170	Side-by-side stroller for two. Navy with three wheels. 16-inch front wheel, 16-inch rear wheels, five-point harness, 100-pound capacity, two-position reclining seat, canopy, basket.
Caravan Lite LX	$210	Tandem stroller with navy aluminum frame and blue fabric. Accommodates most Century, Evenflo, Cosco, Gerry, and Kolcraft infant seats. Fully reclining stroller seats, three-point harness, removable, washable seat pads.
Sit-N-Stand LXIII	$150	Midpriced stroller with choice of fabric colors and frame designs. Fits most infant car seats from Century, Cosco, Evenflo, Gerry, Graco, and Kolcraft. Reclining stroller seat. Rear step holds standing toddler. Canopy. Storage bin. Car seat not included.
Trend Tandem	$130	Stadium-seating style stroller for two. Three-point harness. Holds up to 90 pounds. Child tray, three-position reclining front seat and Three-position reclining rear seat, eight-inch wheels, large basket, trigger-fold system.
Transport Side-by-Side	$120	Double stroller, three-position independently reclining seats, two canopies, eight-inch wheels, three-point harness, 90-pound capacity, removable front bumper bar, trigger-fold system.

Continued

LINE/MODEL	PRICE	DETAILS
COMBI *Japanese brand makes a twin version of its Savvy models.*		
Twin Savvy	$340	High-end, lightweight side-by-side stroller with navy or black frame and choice of fabrics. Three-position, fully reclining seats, three-point harness, bonnet-style canopies, shoulder strap, and carrying case.
COSCO *Mass-market brand has tandem strollers in its product line.*		
Cameo Stadium-Seating Tandem Stroller	$100	Tandem stroller with navy or blue frame and navy or blue-plaid fabric. Elevated rear seat, one-handed folding, stands when folded, Two-position reclining seats, three-point harness, individual canopies with mesh sides, snack/toy trays, storage baskets.
Two Ways Twin Tandem, Two Ways Stadium-Seating All-Terrain Tandem Stroller	$130-$150	Midpriced line of tandem strollers with navy or blue frame and choice of fabrics. Front seat is reversible. Stadium has one fully reclining seat, Twin has two. One-handed folding, three-point harness. Pricier Two Ways Stadium has elevated rear seat, larger wheels, extra padding.
GRACO *Mass-market brand makes both tandem and side-by-side models.*		
DuoGlider 3 models	$130-$150	Midpriced line of tandem strollers with choice of fabrics. Elevated rear seat. Reclining seats, three-point harness, removable front and rear arm bars, baskets. Pay more for larger wheel, removable front tray, extra padding, and fit with Graco infant seat (sold separately).
DuoRider	$130	Side-by-side stroller with navy frame and choice of fabrics. One-handed folding, front and rear suspension. Reclining seats, three-point harness, one large canopy, two footrests, large basket, removable washable seat pad.
DuoLite	$160	Side-by-side stroller with navy frame and navy fabric with tan accents, three-point harness, individually reclining seats, individual canopies, one-handed folding, two footrests, large basket, front and rear suspension, cushioned front arm bar, removable washable seat pad.
INSTEP *Relative newcomer to juvenile products has selection of sports multistrollers.*		
5K Double Ultra Double	$230-$250	Three-wheel sports stroller with blue seat. Seats two children weighing total of up to 100 pounds. Folds in half for storage. 12-inch front, 16-inch quick-release rear wheels. Bicycle-style handbrake, dual rear parking brakes. Five-point harness, retractable canopy with storage pockets and window. Pricier Ultra has aluminum frame.
KIDCO *Importer has broad line of side-by-side strollers.*		
KD Line, City Light Double, Maverick Double, Maverick Double Plus, Finale Double.	$250-$390	Mid-priced line of side-by-side strollers with choice of frame colors and fabrics. Basic model has reclining seats, dual canopies, five-point harnesses, removable cushioning. Pay more for fully reclining seats, adjustable-height handles, knobby tires, extra padding, armrests.

LINE/MODEL	PRICE	DETAILS
KOLCRAFT *Mass-market brand has two tandem strollers.*		
Tandems Lil' Limo and Lil' Limo XT	$90–$100	Basic line of tandem strollers with navy or brushed-metal frame and choice of fabrics. One-handed folding. Large wheels, elevated, fully reclining rear seat, partially reclining front seat, three-point harness, basket, snack tray, dual canopies. Pricier Lil' Limo XT adds extra padding and larger tires.
MACLAREN *High-end British brand has two side-by-side models.*		
Twin Traveller	$380	High-end side-by-side carriage/stroller with umbrella-style handles. Reclining five-position seats, five-point harnesses, individual canopies, pull-out leg rests.
Twin Traveller and Opus Duo	$430	High-end side-by-side carriage/stroller with navy aluminum frame and choice of fabrics. Umbrella-style handles, reclining, five-position seats, five-point harnesses, single canopy, pull-out leg rests, extra padding, and head bumper.
PEG-PÉREGO *High-end Italian brand has two tandem models and a triple.*		
Tender Twin	$370	Heavyweight tandem stroller with navy frame and navy-and-red fabric. Large wheels. Fully reclining rear seat, three-point harnesses, footrests, individual canopies, basket.
Duette	$430	Heavyweight tandem stroller with navy frame and navy-and-red fabric. Front seat can face forward or backward. Three-point harnesses, fully reclining rear seat, footrests, individual canopies, large wheels, basket.
Triplette	$550	Heavyweight tandem triple stroller with navy frame and fabric: Front seat can face forward or backward. Large wheels. Fully reclining rear seat, three-point harnesses, footrests, individual canopies, basket.

STROLLERS

Strollers range from lightweight, inexpensive umbrella strollers to basic midweight to the more expensive lightweights and pramlike carriage/strollers. Features that make a stroller cost more include an aluminum (instead of steel) frame, a fully reclining seat, a reversible handle, or generous padding. Jogging strollers, with bicycle-style wheels and brakes, let parents cover rougher terrain than a mall or a sidewalk. The larger the wheels, the easier it is to push the unit and run. Multistrollers are worth considering if you have twins, triplets, or closely spaced siblings. See "Multiseat strollers" page 163.

• **Related article** page 41

LINE/MODEL	PRICE	DETAILS
APRICA		*High-end Japanese brand known for products that combine the lightness and maneuverability of an umbrella stroller with the generous cushioning and adjustable seating of a carriage/stroller.*
Sprint Royale 4 models	$240	Midpriced line of strollers in choice of fabrics. Steel frame that stands when folded. One touch open and close handle. Multiple reclining positions, three-point harness, bonnet-style hood.
Quantum Royale 3 models	$280–$300	Midpriced line of carriage/strollers in choice of fabrics. Steel frame that stands when folded. Reversible, height-adjustable handle. Fully reclining seat, three-point harness, bonnet-style hood, protective foot covering. Pay extra for more-adjustable handle.
Flash Prestige 5 models	$350–$400	High-end line of strollers in two fabric choices. Aluminum frame that stands when folded. Height-adjustable handle. Multiple reclining positions, three-point harness, bonnet-style hood. Pay more for five-layer cushioning.
Windsor Prestige 7 models	$400–$500	High-end line of carriage/strollers in choice of fabrics. Aluminum frame that stands when folded. Reversible, height-adjustable handle. Stands when folded. Fully reclining seat, three-point harness, bonnet-style hood, protective foot covering. Pay more for five-layer cushioning, more adjustable handle.
Super Zap Prestige 10 models	$450–$500	High-end line of lightweight strollers in choice of fabrics. Aluminum frame that stands when folded. Height-adjustable handle. Fully reclining seat, three-point harness, bonnet-style hood, protective foot covering. Pay more for five-layer cushioning.
Super-Mini Prestige 4 models	$550–$600	High-end line of lightweight carriage/strollers in choice of fabrics. Aluminum frame that stands when folded. Reversible, height-adjustable handle. Fully reclining seat, three-point harness, bonnet-style hood, protective foot covering. Pay more for five-layer cushioning.
BABY TREND		*Along with its Snap-N-Go frames that support many brands of infant seats (see Travel Systems, page 176), this brand offers a line of conventional strollers.*
Trendsport Lite, Trendsport, Trendsport LX, Trend Carriage LX	$30–$130	Basic line of strollers in choice of fabrics. Double, swivel wheels in front. Reclining seat, three-point harness, bonnet-style canopy, large basket. Pay more for larger wheels and five-point harness.

LINE/MODEL	PRICE	DETAILS
BABY TREND *Continued*		
Snap-N-Go Lite, Lite LX, LX, Sport	$30	Line of basic stroller that fit other brands' infant car seats. Car seat not included. White frame with five-inch wheels positions car seat relatively low to the ground and facing parent. Pay more for navy or brushed-metal frame with navy accents, higher car-seat position, storage basket, larger wheels, cup holder for parent, thicker attachment frame for car seat.
Sit-N-Stand LXIII	$150	Midpriced stroller frame that fits other brands' infant car seats. Car seat not included. Choice of fabric and frame colors. Reclining stroller seat, rear step that holds standing toddler, canopy, storage bin.
COMBI *Japanese brand known for its selection of lightweight strollers. (See also Travel Systems, page 176).*		
SubV	$50	Basic lightweight stroller with choice of frame colors and fabrics. Reclining seat, three-point harness, canopy, large basket, shoulder strap.
Convenience 6100, 6510, 6620	$90-$120	Basic line of lightweight strollers with navy and black frames and choice of fabrics. Pivoting, height-adjustable handle. Three-point harness, canopy with window. Pay more for ability to fit with Century, Evenflo, and Graco infant car seats, car seat cover, larger wheels.
Travel Savvy	$90	Midpriced line of lightweight strollers with choice of frame colors and fabrics. Front swivel wheels. Reclining seat, three-point harness, bonnet-style canopy, large basket.
Savvy Z	$200	High-end line of lightweight strollers with choice of frame colors and fabrics. Aluminum frame, one-handed folding. Front swivel wheels. Three-point harness, reclining seat, large basket, shoulder pack and carrying case.
COSCO *Mass-market brand offers broad selection of strollers as well as travel systems (see page 176).*		
Umbrella	$20	Bare-bones umbrella stroller with navy frame and colored fabric. Simple sling seat, curved umbrella handles.
Comfort Ride	$25	Lightweight stroller with navy frame and blue-and-yellow fabric. Push-release folding. Canopy, mesh storage basket.
Scamper	$40	Basic stroller with blue fabric and frame. Five-point harness. One reclining position, storage bin, canopy.
Contura, Grand Contura, Endeavor, and Grand Endeavor	$50-$80	Midpriced line of strollers with choice of frame colors and fabrics. One-handed folding, double front wheels. Three- or five-point harness, two- or three-position reclining seat. Tray with cup holder, storage bin. Conturas include adapter bar and canopy with window.
Eddie Bauer One-Hand Release Stroller	$90	High-end stroller with designer look: Aluminum frame, one-handed folding. Footrest, snack/toy tray. Three-point harness, two-position reclining seat, bonnet-shaped canopy with window.

LINE/MODEL	PRICE	DETAILS
DELTA/LUV *Mass-market brand has broad selection of strollers.*		
Roadrunner	$20-$40	Basic line of umbrella strollers. Navy or white frames, navy patterned fabric. Relatively tall umbrella-style handle. Seat belt, swiveling front wheels, mesh storage bin. Pay more for reclining seat, extra padding.
Precious Moments D'Lite Stroller	$40	Midpriced stroller with Precious Moments licensed characters. Green frame, aqua fabric. Three-point restraint, bonnet-style canopy, child's feeding tray.
Discovery I 8 models	$50	Basic line of strollers with choice of frame colors and fabrics. Wide one-handed folding, front shock absorbers. Reclining seat, rounded canopy, storage bin, trays for parent and baby.
Bravo II	$60	Midpriced line of strollers with navy or brushed-metal aluminum frame and navy plaids or checks. One-handed folding, five-point harness, relatively large wheels, front shock absorbers. Reclining seat, rear storage bins.
Regency	$70	Basic carriage/stroller with navy frame and navy plaid or print fabric. One-hand folding, telescoping handle, swivel wheels. Fully reclining seat, five-point harness, mesh storage bin.
EVENFLO *Mass-market brand offers broad selection of strollers as well as travel systems (see page 176).*		
Light & Easy	$80	Midpriced, lightweight stroller with navy and brushed-metal frame and choice of fabrics. One-handed folding, and stands when folded. Large basket, retractable canopy.
Easy Comfort Plus and Prodigy	$90-$100	Midpriced, midweight line of strollers with choice of frame colors and fabrics. One-handed folding. Three-point harness, reclining seat, large basket, tray with cup holder. Pricier Prodigy has slightly larger wheels.
GRACO *Largest-selling stroller brand offers a broad variety of options.*		
Breeze Lite Rider, Baby Classics Glider, Cirrus LiteRider, EuroGraco LiteRider, Glider LiteRider, LiteRider Stroller, Sterling Lite Rider	$50-$100	Broad line of midweight strollers in choice of frame colors and fabrics. Front and rear suspension. One-handed folding, two reclining positions. Three-point harness, bonnet-shaped canopy, removable tray, large storage bin. Pay more for five-point harness, multiple reclining positions, removable toys, deeper storage bin, larger wheels, thicker padding, fuller canopy.
Baby Classics Glider	$100	Midweight strollers with tan frame and choice of tan fabrics. Front and rear suspension. One-handed folding. Four-position reclining seat. Five-point harness, bonnet-shaped canopy, removable front and parent tray, large storage bin.

LINE/MODEL	PRICE	DETAILS
GRACO *Continued*		
Ultralite, CitiLite, MetroLite, MetroLite	$90-$130	Broad line of lightweight aluminum strollers in choice of frame colors and fabrics. Front and rear suspension. One-handed folding bonnet-shaped canopy with tinted sun visor, large storage bin. Pay more for adapter for Graco car seats, larger wheels, multiposition reclining seat, removable snack tray with cup holder.
Baby Classics	$150-$160	Heavyweight carriage/stroller with choice of frame colors and fabrics. Front and rear suspension. Fully reclining, five-position seat, three-point harness, adjustable footrest, snack tray, large storage bin, foot-covering boot.
INSTEP *This relative newcomer to juvenile products has three models of stroller.*		
Sport Utility Two models	$40-$90	Lower priced line of umbrella strollers in choice of frame colors and fabrics. Relatively large wheels, telescoping handles, retractable canopy, storage bins. Pricier model seats two children.
Convenience	$90	Midpriced stroller with white-and-blue aluminum frame and blue fabric. Front and rear shock absorbers. Three-position reclining seat, canopy with window, snack tray.
J. MASON *Brand offers two lines of lightweight strollers.*		
Letter Perfect and Skeedaddle	$20-$30	Lower priced line of lightweight strollers that fold into a compact square. Choice of frame colors and fabrics. Three-point harness, storage bin, canopy. Pay more for swivel wheels.
Transport, Limited Edition TransSport, Aluminum TransSport	$50-$70	Lower priced line of lightweight strollers with choice of frame colors and fabrics. Front and rear suspension, removable front trays, canopy, three-point harness, deep storage bin. Pay more for aluminum frame, one-handed folding, swivel wheels, canopy with window, multiposition footrest.
KIDCO *Importer sells selection of high-end umbrella strollers made in Portugal.*		
City Light	$130	High-end stroller with navy aluminum frame and blue fabric with plaid accents. Reclining seat, five-point harness, front swivel wheels, storage bin.
Elan and Maverick Plus	$170-$200	High-end line of strollers with choice of frame colors and fabrics. Aluminum frame, four-position telescopic handle, front swivel wheels. Fully reclining seat, five-point harness, extendable leg rest, storage bin. Pricier Maverick Plus has eight-position, rotating telescoping handles.
Finale, Grand Finale, and Grand Finale Plus	$220-$340	High-end line of carriage/strollers with choice of frame colors and fabrics. Aluminum frame, four-position telescopic handle, front swivel wheels. Fully reclining seat, five-point harness, protective foot covering, bumper bar, storage bin. Fits most brands of infant car seat. Pay more for removable bassinet, eight-position, rotating telescopic handles, knobby tires, reflective trim.

Continued

LINE/MODEL	PRICE	DETAILS
KIDCO *Continued*		
Bébécar Spice	$270	High-end stroller with choice of frame colors and fabrics. Four-position reclining seat, five-point harness. Two-position legrest, bonnet-shaped canopy, storage bin.
Bébécar Unibig	$300	High-end carriage stroller with choice of frame colors and fabrics. Fully reclining, five-position seat. Five-point harness, two-position leg rest, canopy with window, storage bin.
Bébécar Raider A/T and Style A/T	$270-$470	High-end line of strollers with pram-like wheels. Choice of frame colors and fabrics, full suspension, balloon tires with spokes, shock absorbers. Five-point harness. Pay more for front swivel wheels, adjustable-height handle.
KOLCRAFT *Mass-market brand has broad selection of strollers. (See also travel systems, page 176).*		
Umbrella, Reclining Umbrella, and Lil' Sport	$17-$30	Inexpensive line of umbrella strollers with choice of frame colors and fabrics. Umbrella handles, hammock seat, crotch strap. Pay more for reclining seat, canopy, extra padding, shock absorbers, adjustable handlebar, backrest, storage basket.
Sport line Sport About, Grand Sport Xti, and Grand Sport XT	$50-$70	Mid-priced line of strollers that emulate pricier imports. Choice of frame colors and fabrics. One-handed folding mechanism. Three-point harness. Pay more for trays with attached toys, shock-absorbing, larger wheels, extra padding.
Jeep Wrangler	$50	Midpriced umbrella stroller patterned after Jeep vehicles. Brushed-metal frame with navy, green, and tan fabric. Front shock absorbers, three-point restraint. Multiposition reclining seat, and large wheels (front swivel), canopy, large basket, parent cup holder.
Jeep Cherokee and Jeep Grand Cherokee	$80-$110	Midpriced stroller patterned after Jeep vehicles. Choice of frame colors and fabrics. One-handed folding, reclining seat. Removable front tray with play steering wheel, parent tray with lidded compartment, matching saddle bags. Pricier Grand Cherokee has larger wheels, battery-operated play tray toys, and one-handed steering.
MACLAREN *Strollers from this upscale British brand feature the same umbrella-shaped handles and seats. (See also travel systems, page 176.)*		
Daytripper and Mistral	$170-$200	High-end umbrella strollers with navy frame and navy fabric. Lockable, swivel wheels. Five-point harness, canopy, rain cover, basket. Pricier Mistral has blue frame, choice of fabrics, adds three-position reclining seat, pullout leg rest, extra padding.

LINE/MODEL	PRICE	DETAILS
MACLAREN *Continued*		
Vogue 2001 and Techno	$250-$290	High-end strollers with navy, black, or brushed-metal aluminum frame, choice of fabrics. Multiple-position reclining seat, relatively large tires, shoulder straps, five-point harness. Pricier Techno adds spoked wheels and foam grim handles.
PEG PÉREGO *High-end Italian brand offers several models. (See also Travel Systems, page 176.)*		
Pliko Sherpa, Plikomatic	$210	High-end line of strollers with brushed-metal frames and navy/light blue fabrics. Height-adjustable, umbrella-style handles, fully reclining seat, five-point harness, rear footboard for toddler to stand, bonnet-style canopy.
Venezia, Milano, Milano XL	$310-$370	High-end line of carriage/strollers with navy or brushed-metal frame and choice of fabrics. Reversible, height-adjustable handle, swivel wheels, two-hand release. Fully reclining seat, five-point harness, protective foot covering, bonnet-style canopy. Pay more for one-handed release, convertible protective boot covering.

SPORTS STROLLERS

LINE/MODEL	PRICE	DETAILS
BABY JOGGER *Brand that invented the sports stroller has broad selection in this category.*		
Twinkle	$180	Three-wheel all-terrain stroller with choice of fabric colors. Five-point harness, 12-inch wheels, pneumatic tires, sun canopy.
Baby Jogger II	$270-$315	Three-wheel sports stroller with choice of fabrics. Aluminum frame, 75-pound capacity. Five-point harness, bicycle-style hand brake, canopy, and basket. Choice of 16- or 20-in. alloy wheels.
Joggeroo	$380	Three-wheel sports stroller with choice of fabric colors. 16-inch wheels, aluminum frame, 75-pound capacity, one-handed folding, five-point harness, bicycle-style hand brake, canopy, and basket.
Twinner II	$450-$490	Three-wheel side-by-side sports stroller with choice of fabrics. Seats two children weighing total of up to 100 pounds. Aluminum frame, 100-pound capacity, bicycle-style hand brake. Three-point harness, canopy, and basket. Choice of 16-, or 20-in. alloy wheels.
Triple	$570	Four-wheel side-by-side sports stroller with choice of fabrics. Seats three children weighing total of up to 100 pounds. Has two 16-in. front wheels, two 20-in. rear wheels, dual, bicycle-style brakes, five-point harnesses.
BABY TREND *Mass-market brand has selection of sports strollers.*		
Expedition 3 models	$110	Three-wheel sports stroller in choice of colors. 16-inch front wheel, 16-inch rear wheels, 50-pound capacity, two-position reclining seat, canopy, basket.

Continued

LINE/MODEL	PRICE	DETAILS
COSCO *Mass-market brand has one model of sports stroller.*		
Two Ways	$170	Three-wheel sports stroller with navy frame, navy-plaid fabric, stands when folded. Reversible seat allows infants to face parent, toddlers to face forward. Handlebar adjusts to multiple angles and heights. Has bicycle-style wheels, five-point harness, large storage bin, mesh-sided canopy, covered parent tray, odometer.
DELTA/LUV *Mass-market brand sells inexpensive sports strollers.*		
Jog-N-Go, Jog-N-Go II	$70-$120	Three-wheel sports stroller with navy or brushed-metal frame and choice of fabrics. 11-inch wheels. Five-point harness, long canopy, storage bins. Pricier models adds larger frame, hand brakes, and pneumatic (air-filled) tires.
INSTEP *Relative newcomer to juvenile products has selection of sports strollers.*		
EZ Strider and Z11 Single	$80-$100	Three-wheel sports stroller with blue seat. Folds in half for storage. 12-inch front, 16-inch rear wheels, 50-pound weight capacity. Five-point harness, retractable canopy, drawstring storage pouch. Pricier Z11 Single adds bicycle-style hand brake, adjustable reclining seat, rear mesh panel for ventilation.
5K	$100	Three-wheel sports stroller with blue seat. Folds in half for storage. 16-inch quick-release wheels, 50-pound weight limit. Five-point harness, bicycle-style handbrake, retractable canopy with storage pockets and window, dual rear parking brakes.
10K, Ultra, and Elite	$150	Three-wheel sports stroller with blue seat and aluminum frame. Folds in half for storage. 16-inch quick-release aluminum wheels, 50-pound weight limit, bicycle-style handbrake, dual rear parking brakes. Five-point harness, retractable canopy with storage pockets and window.
5K Double Ultra Double	$230-$250	Three-wheel sports stroller with blue seat. Seats two children weighing total of up to 100 pounds. Folds in half for storage. 12-inch front, 16-inch quick release rear wheels. Bicycle-style handbrake, dual rear parking brakes. Five-point harness, retractable canopy with storage pockets and window. Pricier Ultra has aluminum frame.
J. MASON BRAND *Offers one line of sports strollers.*		
StrollAire Five models	$110-$130	Four-wheel sports strollers with navy frame and a choice of fabrics including exotic navy jungle and leopard prints. 9-inch front wheels, 12-inch rear wheels, 40-pound weight capacity, bicycle-style handbrake, foot-activated brake, cushioned handlebars. Five-point harness, removable front trays, large storage bin, multiposition footrests.

SWINGS

A baby swing is typically a seat suspended from a wide-standing frame of tubular metal legs. Its rhythmic motion can help soothe a fussy baby and allow you to free your hands for a few moments. There are two major types available: manual and automatic. Manual models require you to wind them up and will operate as long as 30 minutes before you have to rewind them. (You shouldn't place a baby in a swing much longer than that anyway.) Automatic models run on D batteries and may have several speeds. A crotch post, which can help prevent the baby from sliding out, is an important safety feature. Manufacturers differentiate their swings from other brands by including features such as recorded lullaby music and attached toys or mobiles. A swing takes up a lot of floor space. A more compact alternative is an infant activity seat with motorized vibration.

● **Related article** page 69

LINE/MODEL	PRICE	DETAILS
EVENFLO *Mass-market brand offers a line of automatic swings.*		
Soft and Sturdy, Soft and Sturdy Plus, Soft and Sturdy Ultra	$70-$90	Automatic swing has foldable, A-shaped frame, variable speed, crotch post, three-point restraint, four reclining positions, washable seat pad. Uses four D batteries. Pay more for recorded lullaby music and two-speed vibration.
FISHER-PRICE *Mass-market brand offers two automatic models, one a combination swing and high chair.*		
Cradle Swing	$80	Automatic swing has foldable frame with L-shaped legs, crotch post, two swing directions (front-to-back or side-to-side), two reclining positions, three speeds. Uses three D batteries.
Swing 'n Meals	$110	Automatic swing and high-chair combination has foldable A-shaped frame, crotch post. As a swing, the seat reclines. As a high chair, it adjusts up and down. High chair footrest. There's a small, removable tray for the swing, larger one for the high chair. Uses three D batteries.
GRACO *Mass-market brand offers a broad selection of swings and is the leader in the category.*		
Wind-Up Swing, Recliner, Easy Entry	$40-$60	Wind-up manual swing has A-shaped frame, reclining seat, crotch post, washable cloth seat pad, 15- and 30-minute settings. Pay more for larger Easy Entry swing with additional reclining position.
OpenTop Swing, Three models	$70-$120	Automatic swings with foldable, "U"-shaped frame, multiple swing speeds, four-position reclining seat, tray with one-handed opening mechanism. Uses four D batteries. Pay more for more speeds, timer, recorded lullaby music, toy attachments.
KOLCRAFT *Mass-market brand offers one model of automatic swing.*		
Perfect Height Swing	$80	Automatic swing has foldable A-shaped frame, two height positions, crotch post, newborn head roll, two position recline, variable speed control, toys. Uses four D batteries.

PLAY YARDS

Play yards are designed for portability, whether that means simply fitting through a door to move from one room to the next or folding up completely to fit in the trunk of a car. They are typically 28 inches wide and 40 inches long, and fold to fit into a golf bag–sized carrying tote. Most weigh between 20 and 25 pounds (between 30 to 35 with bassinet or changing station insert). Most models hinge at the center of the side rail for folding. An alternative design (from J. Mason) uses screw-in legs, which CONSUMER REPORTS judged excellent in recent tests. Mesh on all four sides provides ventilation but little protection from sun and wind. Canopies may help to keep insects out, but they also can concentrate heat. Some models include bassinet inserts that slide over the play yard's frame. These shouldn't be used once the baby reaches 3 months or weighs 15 pounds. Changing-station inserts usually include safety harnesses. CONSUMER REPORTS tests found that some brands are more difficult to assemble than others.

• **Related article** page 70   • **Ratings** page 198

LINE/MODEL	PRICE	DETAILS
BABY TREND *This mass-market brand is a relative newcomer to this product category.*		
Trend Traveler 6 models	$50-$110	Broad line of models in choice of fabrics. Basic model has mesh on four sides but no wheels or casters. Pay more for locking wheels, mesh on three sides and fabric on fourth, bassinet, and toy bag. Trend Traveler weighs 22 pounds.
CENTURY *This mass-market brand recently added the Fold 'N Go Élan line.*		
Fold 'N Go Bassinet, Care Center Lite, Lullaby Center, Plush Bassinet	$70-$120	Broad line of models in choice of fabrics. Mesh on two or four sides, bassinet, but no wheels. Pay more for wheels that lock, changing station, extra padding. All models in this line weigh 24 pounds.
Fold 'N Go Élan Care Center Deluxe, Deluxe Bassinet	$100-$120	Models in this line are similar to Fold 'N Go but with curved geometry. Choice of fabric. Mesh on two sides, autolocking wheels, bassinet. Care Center has changer and storage. Deluxe Bassinet model has canopy; bassinet can be used in play yard or independently. Fold 'N Go Elan weighs 24 pounds. Deluxe model weighs 31 pounds.
COSCO *This mass-market manufacturer sells play yards under the Funsport and Eddie Bauer names.*		
Eddie Bauer Travel Play Yard with Bassinet 3 models	$100-$110	Upscale line with designer look and choice of fabrics. Mesh on two sides, roll-down sunshade, locking wheels, bassinet, toy bag. Pay more for a model with changing station or canopy. Weighs 30 pounds.
Eddie Bauer Sport Travel Play Yard	$120	Upscale line with choice of fabrics. Has bassinet, changing station, and canopy. Canopy has mesh ventilation. Padded floorboard with carry bag, two wheels, toy bag, two mesh sides, sun shade. Weighs 38 pounds.

LINE/MODEL	PRICE	DETAILS
EVENFLO *This major baby-products manufacturer offers many fabric options within several lines.*		
PlayCrib	$70	Broad line in choice of fabrics. Mesh on four sides, toy storage bags, but no wheels. Weighs 29 pounds.
Roll & Go **With Bassinet** **With Bassinet and** **Cabana**	$90-$110	This line is similar to PlayCrib but offers choice of fabric, full-sized bassinet locking wheels, mesh on three sides and fabric and deep pocket on fourth side. Pay more for cabana-style cover. Weighs 29 pounds.
GRACO *Offering a broad selection of units, this mass-market brand is the category leader.*		
Pack 'N Play	$60-$70	Basic line with choice of fabrics. Mesh on four sides, changing station. Weighs 25 pounds.
3-Way Pack 'N Play **Portable Play Yard** Three models	$100-$130	High-end line with choice of fabric designs: mesh on four sides, bassinet, and changing station. Pay more for lockable casters, parent organizer basket, canopy with attached toys. Weighs 30 pounds.
5-Way Pack 'N Play Three models	$140-$150	Choice of checked fabric, mesh on four sides, bassinet, changing station, locking wheels on one end. Pay more for roll-down sunshade, parent organizer basket, canopy, full-sized bassinet, changing-supply bag, toy bag. Weighs 31 pounds
Bassinet Pack 'N Play Four models	$80-$90	Mesh on four sides, removable bassinet, toy bar.
INSTEP *This brand is best known for jogging strollers and bicycle trailers.*		
Playyard Plus	$95	Two mesh sides, both with roll-down sunshades, locking wheels, bassinet, changing table. Packed bag can be rolled. Frame can be rolled after it's placed in bag.
J. MASON *Known for its basic line of strollers, this brand's play yards use a unique folding design.*		
Safe Surround **Play Yard** Five models	$80-$110	Broad line in choice of fabrics. Supporting legs screw in and out of the frame. Two mesh sides. Pay more for bassinet, mesh canopy, built-in pouch for unit's legs. Two round models available, one with bassinet. Weight: 24-39 pounds.
KOLCRAFT *This mass-market brand has several models*		
Travelin' Tot **Entertainer,** **Entertainer with** **Bassinet, Deluxe**	$70-$100	Broad line in choice of fabrics. Mesh on four sides, locking casters. Pay more for bassinet, changing table, parent organizer, attached mirror, rattle, and activity panel. Weighs 17-25 pounds.

TRAVEL SYSTEMS

These two-in-one products usually consist of a rear-facing infant seat that snaps into a stroller or car-seat base. This design lets you move a sleeping baby from a car to a stroller undisturbed. The drawback is they only work for infants. Once the child reaches the travel-system seat's maximum weight limit (usually 20 or 22 pounds), you have to buy a front-facing car seat and a stroller. Strollers that come with travel systems are relatively bulky. An alternative to buying an entire travel system is getting a bare-bones stroller frame especially designed to accommodate almost any infant car seat. There are also a few expensive lightweight strollers that can accommodate other brands' infant car seats.

• **Related article** page 42   • **Ratings** page 197.

LINE/MODEL	PRICE	DETAILS
BABY TREND *It's marquee products: Snap-N-Go stroller frames, accommodate Century, Cosco, Evenflo, Gerry, Graco, and Kolcraft car seats.*		
Snap-N-Go **Lite, Lite LX, LX, Sport**	$30-$100	Line of basic stroller that fits other brands' infant car seats. Car seat not included. White frame with 5-inch wheels positions car seat relatively low to the ground and facing parent. Pay more for navy or brushed-metal frame with navy accents, higher car-seat position, storage basket, larger wheels, cup holder for parent, thicker attachment frame for car seat.
Sit-N-Stand LXIII	$150	Midpriced stroller frame that fits other brands' infant car seats. Car seat not included. Choice of fabric and frame colors. Reclining stroller seat, rear step that holds standing toddler, canopy, storage bin.
COMBI *Known for lightweight strollers, this Japanese brand has stroller frames that accommodate Century, Evenflo, and Graco infant car seats.*		
Perfect Match **6510, 6620**	$90-$300	Midpriced line of lightweight stroller frames that fit other brands' infant car seats. Car seats not included. Choice of frame colors and fabric designs, three-point restraint, removable, washable cushion, swiveled front wheels, pivoting, height-adjustable handle, canopy with window, car-seat cover. Pay more for a wider frame and larger wheels.
Ultra Savvy 2720 Series	$290	High-end lightweight stroller frame that fits other brands' infant car seats. Choice of frame colors and fabrics. Aluminum frame, one-handed folding. Front swivel wheels. Three-point harness, fully reclining seat, large basket, car seat cover, shoulder strap and carrying case.
COSCO *Mass-market brand whose low- and midpriced travel systems complement its lines of strollers and car seats.*		
Enterprise	$100	Basic system combining Cosco stroller and infant car seat. Stroller has blue frame, blue-and-white plaid fabric, one-handed folding, three-point restraint, car base, basket, and is self-standing. Car seat fits baby up to 22 pounds, has three-point restraint, car base.
Pathfinder	$150	Midpriced system combining Cosco stroller and infant seat. Stroller has one-handed folding, five-point restraint, three reclining positions, basket, console tray, large wheels. Car seat fits baby up to 35 pounds, has five-point restraint, four-position buckle, car base.

LINE/MODEL	PRICE	DETAILS
EVENFLO *Mass-market brand offers a broad selection of travel systems.*		
Discovery **Discovery and** **Discover Deluxe V**	$130-$160	Midpriced line combining Evenflo stroller and infant car seat. Stroller has blue frame, blue plaid fabric, one-handed folding, one-touch brake, three-point restraint, large basket, cup holder for parent. Car seat fits baby up to 20 pounds, has three-point restraint, car base. Pay more for stroller with larger wheels and for car seat with five-point restraint.
Easy Comfort **Deluxe, Advantage V,** **Ultra V, Premier**	$160-$200	Midpriced line combining Evenflo stroller and infant car seat. Stroller has blue-and-gray frame, blue plaid fabric, one-handed folding, one-touch brake, cup holder for parent. Car seat fits baby up to 20 pounds, models have either a 3- or 5-point restraint, car base. Pay more for stroller with larger wheels and five-point restraint, additional head and neck support, adjustable car-seat base.
Comfort Dimensions	$230	High-end system combining Evenflo stroller and infant car seat. Line adds extra padding, slide-out basket and larger wheels than Easy Comfort models. Fully reclining stroller has navy or taupe frame, blue plaid fabric, one-handed folding, one-touch brake, three-point restraint, cup holder for parent. Car seat fits baby up to 20 pounds, has five-point restraint, adjustable car base.
GRACO *Mass-market brand offers broad selection of travel systems.*		
LiteRider **Breeze, Cirrus,** **EuroGraco, Glider,** **LiteRider, and Sterling**	$120-$200	Graco's lowest-priced line, combining Graco stroller and car seat. Stroller has choice of frame colors and fabric designs, one-hand folding, three-point restraint, two reclining positions, removable pad, child's snack tray with cup holder, removable parent organizer, storage basket, rounded canopy. Car seat fits baby up to 20 pounds, rear-facing only. Three-point restraint, canopy, car base. Pay more for stroller with additional reclining positions, parking stand enabling unit to stand upright when folding, and for car seat with five-point restraint, adjustable car base, head cushion.
MetroLite **Travel System**	$190	High-end system that combines Graco aluminum stroller with car seat. Stroller has lightweight aluminum frame, gray fabric, one-handed folding, five-point restraint, front swivel wheels, height-adjustable handlebar, swivel-release child tray, parent tray, canopy. Car seat fits baby up to 20 pounds, has five-point restraint, car base, canopy.
CoachRider Chauffeur	$230	Midpriced system that combines Graco carriage/stroller and car seat. Carriage/stroller fully reclines, has choice of frame colors and fabric designs, one-handed folding, three-point restraint, front swivel wheels, reversible seat, trays for parent and child, storage basket, foot-covering boot. Car seat fits baby up to 20 pounds, has five-point restraint, adjustable car base.

Continued

LINE/MODEL	PRICE	DETAILS
GRACO *Continued*		
DuoGlider Travel System	$230	Midpriced system combining Graco tandem stroller and infant car seat. Use one infant seat in rear or two infant seats in front and rear. Stroller frame has metal-and-navy frame, tan plaid fabric, stadium-style seating (back seat higher than front seat), three-point restraint, front tray, rear arm bar, rear storage bin, dual canopies. Car seat fits baby up to 20 pounds, has three-point restraint, car base.
KOLCRAFT *While no longer making car seats, Kolcraft still offers a stroller frame that accommodates car seats from Britax, Century, Cosco, Evenflo, Fisher-Price, and Graco.*		
Universal Car Seat Carrier	$40	Basic stroller frame that fits most brands' infant car seats. Car seat not included. Navy frame with large basket, cup holder for parent.
MACLAREN *High-end British brand has an umbrella-handled stroller that can accommodate car seats from Century, Evenflo, and Graco.*		
Global Buggy	$300	Maclaren's stroller allows attachment of other brands' infant car seats. Car seat not included. Brushed-metal frame with navy and light blue plaid fabric, five-position stroller seat, five-point restraint, dual wheels on front and back, large mesh storage bin
PEG PÉREGO *This high-end Italian brand is new to the category.*		
Pliko Travel System	$310	High-end system combines Peg Pérego umbrella stroller and infant car seat. Stroller has brushed-metal aluminum frame, choice of fabrics (including gray-and-white snakeskin), five-point restraint, four double wheels, front swivel wheels, four reclining positions, height-adjustable handles, swing-open front bar, rear foot board for second child to stand. Car seat fits baby up to 20 pounds, has five-point restraint.
Primo Viaggio Travel System	$360	High-end system combines Peg Pérego lightweight stroller and infant car seat. Stroller has brushed aluminum frame, choice of fabrics, three reclining positions, canopy, rain cover. Car seat fits baby up to 20 pounds, has five-point restraint.
Converse Travel System	$420	High-end system combines Peg Pérego carriage/stroller and infant car seat. Stroller has brushed aluminum frame, fully reclining, reversible seat, protective boot covering. Car seat fits baby up to 20 pounds, has five-point restraint.

BRAND LOCATOR

NAME	CUST. TEL. #	WEB ADDRESS
Ameda (see Hollister)	–	–
Ansa Co.	800-527-1096	www.theansacompany.com
Aprica U.S.A.	310-639-6387	www.apricausa.com
Baby Bjorn/Regal Lager, Inc.	800-593-5522	www.babybjorn.com
Baby Jogger Company	509-457-0925	www.babyjogger.com
Baby Trend	800-328-7363	www.babytrend.com
Baby Luv (see Delta Enterprises)	–	–
Beech-Nut Nutrition Corp.	800-BEECHNUT	www.beech-nut.com
Britax Child Safety	888-4BRITAX	www.childseat.com
Carnation "Good Start" (See Nestlé)	–	–
Century Products Company	800-837-4044	www.centuryproducts.com
Chicco USA	877-4CHICCO	www.chiccousa.com
COMBI International Corp.	800-992-6624	www.comi-intl.com
Cosco/Dorel Juvenile Group	800-457-5276	www.conscoinc.com
Crown Crafts	800-421-0526	www.crowncraftsinfantproducts.com
Delta Enterprises	718-385-1000	www.deltaenterprise.com
Discovery Toys	800-426-4777	www.discoverytoysinc.com
Dr. Brown's (see Handi-Craft Co.)	–	–
Eddie Bauer (see Cosco)	–	–
Evenflo Co.	800-233-5921	www.evenflo.com
The First Years	800-225-0382	www.thefirstyears.com
Fisher-Price	800-432-5437	www.fisher-price.com
Gerber Products Company	800-4-GERBER	www.gerber.com
Graco Children's Products	800-345-4109	www.gracobaby.com
Handi-Craft Co. (Dr. Brown's)	800-778-9001	www.handi-craft.com
Heinz, H.J.	800-565-2100	www.hjheinz.com, www.heinzbaby.com
Hollister, Inc. (Ameda)	877-323-4060	www.hollister.com
Huggies (see Kimberly-Clark Corp.)	–	–
Infantino	800-365-8182	–
Inglesina USA	877-486-5112	www.inglesina.com
InSTEP LLC	800-242-6110	www.instep.net
International Playthings	800-631-1272	www.intplay.com
Jeep (see Kolcraft)	–	–
Johnson & Johnson	800-526-3967	www.jnj.com

NAME	CUST. TEL. #	WEB ADDRESS
J. Mason Products	800-242-1922	www.jmason.com
Kelty K.I.D.S.	800-535-3589	www.kelty.com
KidCo	800-553-5529	www.kidcoinc.com
Kids II	770-751-0442	www.kidsii.com
Kimberly-Clark (Huggies)	800-544-1847	www.huggies.com
Kolcraft	800-453-7673	www.kolcraft.com
Kool-Stop International	800-586-3332	www.koolstop.com
Learning Curve International	800-704-8697	www.learningcurve.com
Lego Baby/Lego Systems	800-422-5346	www.lego.com
Little Tikes	888-832-3203	www.littletikes.com
Luv 'n Care	318-388-4916	–
Maclaren USA, Inc.	877-442-4622	www.maclarenstrollers.com
Mead Johnson Nutritionals	800-222-9123	www.enfamil.com
Nestlé USA (Carnation "Good Start")	800-547-9400	www.nestleusa.com, www.verybestbaby.com
North American Bear Co.	800-662-3427	www.nabear.com
Over the Shoulder Baby Holder	800-637-9426	www.babyholder.com
Peg Pérego U.S.A.	800-671-1701	www.perego.com
Procter & Gamble (Luvs and Pampers)	800-285-6064	www.pampers.com
Prince Lionheart	800-544-1132	www.princelionheart.com
R.E.I.	800-426-4840	www.rei.com
Ross Products	800-986-8510	www.ross.com, www.welcomeaddition.com
Safeline Kids	800-829-1625	www.safelinekids.com
Safety 1st	800-962-7233	www.safety1st.com
Sassy	616-243-0767	www.sassybaby.com
The Step 2 Company	800-347-8372	www.step2.com
Theodore Bean Adventure Company	800-68-BEAN	www.theodorebean.com
Tiny Love	800-843-6296	www.tinylove.com
Tot Tenders Inc.	800-634-6870	www.babycarriers.com
Tough Traveler	800-GO-TOUGH	www.toughtraveler.com
Weego	800-676-0352	www.weego.com

Shopping guide

Contents

Where to buy baby gear

New parents have more shopping options than ever as they prepare for baby's arrival. Stores galore cater to expectant parents, with aisle after aisle of baby gear. Some retailers that once focused solely on adult apparel and gear now have divisions—or even entire stores—devoted to children and babies. L.L. Bean, Gap, and Ethan Allen are a few prominent examples. Catalogs offer everything from organic cotton diapers to hospital-grade breast pumps. Then there are online venues. Some pure-play (web-only) sites are still around, but increasingly, online merchants are the same names you see in the mall or in your mailbox. With such "multichannel" retailers, you can often return online purchases to the retail store, a real convenience.

Here's an overview of places to buy baby gear, from major retailers to more specialized outlets. Listed alphabetically.

COMPANY/WAYS TO SHOP	WHAT YOU'LL FIND
BABIES 'R' US *www.babiesrus.com*	
In store **Online**	Babies 'R' Us is the baby-outfitting component of the toy superstore, Toys 'R' Us. You can pretty much get everything you need to clothe and care for baby here, except for the fanciest merchandise. Babies 'R' Us offers a baby registry, as well as an online health/behavior resource guide. No customer-service number is listed on the web site, but you can e-mail for help.
BABY AGE *www.babyage.com*	
Online	This web site sells a wide, though not very deep, range of baby products, from cribs to nursing accessories. They also sell bedding and feature an online gift registry.
BABYANT.COM *www.babyant.com*	
Online	This web site sells apparel, toys, and a large variety of gear from well-known manufacturers, such as Aprica and Carters. You'll also find a baby registry and baby-care articles. It also has a "baby gallery" to which you can post a photo of your new family member. No customer-service number is listed on the web site, but you can e-mail for help.
BABY BEST BUY *www.babybestbuy.com*	
Online	Essentially a discount baby store online, you can find good prices, but the selection is fairly limited. The site sells apparel, diapering accessories, furniture, and assorted baby gear. There's also a closeout section.

COMPANY/WAYS TO SHOP	WHAT YOU'LL FIND

BABYBOX.COM *www.babybox.com; 800-373-8216*

Online	A web-only venue that sells high-end infant and toddler apparel, as well as linens and toys. The selection is not very wide.

BABY CATALOG OF AMERICA *www.babycatalog.com; 800-752-9736*

Catalog Online	Savings on pregnancy, baby, and toddler products. Added information on how to select products by categories, and a closeout page for bargains. Discounts for club members.

BABY EINSTEIN *www.babyeinstein.com; 800-793-1454*

Catalog Online	This company sells educational products with an emphasis on language, poetry, art, and music. Their line includes videos, musical recordings, books, DVDs, and puppets. The Learning Lab provides online access to language flash cards and a Van Gogh coloring book.

BABY DEPOT *www.babydepot.com; 888-223-2628*

In store (Burlington Coat Factory) Online	Baby Depot is the online component of the Burlington Coat Factory, a nationwide chain of stores that carry baby apparel and gear. When Consumer Reports Online rated the Baby Depot web site in Spring 2001, it received a poor rating due to limited selection and difficult ordering and searching.

BABY GAP *www.babygap.com*

In store Online	You'll find a good selection of baby basics (sleepers, T-shirts, booties) as well as mini versions of Gap's trademark khakis, oxford shirts, and jeans. There's a link to Maternity Gap, the retailer's web-only line for moms-to-be.

BABY GUARD *www.babyguard.com*

Catalog Online	This company sells a basic selection of latches (for everything from VCRs to refrigerators), locks, and accessories to babyproof your home. It also carries guards for fireplace hearths and a wide variety of safety gates.

BABY SHOP *www.mommy-mall.com*

Online	An online mall with direct links to manufacturers of baby apparel, furniture, toys, and maternity needs.

BABYSTYLE.COM *www.babystyle.com; 877-378-9537*

Online	A hip-looking web site affiliated with estyle.com, it offers a large selection of baby and toddler apparel, with links to "boutique" baby collections. When Consumer Reports Online rated the BabyStyle web site in Spring 2001, it received a good rating, with a large selection and easy ordering.

BABY SUPER CENTER *www.cribstogo.com*

Online	A very large selection of baby gear, furniture, and accessories are available on this web site. There's also a parenting information section, links to baby-related news and magazine articles, and a gift registry.

COMPANY/WAYS TO SHOP	WHAT YOU'LL FIND

BABY ULTIMATE *www.babyultimate.com; 877-724-4537*

Online	This web-only retailer sells all types of apparel, including special-occasion clothing, costumes, and christening outfits. There's also a layette section, and a small selection of toys, mobiles, and photo frames.

BABY UNIVERSE *www.babyuniverse.com; 954-523-9892*

Online	Online superstore with a wide range of gear, from cribs to high chairs. Note that the site can take a long time to load.

BABY WAREHOUSE *www.thebabywarehouse.com*

Online	This web site sells a range of basic baby gear, including car seats, high chairs, carriers, and feeding accessories. You'll find a number of high-end brands available.

BABYWORKS *www.babyworks.com; 800-422-2910*

Catalog Online	This retailer's focus is on cloth diapering systems, including covers, with a variety of diapers (including unbleached flannel) and accessories. You'll also find a small selection of cotton apparel, bedding, and some natural skin-care products.

BACK TO BASICS TOYS *www.backtobasicstoys.com; 800-356-5360*

Catalog Online	This web address brings you directly to Amazon.com, which hosts the Back to Basics web site. There is a wide selection of colorful toys, searchable by age and type of toy. Call the 800 number for a catalog.

BAREFOOT BABY *www.barefootbaby.com; 800-735-2082*

Catalog Online	You'll find mostly diapers, diaper accessories, toilet-training items, and linens (cleaning cloths, bibs, etc.) from this company, as well as a selection of skin-care items for nursing moms and babies.

BJ'S WHOLESALE *800-BJS-CLUB*

In store	This warehouse store often stocks child safety seats, strollers, and other large baby items, as well as a limited, seasonal selection of apparel. Source for disposable diapers and wipes in big quantities at a discount price. Membership required.

BREASTFEEDING.COM *www.breastfeeding.com*

Online	Primarily an information center for breastfeeding with a variety of nursing-related products available for sale, including bras, breast pumps, and maternity wear.

BUY BUY BABY *www.buybuybaby.com*

In Store Online	Retail outlets of this baby superstore can be found in New York, New Jersey, and Maryland. Residents of other states can browse the store's online inventory of car seats, strollers, high chairs, bedding, toys, and more. Web site has store locator and online registry.

COMPANY/WAYS TO SHOP	WHAT YOU'LL FIND

THE CHILDREN'S PLACE *www.childrensplace.com; 877-PLACE-USA*

In store Online	A nationwide chain that sells its own line of casual clothing for kids from infants through adolescents. There's a wide selection of layette and infant apparel, including pajamas and booties.

CONSTRUCTIVE PLAYTHINGS *www.constplay.com; 800-832-0572*

Catalog Online	This company sells mostly to schools and day-care centers, but anyone can buy from its web site or catalog. You'll find soft and wooden toys, ride-on toys, puzzles, and games, categorized by age.

COSTCO *www.costco.com*

In store Online	A warehouse-store source for discount prices on disposable diapers and wipes, with occasionally good deals on larger items such as child safety seats, carriers, and strollers. You must be a member to shop in the store or online.

DECENT EXPOSURES *www.decentexposures.com; 800-524-4949*

Catalog Online	You'll find organic cotton baby accessories, such as caps and T-shirts, as well as a wide selection of stretchy bras that can be used for nursing.

DISCOVERY TOYS *www.discoverytoysinc.com; 800-426-4777*

Catalog	Toys from this company are sold by representatives, in much the same manner as Avon or Pampered Chef products. Discovery Toys has a wide range of quality toys, and books, for infants through age 5. You can preview a selection of toys on its web site, but not order directly.

EBABYBABIES *www.ebabybabies.com*

Online	This web site offers a large range of gear, including car seats, carriers, strollers, and more. It's very easy to browse each category by manufacturer.

EBABY SUPERSTORE *www.ebabysuperstore.com; 877-253-7717*

Online	The focus here is on gear, with a very large selection of strollers, play yards, nursery accessories, and car seats. There's also an interactive "safety center," with suggested items depending upon the room you wish to babyproof.

ECO BABY *www.cloth-diapers.com; 800-596-7450*

Catalog Online	You'll find a wide selection of organic cotton or flannel baby items, including diapers, cov-ers, apparel, fabrics, and bedding. The company also sells nursing tops and bras, toys, and skin-care items.

EDDIE BAUER HOME *www.eddiebauer.com; 800-625-7935*

In store Online	This retailer of casual clothes and home furnishings has a line of bedding, furniture, and nursery furnishings (lamps, rugs, and curtains) for babies. You'll find a wider selection of baby gear on the web site than in the store.

COMPANY/WAYS TO SHOP	WHAT YOU'LL FIND

EA KIDS *www.ethanallen.com; 888-EAHELP-1*

In store **Catalog**	Home-furnishings retailer Ethan Allen entered the children's marketplace with a line called EA Kids, featuring cribs and other nursery furnishings. Although you can access EA Kids on the main Ethan Allen web site, not much is offered online. Better to request a catalog.

GYMBOREE *www.gymboree.com; 877-4-GYMWEB*

In store **Online**	Known initially for its chain of activity centers offering play groups and music classes for babies and toddlers, Gymboree stores often feature "activity corners" where little ones can catch a video while mom shops within sight. Merchandise includes apparel for newborn to 7 years, as well a Gymboree line of toys, music, and videos.

HANNA ANDERSSON *www.hannaandersson.com; 800-222-0544*

In store **Online** **Catalog**	This company sells what it calls "European quality" apparel for babies and toddlers. It has a selection of basics, outerwear, and layette. Hanna Andersson includes a primer on its web site to help parents convert its unorthodox sizing method.

IMATERNITY *www.imaternity.com; 888-847-2229*

In store **Online**	Primarily a maternity shop that also offers a decent range of baby gear (no apparel). It has a large number of strollers, including joggers and multistrollers. The web site also has an information section and advice on on pregnancy, childbirth, and breastfeeding.

JCPENNEY *www.jcpenney.com; 800-322-1189*

In store **Online** **Catalog**	This department store offers a wide range of baby apparel, gear, and furniture. It sell its own apparel label, as well as other well-known brands. You'll find a good selection of child safety seats, strollers, high chairs, and more. When Consumer Reports Online rated the JCPenney web site in Spring 2001, it received a good rating, with a wide selection and good policies.

KMART *www.bluelight.com; 866-KMRT-4U*

In store **Online**	The retail oulets of this national chain feature a better selection than its web site, though you can find a limited number of baby products online, including the Martha Stewart "baby baby" line of bedding and nursery items.

L.L. BEAN *www.llbean.com; 800-441-5713*

Catalog **Online**	Both the catalog and web site of this outdoor/casualwear outfitter offer baby carriers, bicycle seats, trailers, and a limited selection of bedding and apparel. When Consumer Reports Online rated the web site in Spring 2001, it got a very good rating, with good design, search feature, and content.

LANDS' END *www.landsend.com; 800-963-4816*

Catalog **Online**	You'll find more for baby in this retailer's catalog than on the baby-dedicated section of their web site called "The Baby Store." Both offer bedding, apparel, diaper bags, and footwear. When Consumer Reports Online rated the web site in Spring 2001, it received a very good rating, with good policies and content.

COMPANY/WAYS TO SHOP	WHAT YOU'LL FIND

LOTS 4 TOTS *www.lots4tots.com*

Online	This site offers strollers, diapers, and other goods, plus a classified section for registered members that sells used baby gear.

MACY'S *www.macys.com; 800-289-6229*

In store Online	Macy's sells apparel, including layette and special occasion outfits, and small selection of bedding items. While you can find some baby items on Macy's web site, you have to use the search feature, as no direct link to their babies section exists on the home page.

NATURAL BABY *www.kidsstuff.com*

Catalog Online	This company sells all-cotton bedding, clothing, and diapering items, as well as selection of educational toys.

NETKIDSWEAR.COM *www.netkidswear.com; 732-264-7800*

Online	Essentially a large online discount store, it sells name-brand baby gear from high chairs to car seats, as well as clothing, bedding, and nursery accessories.

ONE OF A KIND KID.COM *www.oneofakindkid.com; 540-725-5909*

Online	This web site labels itself an online discount boutique, and offers clothes from a number of designers for infants through teens. There's also a link to an affiliated site, Snips and Snails.com, which sells clothes just for boys.

ONE STEP AHEAD *www.onestepahead.com; 800-274-8440*

Catalog Online	This company sells all kinds of baby gear, including diapering systems, potty-training aids, stroller accessories, and some clothing.

PEAPODS *www.peapods.com*

Online	Peapods sells a wide selection of slings, as well as cloth diapers and diaper covers. It also has toys and organic cotton diapers.

PERFECTLY SAFE *www.perfectlysafe.com; 888-373-4044*

Catalog Online	This company offers myriad products for babyproofing your home: all kinds of locks, latches, gates, shields, and outdoor safety equipment. The web site features a safety newsletter.

POTTERY BARN KIDS *800-922-9934*

Catalog	This housewares and home furnishings retailer launched its kids' line a few years ago, featuring bedding, window treatments, and furniture. The company plans to open Pottery Barn Kids stores and launch a web site late 2001.

RAINBEE *www.rainbee.com*

Online	A wide range of upscale bedding, apparel, furniture, toys, and nursery accessories is offered on this site.

COMPANY/WAYS TO SHOP	WHAT YOU'LL FIND

THE RIGHT START *www.therightstart.com*

In store Online	A specialty store and web site that features a wide variety of clothing, toys, nursery items, and furniture. When Consumer Reports Online rated The Right Start web site, it received a fair rating due to less-than-satisfactory policies.

SAFE BEGINNINGS *www.safebeginnings.com; 800-598-8911*

Catalog Online	This company sells babyproofing items, baby gear, nursing and feeding paraphernalia, and parenting books and videos.

SAFE 'N SOUND KIDS *www.safensoundkids.com*

Online	Room-by-room childproofing items, including locks, shields, latches, and bathtime safety products can be found here. The site also features a list of recent product recalls.

SEARS *www.sears.com; 800-MY-SEARS*

In store Catalog Online	You'll find the wide range of baby products you'd expect from a department store. Apparel, layette, furniture, monitors, and more are offered through all of Sears's shopping venues. Its web site has a special section called "BabyMe," which allows you to browse its inventory of baby items.

TARGET *www.target.com*

In store Online	Target stocks a huge variety of baby items in store and online. Furniture, strollers, child safety seats, apparel, and bedding are among its offerings. Its selection of medicine-cabinet basics and accessories is what you'd expect from a discount drug store—wide and plentiful.

THIS BABY OF MINE *www.thisbabyofmine.com*

Online	A baby-information site that also sells diapering systems, nursing apparel and accessories, toys, slings, and car-seat covers.

TWINS HELP! *www.twinshelp.com*

Catalog Online	Very specialized retailer of twins-related merchandise, novelty items, and some helpful nursery accessories.

USA BABY *www.usababy.com; 800-323-4128*

In store Catalog	This nationwide chain sells primarily furniture, including nursery ensembles, rockers and gliders, and traveling essentials, such as strollers, child safety seats, and play yards. You can't purchase directly from its web site, but you can preview merchandise, find a nearby store, or order a catalog. There's also a baby registry available online.

WAL-MART *www.walmart.com*

In store Online	You'll find what you'd expect at both the stores and the web site—baby basics at discount prices. The selection of furniture, gear, and apparel is neither broad or deep.

Baby-gear inventory worksheet

Use this space to write down the brand and model name for each piece of baby gear.
You can then refer to it to check recalls.

ITEM	BRAND	MODEL
Baby bathtub	_____	_____
Baby monitor	_____	_____
Bicycle trailer	_____	_____
Booster seat	_____	_____
Car seat	_____	_____
Changing table	_____	_____
Crib	_____	_____
Doorway jumper	_____	_____
Framed back carrier	_____	_____
Gate	_____	_____
High chair	_____	_____
Infant activity seat	_____	_____
Infant swing	_____	_____
Mini-crib or cradle	_____	_____
Nursery furniture	_____	_____
Play yard	_____	_____
Sling or soft carrier	_____	_____
Stationary entertainer	_____	_____
Stroller	_____	_____

Contents

Ratings

For 65 years, CONSUMER REPORTS has bought products and tested them so consumers can make informed buying decisions. From methodical, scientific evaluations, it develops its Ratings, including the Ratings of baby products included in this book.

To determine what to test, our engineers, market analysts, and editors attend trade shows, read trade publications, and look at what's in stores to spot the latest products and trends. Our market analysts query manufacturers about product lines and update in-house databases listing thousands of models. Eventually, staff shoppers visit dozens of stores or go online to buy the selected models.

Next, a test plan is prepared to evaluate performance and other aspects of the product. With baby products such as car seats, play yards, baby carriers, and travel systems, safety is the key consideration, followed by convenience and usability. Then products are put to the test in CONSUMER REPORTS' own labs in Yonkers, N.Y. As was the case with car seats, some tests are carried out under the auspices of CONSUMER REPORTS at an outside laboratory specially suited for the purpose.

Car seats

Buy the right type for your child—infant, convertible, toddler/booster, or booster. Start fresh. Don't buy a used car seat at a yard sale or accept a hand-me-down. Older models may not meet current safety standards or may have been recalled (see page 257 for more on recalls). Never use a seat that has been in an accident—its protective capability is apt to be compromised.

Most of the models we tested in all categories were very good. The booster-seat category had a few excellent models, including the Evenflo Right Fit, a CR Best Buy. Because of potential problems securing a safe fit for the child with the shoulder-belt guide on some toddler/booster seats, we recommend against using them in the toddler mode when a child's size requires the use of a seat belt. Fisher-Price stopped making car seats in 2001. The company's models listed in these Ratings, however, may still be available in some stores.

Overall Ratings — Infant seats — In performance order

Excellent ⊖ Very good ◒ Good ○ Fair ◔ Poor ●

KEY NO.	BRAND & MODEL	PRICE	OVERALL SCORE	CRASH PROTECTION [1]	EASE OF USE	FIT TO CAR WITH BASE	FIT TO CAR NO BASE
1	**Graco** SnugRide DX5 8458	$80		⊖	⊖	⊖	⊖
2	**Cosco** Designer 35	70		⊖	⊖	⊖	⊖
3	**Century** Avanta SE V 41580	80		○	⊖	⊖	⊖
4	**Fisher-Price** Stay In View 79052	70		⊖	◔	⊖	○
5	**Century** SmartFit Plus 22 41310	65		⊖	⊖	⊖	⊖
6	**Evenflo** On My Way Position Right V 282	70		⊖	○	⊖	●
7	**Evenflo** Discovery AdjustRight V 214	60		⊖	⊖	○	◔
8	**Britax** Handle With Care 191	150		⊖	⊖	-	●
9	**Cosco** Arriva 02-727	50		⊖	◔	-	●

OVERALL SCORE scale: 0 — P F G VG E — 100

Based on tests published in CONSUMER REPORTS in July 2001

The tests behind the Ratings (all car-seat categories)

Overall score is based mainly on a seat's performance in crash tests plus our judgment of the ease of use and fit to car. To judge **crash protection,** we had an outside laboratory perform crash tests similar to those used by NHTSA. Dummies of various sizes and weights were strapped into seats mounted on sleds and run through a course simulating a head-on collision at 30 mph. Electronic sensors measured forces to the head and chest, and video cameras showed how far forward the head moved. Crash scores shown for the infant seats are without base. With base, all scored Good, except Century SmartFit Plus, which scored Fair. Convertible seats were tested in the rear-facing infant installation and forward-facing toddler installation, front-facing with and without tether. For toddler/booster seats, scores are given for use with harness (with and without tether), and as a booster seat using vehicle safety belts. **Ease of use** reflects the installation of seat and tether, and harness and tether adjustments. **Fit to car** scores are based on the stability of a seat in vehicles with different seat configurations and safety-belt designs. **Price** is approximate retail.

Recommendations and notes

Unless otherwise noted, all infant seats listed here have a five-point harness and hold babies up to 22 pounds.

1 > **GRACO** SnugRide DX5 8458 **A safe and easy-to-use seat.** Convenient harness and leveling adjustments. Available in travel system Sterling 7429, $200.

2 > **COSCO** Designer 35 **The best infant seat for keeping bigger babies—up to 35 lb.—facing rear. 3-position leveling adjustment.** Harness does not require rethreading belts to adjust height, a convenience. But 3-point harness is not best design. Available in travel system with 5-point harness, Pathfinder, $175.

3 > **CENTURY** Avanta SE V 41580 **A very good choice.** 2-position leveling adjustment. Available in travel system Lifestyle Avanta, $180.

4 > **FISHER-PRICE** Stay in View 79052 **Adequate protection but not the easiest to use.** Convenient harness adjustment. Base with mirror lets driver see child's face in rearview mirror. But 3-point harness is not best design. Difficult handle adjustment. Requires assembly.

5 > **CENTURY** SmartFit Plus 22 41310 **Decent and economical.** But 3-point harness not best design. 4-position leveling adjustment.

6 > **EVENFLO** On My Way Position Right V 282 **A good seat, but unstable without base.** Convenient harness and leveling adjustment. Available in travel system Comfort Dimensions 4621236, $270.

7 > **EVENFLO** Discovery AdjustRight V 214 **A good seat with 2-position level adjustment.** Convenient harness adjustment.

8 > **BRITAX** Handle with Care 191 **Too expensive for what you get.** Lacks base, but carrier has stabilizer stand. Locking device did not hold vehicle safety belt securely. Convenient harness adjustment. Has front tether.

9 > **COSCO** Arriva 02-727 **Inexpensive, but too many compromises.** Lacks base. Difficult carrier-handle adjustment.

Putting car seats to the test

To evaluate the crash protection of car seats, CONSUMER REPORTS works with an outside lab to do "sled tests," which simulate the effect of a head-on collision. The tests are somewhat more rigorous than those carried out by the federal government. The sled used in the tests operates on a rebound principle, achieving a desired velocity change by reversing its direction during the "impact event." If a seat performs poorly in those tests, it's tested again according to the government's criteria.

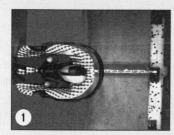  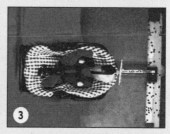

Here, the Graco SnugRide DX5 8458, which was our top-rated infant car seat, undergoes a simulated head-on collision, with electronic sensors measuring forces to the head and chest, and video cameras showing how far forward the head moves. 1) The test run begins with the infant seat attached to the test sled. 2) The point of simulated impact is attained with the maximum severity of a 30-mph frontal crash. 3) The sled comes to a stop and the test ends.

Overall Ratings — Convertible seats — In performance order

Excellent ⊖ Very good ⊖ Good ○ Fair ◑ Poor ●

KEY NO.	BRAND & MODEL	PRICE	OVERALL SCORE (0 P F G VG E 100)	CRASH PROTECTION INFANT	CRASH PROTECTION TODDLER WITH TETHER	CRASH PROTECTION TODDLER NO TETHER	EASE OF USE	FIT TO CAR
1	**Fisher-Price** Safe Embrace II 79704 (with LATCH)	$140	▬▬▬▬▬	○	⊖	○	⊖	⊖
2	**Fisher-Price** Safe Embrace 79705	100	▬▬▬▬	⊖	⊖	○	⊖	⊖
3	**Cosco** Triad 02-935 (with LATCH)	100	▬▬▬▬	○	⊖	○	⊖	⊖
4	**Britax** Roundabout	210	▬▬▬▬	○	⊖	◑	⊖	⊖
5	**Century** 1000 STE Classic 44161	70	▬▬▬	⊖	⊖	○	⊖	⊖
6	**Century** 2000 STE 44261	72	▬▬▬	⊖	⊖	○	⊖	⊖
7	**Cosco** Touriva 02-519	50	▬▬▬	○	⊖	○	⊖	⊖
8	**Century** Bravo SE 44620	135	▬▬▬	○	⊖	◑	⊖	⊖
9	**Evenflo** Horizon V 4251101	85	▬▬	⊖	⊖	○	⊖	⊖
10	**Evenflo** Odyssey 5 point Comfort Touch	100	▬▬	○	⊖	○	⊖	⊖
11	**Century** Accel DX 45200	70	▬▬	○	⊖	—	⊖	⊖
12	**Safeline** Sit 'n Stroll	190	▬▬	⊖	○	○	◑	○
	Not recommended as booster when child's size requires use of shoulder-belt guide.							
13	**Cosco** Alpha Omega 02-531	130	▬▬	○	⊖	○		⊖

Based on tests published in CONSUMER REPORTS in July 2001

Recommendations and notes

Except as noted, all convertible seats listed here have a five-point harness and hold infants up to 30 pounds rear-facing, toddlers roughly 20 to 40 pounds front-facing.

1▷ **FISHER-PRICE** Safe Embrace II 79704 (with LATCH) **Excellent but expensive.** Padded for extra protection in side-impact accidents. Requires assembly. Color-coded for belt-routing. Has locking device for vehicle belts.

2▷ **FISHER-PRICE** Safe Embrace 79705 **Outstanding crash protection.** Padded for extra protection in side-impact accidents. Requires assembly. Color-coded for belt-routing. Has locking device for vehicle belts.

3▷ **COSCO** Triad 02-935 (with LATCH) **One of the best convertible seats for keeping bigger babies—up to 35 lb.—facing rear.** Cumbersome tether installation and adjustment.

4▷ **BRITAX** Roundabout **Priciest seat tested.** Padded for extra protection in side-impact accidents. Has locking device for vehicle belts.

5▷ **CENTURY** 1000 STE Classic 44161 **A very good seat for infants and toddlers at a competitive price.** Holds babies up to 22 lb.

6▷ **CENTURY** 2000 STE 44261 **Very good protection.** T-shield harness. Holds babies up to 22 lb. rear-facing.

7▷ **COSCO** Touriva 02-519 **One of the best convertible seats for keeping bigger babies—up to 35 lb.—facing rear.** Low priced. Cumbersome tether installation and adjustment.

8▷ **CENTURY** Bravo SE 44620 **A very good seat.** Convenient front-facing installation. 3-position recliner. DISCONTINUED, but may still be available.

9▷ **EVENFLO** Horizon V 4251101 **Very good protection for infants and toddlers.** Convenient front-facing installation.

10▷ **EVENFLO** Odyssey 5 point Comfort Touch **A fine choice.** Convenient front-facing installation. 3-position recliner.

11▷ **CENTURY** Accel DX 45200 **A very good seat.** Convenient front-facing installation.

12▷ **SAFELINE** Sit n' Stroll **Expensive but versatile.** Converts to stroller. Excellent fit to car in infant mode.

The following model is not recommended as a booster when child's size requires use of shoulder-belt guide:

13▷ **COSCO** Alpha Omega 02-531 **Cumbersome tether installation and adjustment.** Also serves as booster but not recommended for that use. Had same performance problem as Cosco Adventurer toddler/booster seat.

Overall Ratings — Toddler/booster seats — In performance order

	Excellent	Very good	Good	Fair	Poor
	⊖	⊖	○	⊖	●

KEY NO.	BRAND & MODEL	PRICE	OVERALL SCORE	CRASH PROTECTION — TODDLER WITH TETHER	TODDLER NO TETHER	BOOSTER	EASE OF USE	FIT TO CAR
1	**Fisher-Price** Grow with Me 79711	$100	⊖ (P F G VG E)	⊖	○	⊖	⊖	⊖
	Use these models with care when child's size requires use of shoulder-belt guide in booster mode.							
2	**Century** NextStep SE 44905	110	⊖	⊖	○	⊖	⊖	⊖
3	**Century** Breverra Classic 44865	50	⊖	⊖	○	⊖	○	⊖
4	**Century** Breverra Metro 44850	66	⊖	⊖	○	⊖	○	⊖
	These models are not recommended as boosters when child's size requires use of shoulder-belt guide. (In alphabetical order.)							
5	**Cosco** Adventurer II 02-448	50	Not scored	⊖	⊖	—	⊖	⊖
6	**Cosco** High Back Booster 02-442	55	Not scored	⊖	⊖	—	⊖	⊖
7	**Evenflo** Express Comfort Touch 2481183	60	Not scored	⊖	⊖	—	○	⊖
8	**Graco** Cherished CarGo 8480	60	Not scored	⊖	—	—	⊖	⊖

Based on tests published in CONSUMER REPORTS in July 2001

Recommendations and notes

All toddler/booster seats listed here have a five-point harness for toddlers weighing roughly 20 to 40 pounds. As booster seats, they use the car's seat belt and hold children roughly 30 to 80 pounds.

1 **FISHER-PRICE** Grow with Me 79711 **The only seat we recommend without reservation.** Convenient belt positioners for use as booster. But assembly required.

Use these models with care when child's size requires use of shoulder-belt guide in booster mode.

2 **CENTURY** NextStep SE 44905 **Locking guide can easily allow a parent to lock safety belt with slack.** Child can also introduce slack if shoulder belt is threaded through only one side of guide and jams when pushed. Be sure to follow manufacturer directions for proper use of guide.

3 **CENTURY** Breverra Classic 44865 Same comments as NextStep SE.

4 **CENTURY** Breverra Metro 44850 Same comments as NextStep SE.

The following models are not recommended as boosters when child's size requires use of shoulder-belt guide:

5 **COSCO** Adventurer II 02-448 **Seatbelt guide can cause belt to derail or jam, allowing slack, if a child pushes and releases the belt.** A safety belt with an automatic locking retractor may minimize problem if used correctly. With this seat and Cosco High Back Booster, a child can slide under lap belt in a crash.

6 **COSCO** High Back Booster 02-442 Same comments as Adventurer.

7 **EVENFLO** Express Comfort Touch 2481183 Same comments as Adventurer.

8 **GRACO** Cherished CarGo 8480 Same comments as NextStep SE. In addition, cover is easily pulled off seat shell, which can cause slack. A safety belt with an automatic locking retractor may minimize problem if used correctly.

Overall Ratings — Booster seats

In performance order

			Excellent	Very good	Good	Fair	Poor
			⊖	⊖	○	◖	●

KEY NO.	BRAND & MODEL	PRICE	OVERALL SCORE	CRASH PROTECTION	EASE OF USE	FIT TO CAR
			P F G VG E (0–100)			
1	**Evenflo** Right Fit **A CR Best Buy**	$25	▬▬▬▬	⊖	⊖	⊖
2	**Fisher-Price** Safe Embrace 79752	60	▬▬▬▬	⊖	⊖	⊖
3	**Britax** Star Riser Comfy	120	▬▬▬▬	⊖	⊖	⊖

Based on tests published in CONSUMER REPORTS in July 2001

Recommendations and notes

All booster seats listed here use the car's seat belt and typically hold children between 30 and 80 pounds.

1> **EVENFLO** Right Fit **A CR Best Buy An excellent booster at an excellent price.** Backless; recommended only if car's seat provides adequate support. Older models previously certified to 60 lb., now certified for 40 to 80 lb.

2> **FISHER-PRICE** Safe Embrace 79752 **Excellent across the board.** Convenient shoulder-belt positioners.

3> **BRITAX** Star Riser Comfy **Another excellent choice.** Expensive, but removable back and width-adjustable seat add to versatility. Convenient shoulder-belt positioners.

Using a booster seat correctly

Wrong: No Booster

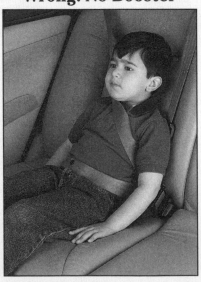

Right: With Booster

Belt-positioning booster seats dramatically reduce injuries caused as a result of ill-fitting adult safety belts, which cross a child's neck and abdomen (left). A booster seat positions children so that the car's safety belts restrain them safely (right).

Travel systems

Travel systems are strollers that work with a companion infant car seat. Convenient and easy-to-use brakes, latches, and harnesses are vital for the stroller component of a travel system. For more on car seats, see the Ratings on page 192. All but one of the travel systems we tested were very good. The best, the Graco Sterling 7429 LiteRider, includes our top-rated infant car seat, the Graco SnugRide.

| Excellent | Very good | Good | Fair | Poor |

Overall Ratings   Travel systems   In performance order

KEY NO.	BRAND AND MODEL (CAR SEAT MODEL)	PRICE	OVERALL SCORE	CRASH PROTECTION OF CAR SEAT	EASE OF USE	FIT TO CAR WITH BASE	FIT TO CAR NO BASE	TRAVEL SYSTEM STROLLER SAFETY	TRAVEL SYSTEM STROLLER EASE OF USE
			0 P F G VG E 100						
1	**Graco** Sterling 7429 LiteRider (SnugRide DX5 8458)	$200		⊖	⊖	⊖	⊖	⊖	⊖
2	**Evenflo** Comfort Dimensions 4621236 (On My Way Position Right V 282)	230		⊖	○	⊖	●	⊖	⊖
3	**Century** LifeStyle Series Avanta (Avanta SE V 41580)	180		○	⊖	⊖	⊖	○	○
4	**Cosco** Pathfinder (Designer 35)	150		⊖	⊖	⊖	⊖	◡	◖

Based on tests published in CONSUMER REPORTS in July 2001

The tests behind the Ratings

Overall score is based on safety and ease of use. **Crash protection** was tested as for car seats. Car seat **ease of use** includes installation, adjusting harness positions, placing the child in, securing the harness, and removing the child. Seats were installed in cars with various seat configurations and safety-belt designs to assess **fit to car**. **Stroller safety** includes our judgment of safety features and tested stability, brake effectiveness, and strength. **Stroller ease of use** reflects convenience of brakes, latches, harness, steering, and more. **Price** is the approximate retail.

Recommendations and notes

1 **GRACO** Sterling LiteRider 7429. **Very good system with highest-rated infant seat.** Convenient harness and leveling adjustments on car seat. Stroller has five-point harness, single-action brakes. Backrest doesn't fully recline.

2 **EVENFLO** Comfort Dimensions 4621236. **Very good system.** Convenient harness and leveling adjustment on car seat. Stroller has three-point harness, single-action brakes. Backrest can recline fully.

3 **CENTURY** LifeStyle Series Avanta. **A very good choice.** Car seat has two-position leveling adjustment. Stroller has five-point harness; brake requires two actions. Backrest doesn't fully recline.

4 **COSCO** Pathfinder. **Generally good system.** Car seat harness does not require rethreading belts to adjust height, a convenience. Stroller has three-point harness; brake requires two actions. Backrest doesn't fully recline. Steers like bad shopping cart when you let front wheels swivel.

Play yards

As a portable place for baby to play and nap, play yards have pretty much taken the place of playpens.
One standout among the models we tested was the J. Mason Safe Surround J5010, with an unusual
design that gave it an excellent score for rail-safety—an area in which play yards have been
troublesome in the past. For this reason, be sure to buy a play yard manufactured after late
2000 to ensure it complies with recently instated safety standards. (Look for the date of
manufacture on the play yard or the box it came in. Also check for a JPMA certification seal.) Most of
the models we tested were easy to set up and take down. Models with wheels are a bit pricier, but the
added convenience is worth it.

Overall Ratings Play yards — In performance order

Excellent	Very good	Good	Fair	Poor
⊖	⊖	○	◒	●

KEY NO.	BRAND & MODEL	PRICE	WEIGHT (LB.)	OVERALL SCORE	RAIL SAFETY	EASE OF USE
1	**J. Mason** Safe Surround J5010	$100	22		⊖	○
2	**Baby Trend** Nursery Center & Playard 8146 BT	90	25		⊖	○
3	**Graco** Pack 'N Play 9742	110	31		○	⊖
4	**Kolcraft** Travelin' Tot 18725 CG FR	80	28		○	⊖
5	**OshKosh B'gosh** by Evenflo PlayCrib 3633T8	125	30		○	⊖
6	**Century** Fold 'N Go élan Deluxe 10-747	110	31		○	○
7	**InStep** Playard "Plus" PY300BP	95	30		○	○
8	**Cosco** Funsport 05-372	100	29		●	○
9	**Cosco** Eddie Bauer 05-074	120	30		●	○

Overall score scale: 0 (P F G VG E) 100

Based on tests published in CONSUMER REPORTS in July 2001

The tests behind the Ratings

Overall score combines safety and ease of use. **Weight** is of the packed play yard with accessories. **Rail safety** was
judged largely on the basis of the ASTM side strength and deflection test for play yards. **Ease of use** reflects ease of
setup, pack-up, and portability, among other things. **Price** is approximate retail.

Recommendations and notes

All models listed here are about 40 inches long, 28 inches wide, and at least 22 inches deep. All have a bassinet. Most have two mesh sides and a mattress pad that folds to form a carrying case.

1 > **J. MASON** Safe Surround J5010 **The safest model tested.** Unusual design: nonfolding top rail eliminates the risk of rail collapse, but makes packed unit bulkier than most. No wheels. Screwing legs into rail judged difficult when new. Nonfolding mattress pad. Has toy bag.

2 > **BABY TREND** Nursery Center & Playard 8146 BT **Rails bent less in strength test than models listed below.** Has 4 mesh sides, no wheels. Has diaper-changing station, but pad insert creates an unsteady surface. Discontinued, but may still be available.

3 > **GRACO** Pack 'N Play 9742 **Easy to use.** Has 4 mesh sides, locking swivel casters, diaper-changing station, and parent supply-organizer basket.

4 > **KOLCRAFT** Travelin' Tot 18725 CG FR **Easy to use and a good buy.** Has 4 mesh sides, locking swivel casters.

5 > **OSHKOSH B'GOSH** by Evenflo PlayCrib 3633T8 **Easy to use.** Has 3 mesh sides, removable toy bag, nonlocking wheels. Packed bag can be wheeled.

6 > **CENTURY** Fold 'N Go Élan Deluxe 10-747 **A decent choice.** Has nonlocking wheels; packed bag can be wheeled. Bassinet doubles as a diaper-changing station, but hard to insert floor pad. Has canopy, but hard to assemble.

7 > **INSTEP** Playard "Plus" PY300BP **A decent choice.** Wheels lock but can disengage if unit is pushed from opposite end. Packed bag can be wheeled. Roll-down curtain on two sides. Removable toy bag. Center floor handle hard to push flat.

8 > **COSCO** Funsport 05-372 **Rail broke during standard rail-loading test.** There are better choices.

9 > **COSCO** Eddie Bauer 05-074 **Rail broke during standard rail-loading test.** There are better choices.

Why old play yards are unsafe

ILLUSTRATION BY GREG MAXSON

Many play yards made in the 1990s had rails that could collapse into a dangerous V-shaped angle, as shown at left. Those models have been recalled, but many may still be in use. If your child uses a play yard in a day-care facility or a hotel, be sure it meets the 1999 industry safety standard.

Soft carriers

You get what you pay for when buying a soft carrier. The more expensive models, around $80, are also the most comfortable and durable. If you plan to carry an infant under 2 months old in a carrier, pay special attention to the Ratings, which call out models with leg holes that an infant could fall through.

				Excellent	Very good	Good	Fair	Poor
				⊜	⊖	○	◔	●

Overall Ratings Soft carriers In performance order

KEY NO.	BRAND & MODEL	PRICE	CHILD WEIGHT RANGE (LB.)	OVERALL SCORE	EASE OF USE	COMFORT
				0 P F G VG E 100		
1	**Kelty K.I.D.S.** The Kangaroo Soft Infant Carrier	$70	8 to 25		⊖	⊜
2	**Baby Björn** Baby Carrier BB130	90	8 to 33		⊖	⊜
3	**Theodore Bean** Micro-Mesh Carrier 36201	70	8 to 12 with newborn insert; 10 to 40		⊖	⊜
4	**Snugli** (Evenflo) Easy Comfort Front and Back Pack 076063	40	6 to 26		○	⊜
5	**Infantino** 6-in-1 Carrier 150-012	40	up to 35		○	⊜
6	**Weego** Baby Carrier 301	90	up to 30		○	○
7	**Snugli** (Evenflo) Out and About Soft Carrier 5181174	30	7 to 21		⊖	◑
	The following are not recommended for use with infants under 2 months because of leg-hole problems. Overall scores reflect use with infants over 2 months.					
8	**KidCo** Womb with a View W10	70	8 to 26.5		⊖	⊜
9	**Fisher-Price** Deluxe Perfect Support Carrier 79471	40	up to 26		⊖	○
10	**Graco** 3-in-1 Soft Infant Carrier 5077AE	50	8 to 21		⊖	○

Based on tests published in Consumer Reports in July 2001

The tests behind the Ratings

Overall score is based on use as a front carrier and reflects ease of use and comfort (judged with the aid of parents). **Ease of use** considers how well the carriers fit the adult and the child, and ease of loading/unloading the child. **Comfort** considers the comfort of the straps and other parts and how balanced the carrier felt to the adult. **Price** is approximate retail. **Child weight range** is per the manufacturer. Note that we do not recommend three models for use with babies under 2 months, contrary to the manufacturer's guidelines; we judged those models unsafe in leg-hole size or design for that age group. The top seven models were judged safe in leg-hole size and design.

Recommendations and notes

All models listed here are machine washable and allow the child to face forward or toward the parent when used as a front carrier.

1. **KELTY K.I.D.S.** The Kangaroo Soft Infant Carrier **Front carrier only.** Excellent performance, lots of features (pockets, pacifier/toy loops, zip-out hood, reflector strips). Many straps and adjustments; takes time to learn proper use. Well-padded adult shoulder straps, wide waist belt. Infant headrest folds down when not needed.

2. **BABY BJÖRN** Baby Carrier BB130 **Front carrier only.** Simpler than the Kelty. Excellent performance. Wide adult shoulder straps. No waist belt. Infant headrest folds down when not needed. Minimum height 21 in.

3. **THEODORE BEAN** Micro-Mesh Carrier 36201 **Front carrier only.** Must use seat insert to carry young infants. Wide, lightly padded adult shoulder straps. No waist belt. Hooks could catch small fingers.

4. **SNUGLI** (Evenflo) Easy Comfort Front and Back Pack 076063 **Front and back carrier.** Lightly padded adult shoulder straps and waist belt. Has toy loop, snap-out bib, removable infant head bolster. But entry on only one side; buckle difficult to use. Discontinued, but may still be available.

5. **INFANTINO** 6-in-1 Carrier 150-012 **Front and back carrier.** Reverses to convert from infant carrier to use with older child. Padded adult shoulder straps. No waist belt. A few extras (bib, pocket). Comes with instructional video. Hooks could catch small fingers.

6. **WEEGO** Baby Carrier 301 **Front and back carrier.** Covers more of adult's chest area than most; could be warm in summer. Some leg-hole safety concerns. Padded shoulder and waist straps. Comes with 3 bibs.

7. **SNUGLI** (Evenflo) Out and About Soft Carrier 5181174 **Front carrier only.** Unusual design: single, wide adult shoulder strap (padded); waist belt with fanny-pack pocket and reflector strips. Infant headrest folds down when not needed. But side-entry buckles difficult to use.

The following are not recommended for use with infants under 2 months because of leg-hole problems. Overall scores reflect use with infants over 2 months.

8. **KIDCO** Womb with a View W10 **Front carrier only.** Has infant leg straps but easy to use them incorrectly. Wide but unpadded adult shoulder straps. No waist belt. Infant headrest folds down when not needed. Comes with 2 bibs. Minimum height 20 in. facing adult; 23½ in. facing out.

9. **FISHER-PRICE** Deluxe Perfect Support Carrier 79471 **Front carrier only.** Padded shoulder straps and waist belt; many buckles and straps. Has bib, plus a shield for privacy or weather protection. Can also be worn sling-style. Discontinued, but may still be available.

10. **GRACO** 3-in-1 Soft Infant Carrier 5077AE **Front and back carrier.** Padded adult shoulder straps and waist belt. Many straps, snaps, buckles. Infant headrest folds down when not needed. Has pockets, bib, pacifier strap, weather shield. Discontinued, but may still be available.

Parenting & health resources

Contents

Parenting web sites

ABC's of Parenting
www.abcparenting.com
Resources, discussion boards, chat rooms, and information on topics such as infancy, breastfeeding, and single parenting. Also shopping links and a recipe exchange.

Babies Planet
www.thebabiesplanet.com
Lots of information on breastfeeding, teething, colic, and general parenting issue. There are also bedtime stories and a link to myriad sources for coupons.

Baby Center
www.babycenter.com
Articles, chat rooms, and bulletin boards on fertility, pregnancy, birth, babies, and toddlers. Also has a shopping section, link to free offers, and birth announcements.

All Baby Freebies
www.geocities.com/babyfreebies
Links to offers of samples or coupons from manufacturers of diapers, toiletries, formula, and more.

Baby Gear Review
www.babygearreview.com
Parent reviews of products, plus links to shopping sites, reviews of children's books, and classified ads.

Baby Net
www.thebabynet.com
Articles on parenting, as well as baby-photo contests, chat rooms, lullaby lyrics, and birth announcements.

Baby Parenting
www.babyparenting.about.com
Lots of parenting advice and articles on diverse topics such as sleep problems, birth orders, multiples, foster parenting, special-needs children, and more.

Baby Zone
www.babyzone.com
Pregnancy and parenting articles and chat rooms. Special areas include adoption, product recalls, and sleep. Links to coupon sources and freebies.

Breastfeeding.com
www.breastfeeding.com
Tips, advice, and information on breastfeeding, and a national directory of lactation consultants. Also sells some nursing-related items.

Child Magazine
www.childmagazine.com
Articles from the magazine, plus child-related news and parenting advice searchable by age.

ClubMom.com
www.clubmom.com
Chat rooms, advice, customizable calendars, and checklists. Lots of links to and offers from product manufacturers.

Diaper Pin
www.diaperpin.com
Exhaustive information about buying and using cloth diapers, with parent reviews, discussions, and a price calculator.

Expert Parents
www.expertparents.com
Parent-written advice on myriad child-related topics, plus links to resources, books, and more.

First Years
www.firstyears.excite.com
Information on pregnancy, child development, and a state-by-state child-care finder.

Kinderstart.com
www.kinderstart.com
Search engine devoted to parenting, families, children's health, and activities, with links to hundreds of web sites.

Moms Online
www.momsonline.com
Articles, reviews, and bulletin boards on families, parenting, jobs, and more. Part of the Oxygen network.

Momsview
www.momsview.com
Links to thousands of freebies and coupon, for baby products and other items.

National Parent Information Network
www.npin.org
Part of the ERIC (Educational Resources Information Center), with research-based information on parenting, families, and education.

National Parenting Center
www.tnpc.com
Many articles on childhood development, as well as product and service reviews and a parents' chat room.

Parenthood Web

www.parenthoodweb.com

Articles and parent-to-parent advice on myriad topics; children's book, video, and web-site reviews; baby-product recalls; and more.

Parents Magazine

www.parents.com

Covers behavior and health issues for children up to 4 years old. Sections on safety, pregnancy, and a searchable index.

Parents' Choice Foundation

www.parents-choice.com

Reviews and recommendations of children's books, videos, software, periodicals, toys, TV shows, and games.

ParentSoup

www.parentsoup.com

A part of the iVillage web site, with articles and expert advice on pregnancy, infants, toddlers, and families in general.

Health & safety organizations

Alliance to End Childhood Lead Poisoning

202-543-1147 • www.aeclp.org

Information on lead poisoning, its causes and prevention, and guidelines for renovating older houses.

American Academy of Pediatrics

847-434-4000 • www.aap.org

Articles on a wide range of child-health issues. Web site has comprehensive section on car-seat safety.

American Red Cross

Contact nearest Red Cross chapter

www.redcross.org

Web site lists local chapters, many of which offer courses on child care, babysitting, and CPR.

Back to Sleep Campaign

800-505-CRIB • www.nichd.nih.gov

Info on the National Institute of Child Health and Development's SIDS-education program.

Centers for Disease Control & Prevention

888-880-4232 • www.cdc.gov

Site covers vaccine-preventable diseases and the CDC's childhood-immunization schedule.

Consumer Federation of America

202-387-6121 • www.safechild.net

Web site lists recalled products, news, and a setup for e-mail notification of recalls.

Danny Foundation

800-83-DANNY • www.dannyfoundation.org

Aims to prevent injuries caused by unsafe baby products. Has a newsletter listing dangers and recalls.

Depression After Delivery

800-944-4880 • www.depressionafterdelivery.com

Postpartum-depression clearinghouse has information on causes, symptoms, and treatment.

Federal Aviation Administration

800-FAA-Sure or 202-267-3484

www.faa.gov/childinfo.htm

Information on the proper use of child-safety seats in aircraft. Free brochures are available by phone.

Federal Consumer Education Center

800-688-9889 • www.pueblo.gsa.gov

Web site offers numerous online articles on baby safety, health, nutrition, and product recalls.

International Association for Child Safety

888-677-IACS • www.iafcs.com

National organization for professional babyproofers. Web site offers a list for finding professionals by locale.

International Lactation Consultant Assn.

919-787-5181 • www.ilca.org

Provides referrals for professional breastfeeding support. Order lactation-related publications online.

Juvenile Products Manufacturers Assn.

856-439-0500 • www.jpma.org

International trade organization of child-product manufacturers in North America. Web site features baby-safety tips and a list of recalled products.

Kids Health

www.kidshealth.org

Sponsored by the not-for-profit Nemours Foundation, this website-only source carries extensive articles on childhood health and illness.

La Leche League International

800-LA-LECHE • www.lalecheleague.org

Breastfeeding information, support, and education. Website has an international index of local groups.

March of Dimes Birth Defects Foundation

888-663-4637 • www.modimes.org

Information on healthy pregnancy and the prevention and treatment of birth defects.

Mothers at Home

800-783-4666 • www.mah.org

Support and information for at-home mothers. Order books and monthly journal online.

National Association of At-Home Mothers

515-472-3202 • www.at-home-mothers.com

Member organization for at-home mothers. Web site offers mothering tips. Free electronic newsletters.

National Easter Seal KARS (Kids Are Riding Safely)

800-221-6827 • www.seals.com

KARS program provides education, training, and loaner car seats to families with special-needs kids.

National Committee to Prevent Child Abuse

312-663-3520

Advocacy organization offers consultative and educational services. Child-abuse prevention material.

National Highway Traffic Safety Administration

888-327-4236 • www.nhtsa.dot.gov

Information on child-passenger safety, including guidelines for child-seat installation and inspection.

National Lead Information Center

800-424-LEAD • www.epa.gov/lead/nlic.htm

Provides professionals and the general public with information on lead hazards and their prevention.

National Organization of Mothers of Twins Clubs

800-243-2276 • www.nomotc.org

Referrals to local support clubs. Web site has pamphlets, books, and videos on multiple-birth issues.

National Safe Kids Campaign.

202-662-0600 • www.safekids.org

Dedicated to reducing accidental injuries among children.

National Safety Council

630-285-1121 • www.nsc.org

Web site offers information on a range of safety issues, including accident, fire, and poisoning prevention.

National Sudden Infant Death Resource Center

703-821-8955 • www.circsol.com/sids

Devoted to promoting SIDS awareness and information sharing. Web site includes links to related organizations worldwide.

Parents Anonymous

909-621-6184 • www.parentsanonymous.org

Dedicated to breaking the cycle of child abuse. Web site features a local-network locator for parents.

Parents Without Partners

800-637-7974

www.parentswithoutpartners.org

Organizes support groups in the U.S. and Canada. Newsletters and a chapter locator online.

Safety Belt Safe USA Safe Ride Help Line

800-745 7233 • www.carseat.org

Guidelines for proper child-seat installation, as well as information on booster-seat and air-bag safety.

Sudden Infant Death Syndrome Alliance

800-221-SIDS • www.sidsalliance.org

Propagates information on SIDS and provides support for families affected by it.

U.S. Consumer Product Safety Commission

800-638-2772 (Consumer Safety Hotline)

www.cpsc.gov

Web site includes an exhaustive list of recalled and potentially dangerous child and baby products. Consumers can report injuries and unsafe items.

U.S. Department of Agriculture

202-720-2791 • www.usda.gov

Offers information on meats in baby foods and other childhood-nutrition concerns.

U.S. Food and Drug Administration

800-INFO-FDA (general inquiries)
800-FDA-1088 (consumer complaints)
www.fda.gov
www.fda.gov/cder/pediatric/labelchange.htm
(for recent changes in drug labeling)

Information on baby food, skin-care-product safety, preventing food-borne illnesses, and other matters falling within the agency's regulatory purview.

10 things to do before baby arrives

First-time parents may picture the first months with a baby as fairly peaceful—while the newborn snoozes, you have blocks of free time to tackle chores and projects. The reality is that baby's daily demands plus your own fatigue can overwhelm the best-laid plans. Here are projects you'll be glad to have under control:

○ CLEANING. It's a shame that "nesting" instinct doesn't kick in until the third trimester. Expectant moms could get a lot more done earlier! Do your spring (or fall or winter or summer) cleaning well before baby arrives. Donate old clothes, recycle magazines, organize the pantry. You'll be glad when it's out of the way.

○ BIRTH ANNOUNCEMENTS. Address envelopes and adhere the stamps ahead of time so all you'll need to do is slip in the announcements and mail.

○ STOCKING UP. Fill your pantry and storage room with staples such as canned foods, pasta, rice, cereal, peanut butter, laundry detergent, paper goods, and other supplies.

○ HOMEMADE KEEPSAKES. Knitting a sweater, crocheting a blanket, or sewing a stuffed animal? Try to complete it before baby's arrival, or that sweater may be outgrown before you finish it!

○ BIG PROJECTS AT WORK. Try to finish any project that absolutely requires your involvement. Leave clear instructions for supervisors and coworkers on how to find information they'll need in your absence.

○ GARDENING. If the season's right, plant your garden—or start seedlings—now. Watering and harvesting are easy with a baby in tow, digging and planting aren't. Consider a window herb garden instead of a full-blown vegetable garden in baby's first year.

○ SWAP SEASONAL CLOTHES. By the time you fit into your pre-pregnancy clothes, it might be time for warmer (or cooler) garments. Unpack at least some of that clothing now so you won't have to root through boxes or garment bags looking for, say, a warm sweater or a cool T-shirt when you and baby want to go for a walk.

○ PLAN AHEAD FOR SPECIAL EVENTS. Whether you're planning a Fourth of July barbecue, birthday party, or holiday celebrations, take care of as much as possible ahead of time. Shop, wrap gifts, buy supplies, and make and freeze food.

○ BIG HOUSEHOLD PROJECTS. Beyond finishing baby's room, you'll want to take care of any painting, carpeting, drape installation, etc., in any other part of the house. Once baby's home, you won't want workers tromping around.

○ TAKE THAT BIG TRIP. Remember that baby (and any future siblings) will be your traveling companion for years to come. So long as the future mom has her doctor's approval, you might want to take that trip to Europe or Hawaii while it's still just the two of you!

Great baby gifts to request

Friends and family will inevitably ask what you'd like for baby. Now's your chance to speak up. Decide up front what you want to purchase yourself (a crib or changing table, for instance, if you're decorating a nursery in a particular theme) and let people know so they don't choose to "surprise" you with these items.

The sample list below focuses on smaller items you might receive at your baby shower. If you've registered for baby gear at a store, let your shower hostess know so she can pass the information along to guests. If friends would like to pitch in for big-ticket items such as a stroller or car seat, go ahead and give them the exact model number and color you'd like (see the Product guide on page 149 to get started). People would much rather give you exactly what you want than buy you something you don't.

O **ONE PACKAGE EACH OF SIZE-1 AND SIZE-2 DISPOSABLE DIAPERS.** Believe it or not, some newborns are already too big for the smallest size. (Use leftover unused disposables to absorb spills from carpets.)

O **DIAPER SERVICE FOR THE FIRST MONTH.** For cloth-diaper users, this will be a big help while baby gets the new parents used to being "on call."

O **CLOTH-DIAPERING SYSTEM.** If you choose to use cloth instead of disposables, these diaper-and-cover combos are very convenient.

O **DIAPER PAIL.** There are different kinds for for disposable and cloth.

O **DIAPER BAG.** It's got a tough job ahead, so it ought to be tough, too—roomy, rip-proof, stain-resistant, with strong handles and plenty of pockets.

O **BABY MONITOR.** Specify audio or video, depending if you want to simply hear baby's every whimper, or also see each wriggle.

O **BABY CLOTHES.** Babies grow so fast, so ask for clothes mostly in sizes 6 months, 12 months, and even 18 months.

O **SLING OR SOFT CARRIER.** Ask for a lesson or two from an experienced mom in how to put it on and get baby happily inside.

O **BABY BATHTUB.** Fluffy towels and washcloths are nice extras, as is a rubber ducky that baby can someday learn to throw out of the tub.

O **TEETHING RINGS.** Other safe-to-chew-on toys are good to have, too.

O **ACTIVITY GYM.** Noisemakers, mirrors, and toys will help baby stay entertained and active at home or when he travels.

Selecting a babysitter

Ready for an evening out—or just a few hours away from baby during the day?
Then it's time to find a reliable sitter. Here are things to do to find one.

○ **ASK AROUND FOR RECOMMENDATIONS.** Talk to friends, relatives, neighbors, your doctor, and other parents. Each time you get a name, ask about the person's qualifications, and see if your source has any special praise—or reservations.

○ **CHECK BULLETIN BOARDS.** Prospective sitters may post notices at community centers, churches and synagogues, your pediatrician's office, local stores, the gym, the library. Look for those with child-care experience.

○ **GO BACK TO SCHOOL.** Call the guidance office at your local high school, where a counselor might recommend an especially trustworthy student. Schools often offer child-care classes especially for teens who want to get babysitting jobs. Check local colleges, too.

○ **FIND A "BABYSITTER'S CLUB" IN YOUR AREA.** Child-care experts recommend you seek older teens to care for infants—15 or 16 is a good starting age.

○ **LOOK UNDER "BABYSITTING SERVICES" IN THE YELLOW PAGES.** Such agencies prescreen their sitters and usually employ older individuals.

○ **SWAP WITH OTHER PARENTS.** Once a week you can watch your baby and theirs for a few hours; they'll return the favor at another time during the week.

○ **JOIN A BABYSITTING CO-OP—OR FORM YOUR OWN.** A co-op is simply a group of parents who agree to rotate babysitting duties, so it's more like leaving your child with a friend. Just be sure that everyone gives and gets equal time.

○ **ASK FOR REFERENCES.** If the recommendation comes from a trusted source, and you're comfortable with that recommendation alone, you may be able to skip this step. Otherwise, check each reference to confirm the sitter's credentials.

○ **CHECK QUALIFICATIONS.** Best is someone who's been trained in infant CPR, the Heimlich maneuver, and other emergency procedures. Some teens who've gone through a babysitting course may have even been taught these procedures.

○ **SIZE UP THE INDIVIDUAL YOURSELF.** Gauge your gut instincts. Does the person seem mature and competent? Did the sitter arrive on time? Seem pleasant?

○ **DO A TRIAL RUN.** You might ask the sitter to stay with baby for the first time while you're at home. Use the time to catch up on neglected tasks while keeping an eye on how the sitter interacts with your child.

What your babysitter needs to know

Leaving the sitter with very clear instructions will make both you and her or him feel better. Use this list as a starting point and tailor it to your specific needs.

○ CONTACT INFORMATION. Include cell phone and beeper numbers, plus your destination name, address, and phone number.

○ TIME YOU'LL RETURN HOME. If you get delayed, let the sitter know how late you expect to be.

○ BACK-UP CONTACTS. Give the sitter the names and numbers of people to contact if you can't be reached: friends, neighbors, or grandparents, for instance.

○ EMERGENCY NUMBERS. Police, fire department, poison-control center, and local hospital as well as the name, address, and phone number of your child's pediatrician.

○ DEFINE WHAT MERITS A CALL TO YOU. Some parents want to be notified for every little thing. Others might specify only if baby is injured, develops a fever, vomits, or cries for any length of time for no apparent reason, or if a situation develops that the sitter is unable to resolve.

○ FEEDING INSTRUCTIONS. Be clear on how many bottles baby gets, and when. Also indicate whether the sitter can offer water, juice, or snacks. Be especially clear on prohibited foods: hot dogs, celery, raw carrots, grapes, nuts, raisins, popcorn, hard candy, gum, or raw pears or apples—all of which can pose a choking hazard to children under the age of 3.

○ MEDICAL INFORMATION. Include baby's allergies (food or other) and medications, as well as any illness or discomfort baby's experiencing, such as teething or an ear infection.

○ REGULAR ROUTINE. Write out the baby's feeding times, when to put her to sleep, and other details of her routine.

○ SPECIAL REQUESTS. Does baby like his bottle warm or room temperature? What music might soothe him to sleep?

○ EMERGENCY PROCEDURES. List the whereabouts of first-aid kit, flashlight, candles, and circuit breaker box. It's not a bad idea to give the babysitter a quick tour of the house and indicate where these are before you leave.

○ MAPPED ESCAPE ROUTE. Include all possible exits from the house.

○ DIRECTIONS TO YOUR HOUSE. In case the sitter needs to summon help, you'll want to provide clear, written instructions.

10 time-savers for new parents

Plan ahead to simplify those first few weeks or months after your little one arrives. Here are suggestions that can make home life with your new baby less hectic.

○ **STOCK UP.** Invite over a friend who likes to cook, put on some good music, and prepare two weeks' worth of dinners to put in the freezer to have when baby arrives. Soups, stews, pasta dishes, and casseroles are all good candidates. Label each with reheating instructions. Later you can pop in the oven or microwave when you need a quick dinner.

○ **HAVE GROCERIES DELIVERED.** Some stores will deliver. Nonperishables, such as canned goods, rice, and pasta, will keep even if the delivery is delayed. Also look into online ordering, again best for nonperishables.

○ **COLLECT TAKEOUT MENUS.** Go beyond the obvious sources, like Chinese takeout shops and pizzerias. Check with local restaurants. Some may prepare food to go.

○ **STOCK UP ON PAPER PLATES AND CUPS.** You can give yourself a dishwashing break, and prevent kitchen-sink pileups.

○ **HAVE YOUR LAUNDRY DONE.** Many laundromats will wash, dry, and fold your clothes, typically charging by the load or the pound.

○ **RING FOR THE MAID.** Most housecleaning services will do a one-time cleaning, or set up a temporary schedule for you. Rates are usually hourly, based on the number of cleaning people. You might also want to get the house professionally cleaned before baby arrives.

○ **GET PART-TIME HELP.** Find someone reliable who can handle light housework, dishes, and laundry. Contact the local high school or college, check ads in the paper (smaller papers may have more "work wanted" ads), look at local bulletin boards. Ask for references, too.

○ **INVESTIGATE ERRAND SERVICES.** They'll be listed in the Yellow Pages or might advertise in the classified section of your newspaper. Services will grocery-shop, collect dry cleaning—even pick up a package of diapers.

○ **HIRE A PERSONAL CHEF.** This is a growing industry, and is a great gift to request. Check out *www.uspca.com* or *www.personalchef.com* for local referrals.

○ **LINE UP A SITTER NOW.** You may not be planning on an evening out right away. But at some point, you'll welcome the chance to just rest for several hours. Having some names lined up in advance will make it easier. You'll be glad you already know some people to call.

Diaper-bag essentials

Make sure you're fully prepared when you and baby venture away from home. But don't go overboard—you've still got to carry that bag. Restock the bag each time you return home, so you don't forget anything the next time you go out.

- ○ **Diapers**, of course. At least five or six if you'll be out most of the day
- ○ **Changing pad.** Many diaper bags include one. If your doesn't, buy one at a baby store
- ○ Unscented, nonantibacterial **baby wipes**
- ○ Zinc oxide **diaper-rash ointment**
- ○ **Plastic bags** for disposing of soiled disposable diapers
- ○ **Leak-proof bag** for soiled cloth diapers or wet clothes. (Many diaper bags come with one of these.)
- ○ One complete **change of clothes** (including socks), plus a sweater, hat, or jacket
- ○ If bottle-feeding, **extra formula** and **sterilized water**
- ○ **Snacks**, such as cereal and crackers, in lidded plastic containers
- ○ A **bib** or two
- ○ Two clean **pacifiers** if your baby uses one
- ○ A favorite small **toy** or two
- ○ A **book** that baby can hold and/or chew on
- ○ **Teething ring**, if needed
- ○ **Tissues**
- ○ **Cloth diaper** or small towel to mop up spit-ups and spills
- ○ **Sunscreen**
- ○ Baby **pain and fever reliever**
- ○ **Petroleum jelly** to protect from windburn and dryness
- ○ Extra **blanket**
- ○ **Reading material.** If you have a few minutes, you can catch up on that magazine article you never get to read at home

10 rainy-day destinations

Plan in advance for those bad-weather days that threaten to keep you cooped up inside. Have your raingear ready and consider taking these short trips to child-friendly places.

○ THE MALL. One or two errands might be the limit before fussiness sets in. If your baby is at the stage where he can't resist reaching for anything and everything, just window shop. Stop in the food court for snacks and juice, or a bottle for the little one and a latte for you.

○ A MUSEUM. Some offer exhibits that might appeal to children, such as antique toys or events in local history, so check schedules. Most museums allow strollers during the week when visitors are fewer.

○ A FAST-FOOD RESTAURANT. Spilling is almost expected here, so babies and toddlers can feel right at home. If there's a play area, check before you go to see if your child is old enough. Keep them out of the ball pit, if there is one. It's easy for a little one to get jumped on, and it's unlikely the balls are cleaned regularly.

○ A DINER OR COFFEE SHOP. Plan to visit before or after the lunch rush, so you can get a booth. The menu should have plenty of kids' fare, such as pancakes, grilled cheese, and milkshakes. Grandmotherly waitresses are always a plus.

○ AN EXERCISE CLASS. Call around to find one that will accommodate both you and your child. Many health clubs and exercise studios now offer babysitting or a dedicated play place. Or see if there's a class for toddlers in your area.

○ THE LIBRARY. Many libraries offer activities for moms and small children—a story lady or just a get-together. Call to see if you need to register ahead of time.

○ A FRIEND'S HOUSE. Make a "pact" with several other mothers that you'll rotate afternoon meeting places during inclement weather for a BYOS (bring your own snacks) event.

○ THE COMMUNITY CENTER. Get a schedule of activities and keep it handy. If your community center doesn't have much for moms and kids, offer ideas yourself, such as a story time, movement or music class, or crafts class.

○ A BAKERY. Sweet and savory smells can brighten a dark day. Have your toddler pick out a special cookie or cupcake.

○ YOUR OWN LIVING ROOM. For toddlers, create a rainy-day "activity box" with special tapes and toys. Turn a table into a snug tent with a sheet or blanket and tell stories. Put on a puppet show using silly voices. Or snuggle up with baby and watch that movie you recorded two months ago but never got a chance to watch.

Coping with colic

When healthy, well-fed babies cry (and cry and cry and cry) for no apparent reason, the syndrome is called "colic." Colic may begin when baby is about 3 weeks old, reach its peak at the 6- or 8-week mark, start to diminish at 3 months—and most often disappears by the time baby is 4 months old.

If bottle-feeding, investigate a formula allergy. Babies may be allergic to lactose or to a protein in cow's milk. Your doctor can recommend a hypoallergenic formula, if necessary.

It's impossible to predict whether a baby will be colicky. Colic tendencies vary from sibling to sibling. But you'll want to be prepared with possible solutions.

○ GET A DOCTOR'S EVALUATION. There is usually no underlying medical condition—but just knowing your baby is healthy can ease your own anxiety.

○ GIVE HER A MASSAGE. Apply unscented, hypoallergenic lotion to your hands—and make sure your hands are warm! Put baby on her stomach. Using your index and middle fingers only, work gently on her back in a circular motion.

○ CARRY YOUR LITTLE ONE. Both warmth and motion can be calming. Snuggle baby in a sling or soft carrier and keep her with you as you move around the house.

○ CALM WITH A SWING. Manual or automatic, swings provide soothing motion. Limit swing-time to 30 minutes, and use the slow setting.

○ TAKE A WARM BATH. Some colicky babies calm down almost instantly when they get into a warm bath with mom or dad.

○ TAKE HIM OUTSIDE. A change in temperature and atmosphere may bring about a change in mood, too. You can put baby in a sling or stroller for a walk.

○ GO BYE-BYE IN THE CAR. Some parents find that driving around can help calm a crying baby, inducing a much-needed nap.

○ AVOID OVERSTIMULATION BEFORE BEDTIME. Your baby may not be able to make an abrupt shift from interacting with others to falling asleep. Putting her in a play yard for quiet time before settling her in the crib can ease the transition.

○ TAG TEAM. Taking a break from caring for a crying baby is important just to preserve your own energy and concentration. So have your spouse or another family member take over occasionally.

○ POP IN THE EARPLUGS. The high-pitched cry of a colicky baby can be too much for some adult ears. Earplugs can drop the decibel level just enough to keep your nerves from fraying and your patience from giving out.

Reduce parenting stress

Along with being the cutest thing you've ever seen, chances are your newborn is also the most demanding—and sometimes bewildering—little person you've ever met. These techniques can help ease the pressure.

○ **JOIN A PARENTS' GROUP.** Being able to discuss a baby's daily life and lovable quirks with others who understand can be a big help. Beyond informal meetings or excursions, some groups may also have a web site where members can post news and requests, and an e-mail or phone network for special bulletins. Weekly get-togethers also allow you to have conversations with other adults—something new parents really appreciate!

○ **GET A BABYSITTER FOR A FEW HOURS.** Whether you need to nap or simply catch up on household chores, having someone else watch your little one, maybe from 2 to 5 in the afternoon, can provide that almost-forgotten luxury—time to yourself. Having baby get used to someone besides her parents is a good way to socialize her as well, and will make longer separations down the road easier.

○ **FIND FUN FOR SIBLINGS.** When older children are feeling left out—and parents are stressed out—see if a friend, relative, or another parent can take big brother or sister on a special outing for a few hours. A jaunt to the park, a visit to a special store at the mall, or a trip for ice cream may be just the ticket.

○ **WELCOME FOOD DELIVERIES.** If good friends or relatives ask what they can bring when coming to meet baby, you might want to answer, "Dinner." Keep it simple, with takeout or basic fixings, throwaway plates, and plastic utensils. You can share the (easy) kitchen chores, then relax around the table like you did pre-baby.

○ **TRADE ERRAND SERVICES.** See if friends who live close by can help out in a pinch, maybe picking up something you've forgotten at the store. (You can then promise to reciprocate some time in the future.) Need more help than friends can provide? Check out an errand or housecleaning service.

○ **STOCK YOUR NIGHTTIME FEEDING SPOT.** While baby is enjoying that middle-of-the-night meal, don't forget to make yourself comfy, too. A well-padded rocker can soothe both of you. Place a low-wattage light nearby, and perhaps a tape or CD player to provide soft music.

○ **SEARCH OUT A DAY SPA.** An excellent Mother's Day or birthday gift to request is a day or even a few hours at a local day spa. Body treatments such as massage, facials, and wraps can rejuvenate you. Dad can enjoy services at most day spas, too.

○ **DOUBLE UP.** Avoid the stress of realizing you forgot vital baby gear for your trip to Grandma's. Keep an extra play yard, high chair, and toys at her house (or any other place you frequent) as well as at home.

Traveling with baby

Whether you're off to visit grandparents or just taking a long weekend, these tips can help make your getaway smoother. Every trip, short or long, will require a car seat and a stroller or baby carrier, and perhaps a travel play yard. Here are ideas for some other items to make traveling easier.

○ Enough clothes, pajamas, socks, and blankets for the length of your trip—plus two more days so you're prepared for delays.

○ Sufficient diapers to get you to your destination, plus a few more. Unless you're camping or going someplace remote, you can always find a place to buy diapers once you arrive.

○ Well-stocked diaper bag (see the checklist on page 212).

○ Bottles, extra nipples, and formula if you're bottle-feeding.

○ Small first-aid kit, including infant's pain and fever medications, and any prescription medication.

○ Copy of baby's medical records; pediatrician's phone and beeper number; home pharmacy phone number.

○ Favorite toys and books.

If you're flying...

○ DETERMINE THE LEAST BUSY FLYING TIMES. Call the airline to find out. You'll be most likely to snag an empty seat—and a less-crowded flight is easier to negotiate with a child, car seat, carry-on bags, etc.

○ MEASURE YOUR CAR SEAT. One wider than 16 inches is unlikely to fit properly into the frame of an aircraft seat.

○ RESERVE ADJOINING SEATS. If you purchase a ticket, you'll want to get your seat assignments immediately. A baby's car seat must be in a window seat, so it won't block the escape path, and it cannot go in an exit row. (Most airlines offer a half-price fare for children under 2, but you may have to quiz the agent to find out about it.)

○ LEARN THE AIRLINE'S CAR-SEAT RULES. Children under 20 pounds must be in a rear-facing seat; from 20 to 40 pounds, they may use a forward-facing restraint; those over 40 pounds may use an aircraft seat belt.

○ PLAN FOR LOST LUGGAGE. Pack several changes of clothing in a carry-on bag. You don't want to be caught high and dry if your luggage is lost.

Keeping baby safe

Contents

Home, safe home

Keeping baby safe is every parent's key concern. By educating yourself about real risks your baby may face—and how to minimize them—you can enjoy playtime, bedtime, mealtime, and every other time with your baby. For years, CONSUMER REPORTS has been at the forefront in informing consumers about product safety. The information here is based on those years of experience. There are plenty of sources of expert advice. Hospitals, birthing centers, and community groups offer classes on infant CPR and babyproofing your home. You can hire a safety consultant who specializes in in-home babyproofing to come in and make recommendations and do the work. Or become your own expert by culling information from these pages and from web sites that specialize in baby safety (see Parenting and Health Resources, page 203).

Safety basics

Begin to think about creating a safe environment before your baby comes home. It's true that in the first months there is not a whole lot a baby can get into—but that will change in a hurry. Before you know it, your baby will be highly mobile. The general advice that follows will help you with the basics. Then you can concentrate on extensive childproofing (see page 222). Of course, a safe home is no substitute for a watchful parent.

General safety concerns

- **Edges and hinges**

    Thoroughly check toys, strollers, high chairs, play yards, and gates for sharp edges and potentially dangerous hinges.

- **Elevated spaces**

    Anything that elevates a squirming baby —a changing table, a framed carrier, a high chair, or an infant car seat—has injury potential. Make sure these items have safety belts—and use them.

- **Hazardous gaps**

    Beware of gaps in which a baby can get stuck if he slips through, such as the leg openings of strollers or baby carriers, the space between the seat and tray of a high chair, or the area between the bars of a crib or, cradle, or between a gate and the floor.

- **Riding toys**

    Don't purchase a riding toy until you're certain your child is mature enough to use it safely. Attach a tall flag on the back of a tricycle so it's visible to motorists. The lower to the ground, the safer a wheeled toy is. Always supervise a child when riding. Be sure your child can ride without going into traffic, on steep hills, or into the driveway. If there is no safe place to ride, only use a riding toy for visits to the park.

Helmets

Get your toddlers or preschooler into the habit of wearing a helmet when using a tricycle or bicycle. Choose a helmet that carriers a certification sticker. Try on different ones to make sure you've got the right size: Your child should be able to see and hear well, the chin strap should be easy to fasten and release, and it should fit comfortably under the chin without chafing.

Ban balloons

Don't let a small child play with an inflated or deflated balloon. The material poses a choking hazard. Put packages of uninflated balloons safely out of reach.

Around the house

Emergency numbers

Gather emergency telephone numbers, including those of your baby's doctor-to-be and the toll-free poison-control center, as well as all contact numbers for family members. Post an easy-to-read copy next to each telephone.

In case of fire

Install a smoke alarm and a carbon monoxide detector in key locations on each floor of your home. Change their batteries when you set your clocks to standard time each October. Check the detectors every other week to make sure batteries are good. Place large street address numbers at the entrance to your driveway or on the front door for the fire department to see easily. Formulate an escape plan.

Product registration

Mail in registration cards that come with baby products so you can be notified about recalls. Follow manufacturers' age or weight guidelines for use of products. Keep product instruction manuals in an easy-to-find location, such as in a large, sealed plastic bag in a kitchen cabinet or, for car seats, in the car.

Water heater

Reduce the setting of your hot-water heater to 120° F. An infant's skin burns much more easily than an adult's.

Thank you for not smoking

Ban smoking indoors. Secondhand smoke has been associated with Sudden Infant Death Syndrome (SIDS) and baby respiratory ailments.

Pet safety

Consider obedience training for your pet to ensure safe, controlled behavior around baby. Talk to a trainer about easy ways to introduce your baby into a home with pets. Buy a tall gate to keep your dog in the kitchen or other safe area. Move your cat's litter box to a spot that you know your toddler won't be able to reach.

Hazardous substances

Have tap water tested for lead and, if needed, purchase an effective water-purification system. Heirloom furniture such as cribs and chests may have been coated with lead-containing paints, lacquers, or varnishes. You can test antique finishes with a lead-testing kit. If you detect lead in a piece of furniture, store it until baby gets older. Old cribs, besides having possibly malfunctioning parts, may have paint that contains lead.

Household cleaners and deodorizers

Assess household cleaning products. Cleaning ingredients such as ammonia can irritate a baby's nose and throat. Fragrances can irritate a baby's sensitive skin and respiratory passages and can even trigger allergic reactions. So you may want to skip floral or citrus scents once baby arrives. You'll probably want to avoid using plug-in or aerosol room deodorizers as well.

Launder new clothes and bedding

Launder all new baby clothes and bedding in a fragrance-free detergent once or twice to remove chemicals. Don't use liquid fabric softener or dryer sheets. The fragrance can irritate baby's skin and respiratory system. Liquid softener may also increase fabric flammability and reduce absorbency.

Cords and ties

Cords from draperies or blinds can entangle a baby. Cut looped cords in half to form two strings. You can also roll cords up and secure them with rubber bands or twist ties. The ties of crib bumper guards should be no longer than 7 inches. Avoid small cord shorteners, which can be ingested.

Secure windows

Purchase window locks or guards from a hardware or home-supply store and install them according to the manufacturer's instructions.

Buckets and sinks

To avoid a drowning hazard, never leave a bucket or sinkful of water or other liquid unattended when small children are around. It's possible for toddlers to fall in head first.

Backyard play equipment

Don't assume children's play equipment is safe simply because it's made for children. Supervise constantly—toddlers don't understand heights, their own limitations, or the pendulum effect of swings. Don't allow your toddler to use a slat-style swing until her feet firmly touch the ground and you're sure she is mature and strong enough to hold on without losing her balance when she leans backward. Put infants and toddlers between the ages of 9 months and 3 years in specially designed swings with sides, backs, and crotch and waist belts to contain them. Look for smooth edges and surfaces with no ragged seams or corners, and no nooks or crannies that could trap a child's fingers.

Night-lights

Night-lights at floor level attract crawling babies and toddlers to sockets. Instead, place a night-light in a socket out of baby's reach, install a dimmer switch, or use a lamp with a low-wattage bulb.

- **Lawn equipment**

  Keep your tot indoors whenever you use a string trimmer, snow blower, power mower, hedge trimmer, or other outdoor equipment. Pour fuel into this equipment while outdoors—not in the garage, where it could ignite.

- **Old refrigerators**

  If you are discarding an old refrigerator, always remove the doors and store the unit facedown while awaiting trash pickup.

- **Bug spray**

  Avoid using bug sprays in areas where baby spends a lot of time crawling around.

Baby's room

- **Decorating the nursery**

  Allow time for fumes from new paint, wallpaper, drapes, and carpeting to subside before baby comes home. Paint the nursery at least a week before baby's arrival. When possible, use paint that is low in volatile organic compounds, which may be irritating to a baby (and some adults). To reduce fumes, air out new furniture and anything made of plastic or particleboard.

- **Crib bedding**

  Be sure that the crib mattress is firm, that there are no gaps between the mattress and the sides of the crib, and that the mattress cover and sheets fit snugly. Soft bedding—pillows, quilts, comforters, and sheepskins—is a suffocation hazard for infants, so keep those items out of the crib.

Instead, plan to dress baby warmly enough for comfort. If you use a lightweight blanket, it should be pulled up no farther than the baby's underarms.

- **Crib location**

  Place the crib well away from wall hangings, toys, window blinds and curtains, and other furniture so that an adventurous baby can't reach anything dangerous.

- **Toys and mobiles**

  Keep soft toys out of the crib, which are a suffocation hazard for young babies and can be used as stepping stools for climbing out. If you buy a crib mobile, be sure to hang it out of baby's reach. (A mobile should be taken down when baby is able to push up on her hands and knees, at about 6 months.)

- **Toy chests**

  Don't store toys in wooden chests with lids that can slam shut and hurt a child. Chests designed specifically for holding toys have hinges with safety stops and carved-out openings to prevent such an accident. Open shelves or crates are safer and make it easier to find toys.

- **Broken parts**

  Check all baby equipment frequently for broken parts or malfunctioning hardware. Stop using anything, particularly a crib, with broken or missing parts.

Childproofing your home

Childproofing can start before baby is born. At the very least, you need to finish before baby starts to crawl. You can do it yourself, or hire a childproofing service. Such services usually charge $60 to $75 per hour plus the cost of products such as cabinet locks, outlet covers, and safety gates, as well as installation. For a list of companies, see the International Association for Child Safety's web site *(www.iafcs.com)*. You'll want to keep these measures in place until they're no longer needed or effective. For instance, a safety gate's useful life ends at about age 2, or when a child is big enough to be able to climb over it. Other measures can be relaxed as you child shows some judgment, maybe by age 4.

All over the house

● **Electrical outlets**

Block unused electrical outlets with safety covers that screw into the outlet. (Small outlet plugs can be dangerous because exploring babies can remove them and put them in their mouths.) Check that all outlets in places where moisture may be present, such as bathrooms, basements, or outdoors, have a ground fault interrupter, which senses imbalances in the current and immediately trips the circuit.

● **Area rugs**

Secure all area rugs or throw rugs in place with foam carpet backing or double-sided tape. To protect new walkers from stumbling, be sure no edges or corners curl up.

● **Railings**

If railings on staircases and balconies are spaced more than 2⅜ inches apart (the diameter of a soda can), install railing guards made of mesh or clear plastic to prevent your child from falling through or getting stuck.

● **Windows**

Keep baby away from open windows— window screens aren't strong enough to keep a child from falling out. Install window guards if you live in a high rise.

● **Small parts**

Inspect your home for dangerously small objects. Anything small enough to fit through the tube of a toilet-paper roll (about 1¾ inches in diameter) could pose a choking hazard.

● **Fire starters**

Place all matches and lighters on a high surface or in a locking drawer or cabinet.

● **Small items**

Keep small objects out of baby's reach— check toys, pick up clutter, keep your purse out of reach, and stash an older sibling's toys with small parts away from baby.

● **Stairways**

Install a secure, hardware-mounted gate at the top of each staircase (see page 128).

Heavy furniture

Bolt or bracket bookcases and other heavy furniture, such as wall units or armoires, to the wall to prevent tipping if a toddler decides to climb on one of them.

Doorknob covers

Consider buying doorknob covers, which can only be squeezed open by an adult hand.

Padding corners

Add safety padding to the sharp corners of coffee tables, or consider storing them during baby's first few years.

Extension cords

Purchase extension cords equipped with locking plug covers. If your house is overloaded with extension cords, talk to an electrician about having additional outlets installed.

Plastic bags

Plastic bags pose suffocation hazards. Keep plastic garbage bags, laundry bags, food storage or grocery bags, and bags used in packaging everything from dry cleaning to electronics on a high shelf or in a locked cupboard. Tie a plastic bag in knots before throwing it out.

Parked cars

Never leave a little one alone in a parked car. Lock parked cars so children can't play in them. Kids who accidentally lock themselves in won't be unable to unlock the doors.

Kitchen

Harmful items

Anything harmful should be stashed away in drawers or cupboards equipped with child-resistant safety latches. The list includes all kitchen cleaners; plastic wrap, food storage bags, and food-wrap packages with a serrated edge; knives, scissors, and other sharp objects; refrigerator magnets or any small kitchen knickknacks; and any type of liquor.

Small appliances

To prevent baby from tugging down small appliances—coffeemakers, food processors, toaster ovens—wrap up and fasten cords out of reach with twist ties or rubber bands. Or tape cords to the wall with masking tape. Irons are another hazard. Put baby safely in a safety seat or play yard whenever you iron, and don't leave an unattended baby and an iron in a room together.

Kitchen stepstool

Keep your kitchen stepstool in a closet when you're not using it to prevent your little one from climbing into trouble.

Kitchen access

When you cook, use a gate for the kitchen or keep baby in a play yard, swing, or high chair—in view but out of harm's way.

Stove

Pull off front stove knobs and store them safely until it's time to cook. You can also buy childproof knob covers. When possible, cook on the back burners, and always turn all pot handles toward the back of the cooktop.

- ### Microwave risks

  Decide on an alternative to using a microwave to heat bottles of breastmilk or formula or jars of baby food. A microwave can create hot spots in the milk or food that can burn a baby's mouth and throat and may also cause jars, bottles, and nurser liners to explode.

- ### In case of fire

  Keep a box of baking soda near the stove to extinguish grease fires. Purchase a small fire extinguisher and mount it nearby. Familiarize yourself with its use.

Bathroom

- ### Keep baby out

  Keep bathroom doors securely closed or blocked off with a gate. You may also want to cover the inside door lock with duct tape to keep baby from locking you out. Install doorknobs that have a hole on the outside through which you can push a thin rod or screwdriver to disengage the lock.

- ### Medicine safety

  Keep medicine out of the bedside table and install a lock on the medicine cabinet. You might even store medications in a childproof locked box kept on a high shelf outside the bathroom. Put vitamin supplements out of reach, too—iron pills or

vitamins containing iron are leading child poisoners. Choose child-resistant packaging for prescription and over-the-counter drugs and any vitamin supplements.

- ### Diaper pail

  If you use cloth diapers, make sure the pail has a tamper-proof lid with a solid locking device to eliminate a drowning hazard. Don't use deodorizing tablets, which can be ingested.

- ### Toilet lid

  Install a device to lock the lid of the adult toilet to keep baby out.

- ### Poison control

  Post the number of the poison-control center near the medicine cabinet. Keep activated charcoal and syrup of ipecac (available from pharmacies) in case your child swallows anything toxic—but always call a poison-control center before you administer any remedy.

- ### Bathing a baby

  When using a baby bathtub, always keep a hand on baby. Never use a bath seat, or bath ring. There have been numerous reports of babies drowning when their parents turned their back on them momentarily. Never leave a baby alone in water.

- ### Bathing a toddler

  Attach rubber strips to the surface of a regular bathtub to prevent slipping. Get a cover for the bathtub's spout to protect a child from its heat-conducting metal and hard edges.

- **Electricity**

  Store all electrical devices such as curling irons and hair dryers in a high cupboard outside the bathroom.

Living room or den

- **Respect for fire**

  If you have a fireplace or wood-burning stove, teach your toddler to respect the warnings "Hot!" and "Don't touch!"

- **Providing supervision**

  Never leave a child in the room alone with a heat source, even if he seems safely enclosed in a play yard or seat.

- **Screens and padding**

  Consider installing a fireproof safety railing around the fireplace, and always use a fireplace screen. Put fireproof padding around sharp brick edges on raised hearths.

- **TV and VCR placement**

  The TV and VCR should be out of reach. Place them on a wall-mounted stand or a shelf fastened to the wall.

- **Glass**

  Put large stickers on sliding glass doors to avoid collisions. Remove vases and other knickknacks that a baby could break, fall on, or swallow.

- **Houseplants**

  Give away poisonous houseplants (poinsettias, dumbcane, dieffenbacia, philodendrons, calla lilies, mistletoe, and hyacinths, to name a few), or ask friends to keep them until your child is older. Lists of poisonous plants can be found on child-safety web sites (see Resource Guide, page 204). Keep all plants well trimmed, so a child can't reach them.

Baby's room

- **Furniture**

  Avoid high chests or tables. Bolt book cases and chests to the wall so they won't tip if a child climbs on them.

- **A clear path**

  Position furniture and toys so you'll have a clear path when you enter the room at night. Any area rug or throw rug should have a nonskid backing or, better yet, be secured with double-faced tape, so no edges stick up. Run power cords under rugs or secure them along the wall.

- **Crib**

  Remember that a crib is the safest place for baby to nap or sleep. But once your child attempts to climb out of the crib, consider using a bed with child railings or putting the mattress on the floor.

Basement and garage

- **Stairs**

  To prevent falls down basement stairs, install a lock as high as you can reach on both sides of the basement door. Make sure stairs are well lit, and keep all clutter and toys off steps.

- **Laundry supplies**

  Stash detergent, bleach, and other laundry essentials in a locking cupboard. Keep all chemicals in their original containers; never transfer them to soda bottles or other beverage containers.

- **Workbench**

  Put your workbench off-limits, whether you're working there or not. Lock up power tools and all small or sharp objects.

- **Door to house**

  Install a lock on the door leading outside or to the garage. Consider installing a self-locking "Dutch door" that allows you to pass groceries into the house without letting your toddler out.

- **Hazardous substances**

  Store gasoline, oil, barbecue starter, insecticides, antifreeze, paint, car polish, and other hazardous substances behind locked cabinet doors.

- **Ride-on toys**

  To keep children away from the garage, store tricycles and ride-on toys somewhere in the house instead.

- **Garage-door openers**

  Test an electric garage-door opener's sensitivity by placing a 2-inch-high block of wood on the floor in the door's path. If the door doesn't stop, don't use the garage door opener. Open and close the door manually or replace the garage-door opener

with a device equipped with optical sensors that prevent the garage door from closing if a child gets in the way.

Decks, porches, and yard

- **Doors leading outside**

  Install a latch high on the backyard door. Firmly lock sliding patio doors, and secure them with a bar in the door track.

- **Roaming outdoors**

  You may want to purchase a baby monitor that you can clip on to a toddler. Some sound an alarm when the child strays. But nothing replaces adult vigilance.

- **Porch or deck railing**

  Spaces between a porch or deck railing should be no more than 2⅜ inches. If they are wider, install a railing guard made of mesh or plastic.

- **Water containers**

  All outdoor containers of water, including buckets and wading pools, should be emptied after use and stored upside down, preferably in the garage.

- **Pools**

  Surround your pool with a fence (required under most building codes, as well as many insurance companies before they'll issue a policy) and a self-locking gate. Cover the pool during the off-season. Pool alarms for in-ground pools sound if a child falls in, but they are prone to false alarms.

Pediatric drugs

Contents

Common prescriptions for kids

This section presents in one place key information parents need to know regarding medications commonly prescribed for babies and young children. Drugs are listed alphabetically.

Over-the-counter (OTC) medications, such as the pain and fever-reducing medications acetaminophen (Tylenol Infants' Drops, Tylenol Childrens' Chewables) or ibuprofen (Children's Advil, Children's Motrin) are also commonly used in young children. Even though these are "children's" medications, it's important to check with your pediatrician before using any OTC medication.

Dosage and usage of prescription drugs used by adults, of course, must be adjusted for small bodies. For prescription and nonprescription drugs, care needs to be taken in measuring the dose. When using liquid formulations, use the dosing cup, spoon, or dropper included with the product. If one is not available, use a measuring spoon, not a regular teaspoon, since such utensils can vary significantly in how much medicine they can hold. Read package labeling and insert information. Do not use any drug after the expiration date on the label, as it may no longer be effective. And remember, keep all medications, vitamins and minerals, and dietary supplements far out of the reach of young children.

ALBUTEROL
nebulizer solution

Sold under these brand names
Proventil
Salbutamol
Ventolin

Description

Adrenergic bronchodilators are medicines that are breathed in through the mouth to open up the bronchial tubes (air passages) of the lungs. These medicines are used mostly for asthma and also for some cases of chronic bronchitis, emphysema, and other lung diseases.

These medicines are also breathed in through the mouth to prevent bronchospasm (wheezing or difficulty in breathing) caused by exercise.

Before using this medicine

Pregnancy
These medicines are used to treat asthma in pregnant women. Although there are no studies on birth defects in humans, problems have not been reported. Some studies in animals have shown that they cause birth defects when given in doses many times higher than the human dose.

Breastfeeding
It is not known whether these medicines pass into the breast milk. Although most medicines pass into breast milk in small amounts, many of them may be used safely while breastfeeding. Mothers who are using these medicines and who wish to breastfeed should discuss this with their doctor.

Proper use of this medicine

These medicines come with patient directions. Read them carefully before using the medicine. If you do not understand the directions or if you are not sure how to use the medicine, ask your health-care professional to show you how to use it.

Dosing

For inhalation aerosol dosage form:

• Children up to 12 years of age: Dose must be determined by your doctor.

Side effects of this medicine

Check with your doctor immediately if any of the following side effects occur:

Severe dizziness; feeling of choking, irritation, or swelling in throat; flushing or redness of skin; hives; increased shortness of breath; skin rash; swelling of face, lips, or eyelids; tightness in chest or wheezing, trouble breathing, irregular heartbeat

Other side effects

Common: Fast heartbeat; headache; nervousness; trembling

Less common: Coughing or other bronchial irritation; dizziness or lightheadedness; dryness or irritation of mouth or throat

Rare: Chest discomfort or pain; drowsiness or weakness; muscle cramps or twitching; nausea and/or vomiting; restlessness; trouble sleeping

ALLEGRA (fexofenadine)

Description

Fexofenadine (fex-oh-FEN-a-deen) is an antihistamine. It is used to relieve the symptoms of hay fever and hives.

Before using this medicine

Allergies

Tell your doctor if your child has ever had any unusual or allergic reaction to fexofenadine. Also tell your health care professional if you are allergic to any other substances, such as foods, preservatives, or dyes.

Pregnancy

In animal studies, this medicine did not cause birth defects but did cause a decrease in birth weight of the infant. Discuss with your doctor whether or not you should continue to use this medicine if you become pregnant.

Breastfeeding

It is not known whether fexofenadine passes into breast milk. Although most medicines pass into breast milk in small amounts, many of them may be used safely while breast-feeding. Mothers who are taking this medicine and who wish to breastfeed should discuss this with their doctor.

Children

This medicine has been tested in children 6 years of age and older and, in effective doses, has not been shown to cause different side effects or problems than it does in adults. There is no specific information about the use of fexofenadine in children less than 6 years of age.

Dosing

For oral dosage form (capsules, tablets) for symptoms of hay fever

• Children 6 to 11 years of age: 30 mg twice daily

• Children younger than 6 years of age: Use and dose must be determined by your doctor.

For symptoms of chronic hives

• Children 6 to 11 years of age: 30 mg twice daily.

• Children less than 6 years of age: Use and dose must be determined by your doctor.

Side effects of this medicine

Back pain; cough; dizziness; drowsiness; earache; fever; headache; nausea; pain or tenderness around eyes or cheekbones; painful menstrual bleeding; ringing or buzzing in ears; runny or stuffy nose; stomach upset; unusual feeling of tiredness; muscle aches and pains

AMOXICILLIN

Sold under these brand names:

Amoxil
Polymox
Trimox
Wymox

Description

Penicillins are used to treat infections caused by

bacteria. They work by killing the bacteria or preventing their growth. None of the penicillins will work for colds, flu, or other virus infections.

Penicillins are available only with your doctor's prescription, in the following dosage forms:
- Capsules (U.S. and Canada)
- Oral suspension (U.S. and Canada)
- Tablets (U.S.)
- Chewable tablets (U.S. and Canada)

Before using this medicine

Allergies
Tell your doctor if your child has ever had any unusual or allergic reaction to any type of penicillin or to a similar class of antibiotics called cephalosporins.

Pregnancy
Penicillin has not been studied in pregnant women. However, it has been widely used in pregnant women and has not been shown to cause birth defects or other problems in animal studies.

Breastfeeding
Penicillin passes into the breast milk. Even though only small amounts may pass into breast milk, allergic reactions, diarrhea, fungus infections, and skin rash may occur in nursing babies.

Children
Many types of penicillins have been used in children and, in effective doses, are not expected to cause different side effects or problems in children than they do in adults.

Some strengths of the chewable tablets of amoxicillin contain aspartame, which is changed by the body to phenylalanine, a substance that is harmful to patients with phenylketonuria.

Dosing

Newborns and infants up to 3 months of age: Dose is based on body weight and must be determined by your doctor. The usual dose is 15 mg per kg (6.8 mg per pound) or less every 12 hours.

Infants 3 months of age and older and children weighing up to 40 kg (88 lbs.): Dose is based on body weight and must be determined by your doctor. The usual dose is 6.7 to 13.3 mg per kg (3 to 6 mg per

pound) every eight hours or 12.5 to 22.5 mg per kg (5.7 to 10.2 mg per pound) every 12 hours.

Precautions while using this medicine

Penicillins may cause diarrhea in some patients.
- Check with your doctor if severe diarrhea occurs.
- For mild diarrhea, diarrhea medicine containing kaolin or attapulgite (e.g., Kaopectate tablets, Diasorb) may be taken.

Side effects of this medicine

Stop taking this medicine and get emergency help immediately if any of the following side effects occur:

Fast or irregular breathing; fever; joint pain; lightheadedness or fainting; puffiness or swelling around the face; red, scaly skin; shortness of breath; skin rash, hives, itching

Check with your doctor immediately if any of the following side effects occur:

Abdominal or stomach cramps and pain (severe); abdominal tenderness; convulsions (seizures); decreased amount of urine; diarrhea (watery and severe), which may also be bloody; mental depression; nausea and vomiting; pain at place of injection; sore throat and fever; unusual bleeding or bruising; yellow eyes or skin

NOTE: Some of the above side effects (severe abdominal or stomach cramps and pain, and watery and severe diarrhea, which may also be bloody) may also occur up to several weeks after you stop taking any of these medicines.

AUGMENTIN
(amoxicillin plus clavulanate)

Description

Penicillins and beta-lactamase inhibitors (clavulinic acid) are used to treat infections caused by bacteria. They work by killing the bacteria or preventing their growth. The beta-lactamase inhibitor is added to the penicillin to protect the penicillin from certain substances (enzymes made by the very bacteria you're treating) that can destroy the penicillin before it can kill the bacteria.

- Oral suspension (U.S. and Canada)
- Tablets (U.S. and Canada)
- Chewable tablets (U.S.)

Before using this medicine

Allergies

Tell your doctor if your child has ever had any unusual or allergic reaction to any of the penicillins, cephalosporins, or beta-lactamase inhibitors. Also tell your health-care professional if you are allergic to any other substances, such as foods, preservatives, or dyes.

Pregnancy

Penicillins and beta-lactamase inhibitors have not been studied in pregnant women. However, penicillins have not been shown to cause birth defects or other problems in animal studies.

Breastfeeding

Penicillins and sulbactam, a beta-lactamase inhibitor, pass into the breast milk. Even though only small amounts may pass into breast milk, allergic reactions, diarrhea, fungus infections, and skin rash may occur in nursing babies.

Children

Penicillins and beta-lactamase inhibitors have been used in children and, in effective doses, are not expected to cause different side effects or problems in children than they do in adults.

Some strengths of the chewable tablets and oral suspensions of amoxicillin and clavulanate combination contain aspartame, which is changed by the body to phenylalanine, a substance that is harmful to patients with phenylketonuria.

Proper use of this medicine

Amoxicillin and clavulanate combination may be taken on a full or empty stomach. Taking amoxicillin and clavulanate combination with food may decrease the chance of diarrhea, nausea, and vomiting.

For patients taking the oral liquid form of amoxicillin and clavulanate combination:

- Use a specially marked measuring spoon or other device to measure each dose accurately. The average household teaspoon may not hold the right amount of liquid.
- Do not use after the expiration date on the label. The medicine may not work properly after that date. If you have any questions about this, check with your pharmacist.

For patients taking the chewable tablet form of amoxicillin and clavulanate combination:

- Tablets should be chewed or crushed before they are swallowed.

Dosing

For oral dosage forms (chewable tablets and suspension):

- Neonates and infants up to 12 weeks (3 months) of age: Dose is based on body weight and must be determined by your doctor. The usual dose is 15 mg of amoxicillin per kg (6.8 mg per pound) every 12 hours.
- Infants 3 months of age and older and children weighing up to 40 kg (88 pounds): 6.7 to 22.5 mg of amoxicillin per kg (3 to 10.2 mg per pound), in combination with 1.7 to 3.2 mg of clavulanate per kg (0.8 to 1.5 mg per pound), every eight or twelve hours.

For oral dosage form (tablets):

- Infants and children weighing up to 40 kg (88 pounds): The amoxicillin and clavulanate combination tablets are too strong for children weighing less than 40 kg (88 pounds). The chewable tablets or oral suspension are used in those children.

Precautions while using this medicine

- Check with your doctor if severe diarrhea occurs.
- For mild diarrhea, diarrhea medicine containing kaolin or attapulgite (e.g., Kaopectate tablets, Diasorb) may be taken.

Side effects of this medicine

Stop taking this medicine and get emergency help immediately if any of the following side effects occur:

Cough; fast or irregular breathing; fever; joint pain; lightheadedness or fainting; puffiness or swelling around the face; red, irritated eyes; shortness of breath or wheezing; skin rash, hives, itching; sore mouth or tongue; unusual tiredness or weakness; vaginal itching and discharge; white patches in mouth and/or on tongue

Check with your doctor immediately if any of the following side effects occur:

Abdominal or stomach cramps and pain (severe); blistering, peeling, or loosening of skin and mucous membranes; chest pain; cloudy urine; convulsions (seizures); diarrhea (watery and severe), which may also be bloody; general feeling of illness or discomfort; nausea or vomiting; redness, soreness, or swelling of tongue; red skin lesions, often with a purple center; sore throat; swelling of face, fingers, lower legs, or feet; trouble in urinating; unusual bleeding or bruising; weight gain; yellow eyes or skin
NOTE: Some of the above side effects (severe abdominal or stomach cramps and pain, and watery and severe diarrhea, which may also be bloody) may also occur up to several weeks after you stop taking any of these medicines.

BACTRIM, SEPTRA
(sulfamethoxazole plus trimethoprim)

Before using this medicine
Allergies
Tell your doctor if your child has ever had any unusual or allergic reaction to sulfa medicines, foods, preservatives (e.g., sulfites), or dyes.

Pregnancy
Sulfamethoxazole and trimethoprim combination has not been reported to cause birth defects or other problems in humans. However, studies in mice, rats, and rabbits have shown that some sulfonamides cause birth defects, including cleft palate and bone problems. Studies in rabbits have also shown that trimethoprim causes birth defects, as well as a decrease in the number of successful pregnancies. Sulfonamides are not recommended for use at the time of labor and delivery because these medicines may cause unwanted effects in the baby.

Breastfeeding
Sulfonamides and trimethoprim pass into the breast milk. These medicines are not recommended for use during breastfeeding. They may cause liver problems, anemia, and other unwanted effects in nursing babies, especially those with glucose-6-phosphate dehydrogenase (G6PD) deficiency.

Children
Sulfadiazine and trimethoprim combination should not be given to infants less than 3 months of age. Sulfamethoxazole and trimethoprim combination should not be given to infants less than 2 months of age unless directed by the child's doctor.

Proper use of this medicine
Sulfonamide and trimethoprim combinations are best taken with a full glass (8 ounces) of water. Several additional glasses of water should be taken every day, unless otherwise directed by your doctor. Drinking extra water will help to prevent some unwanted effects of sulfonamides.

For patients taking the oral liquid form of this medicine:
- Use a specially marked measuring spoon or other device to measure each dose accurately. The average household teaspoon may not hold the right amount of liquid.

Dosing
For oral dosage forms (suspension, tablets):
- Infants less than 2 months of age: Use is not recommended.
- Infants 2 months of age and older and children up to 40 kg of weight (88 pounds): Dose is based on body weight. The usual dose is 20 to 30 mg of sulfamethoxazole and 4 to 6 mg of trimethoprim per kg (9.1 to 13.6 mg of sulfamethoxazole and 1.8 to 2.7 mg of trimethoprim per pound) every 12 hours.

Precautions while using this medicine
Sulfonamide and trimethoprim combinations may cause skin to be more sensitive to sunlight than it is normally. Exposure to sunlight, even for brief periods

of time, may cause skin itching, redness, rash, or a severe sunburn. When you begin taking this medicine:

- Stay out of direct sunlight, especially between the hours of 10:00 a.m. and 3:00 p.m., if possible.
- Wear protective clothing, including a hat and sunglasses.
- Apply a sun-block product that has a skin protection factor (SPF) of at least 15. Some patients may require a product with a higher SPF number, especially if they have a fair complexion. If you have any questions about this, check with your health-care professional.
- Apply a sun-block lipstick that has an SPF of at least 15 to protect lips.

Side effects of this medicine

Check with your doctor immediately if any of the following side effects occur:

More common: Itching; skin rash
Less common: Aching of joints and muscles; difficulty in swallowing; pale skin; redness, blistering, peeling, or loosening of skin; sore throat and fever; unusual bleeding or bruising; unusual tiredness or weakness; yellow eyes or skin
Rare: Abdominal or stomach cramps and pain (severe); abdominal or stomach tenderness; anxiety; blood in urine; bluish fingernails, lips, or skin; confusion; diarrhea (watery and severe), which may also be bloody; difficult breathing; drowsiness; fever; general feeling of illness; greatly increased or decreased frequency of urination or amount of urine; hallucinations; headache, severe; increased thirst; lower back pain; mental depression; muscle pain or weakness; nausea; nervousness; pain at site of injection; pain or burning while urinating; seizures (convulsions); stiff neck and/or back; swelling of front part of neck
NOTE: Some of the above side effects (severe abdominal or stomach cramps and pain, and watery and severe diarrhea, which may also be bloody) may also occur up to several weeks after you stop using any of these medicines.

Also, check with your doctor as soon as possible if the following side effect occurs:

More common: Increased sensitivity of skin to sunlight

Other side effects may occur that usually do not need medical attention. These side effects may go away during treatment as your body adjusts to the medicine. However, check with your doctor if any of the following side effects continue or are bothersome:

More common: Diarrhea; dizziness; headache; loss of appetite; mouth sores or swelling of the tongue; nausea or vomiting; tiredness

Other side effects not listed above may also occur in some patients. If you notice any other effects, check with your doctor.

BIAXIN
(clarithromycin)

Description

Clarithromycin (kla-RITH-roe-mye-sin) is used to treat bacterial infections in many different parts of the body. It works by killing bacteria or preventing their growth. However, this medicine will not work for colds, flu, or other virus infections.

Before using this medicine

Allergies

Tell your doctor if your child has ever had any unusual or allergic reaction to clarithromycin or to any related medicines, such as erythromycin. Also tell your health-care professional if you are allergic to any other substances, such as foods, preservatives, or dyes.

Pregnancy

Clarithromycin has not been studied in pregnant women. However, studies in animals have shown that clarithromycin causes birth defects and other problems. Before taking this medicine, make sure your doctor knows if you are pregnant or if you may become pregnant.

Breastfeeding

Clarithromycin passes into breast milk.

Children

Studies on this medicine have not been done in children up to 6 months of age. In effective doses, the medicine has not been shown to cause different side effects or problems in children over the age of 6 months than it does in adults.

Proper use of this medicine
Dosing
For oral dosage forms (suspension and tablets):

- Children 6 months of age and older: 7.5 mg per kilogram (kg) (3.4 mg per pound) of body weight every 12 hours for 10 days.
- Infants up to 6 months of age: Use and dose must be determined by your doctor.

Side effects of this medicine
Rare: Abdominal tenderness; fever; nausea and vomiting; severe abdominal or stomach cramps and pain; shortness of breath; skin rash and itching; unusual bleeding or bruising; watery and severe diarrhea, which may also be bloody; yellow eyes or skin

Less common: Change in sensation of taste; diarrhea (mild); headache

CEFTIN
(cefuroxime)

Description
Cefuroxime is used in the treatment of infections caused by bacteria. It works by killing bacteria or preventing their growth. Cefuroxime will not work for colds, flu, or other virus infections.

Before using this medicine
Allergies
Tell your doctor if your child has ever had any unusual or allergic reaction to any of the cephalosporins, penicillins, penicillin-like medicines, or penicillamine. Also tell your health-care professional if you are allergic to any other substances, such as foods, preservatives, or dyes.

Pregnancy
Studies have not been done in humans. However, most cephalosporins have not been reported to cause birth defects or other problems in animal studies.

Breastfeeding
Cefuroxime can pass into breast milk, usually in small amounts. However, it has not been reported to cause problems in nursing babies.

Children
Many drugs of this class have been tested in children and, in effective doses, have not been shown to cause different side effects or problems than they do in adults. However, there are some that have not been tested in children up to 1 year of age.

Proper use of this medicine
Cefuroxime may be taken on a full or empty stomach. If this medicine upsets your stomach, it may help to take it with food.

Dosing
For oral suspension dosage form:

- Infants and children 3 months to 12 years of age: 10 to 15 milligrams (mg) per kilogram (kg) (4.54 to 6.81 mg per pound) of body weight every 12 hours for 10 days.

Missed dose
If you miss a dose of this medicine, take it as soon as possible. This will help to keep a constant amount of medicine in the blood or urine. However, if it is almost time for your next dose, skip the missed dose and go back to your regular dosing schedule. Do not double doses.

Precautions while using this medicine
In some patients, cefuroxime may cause diarrhea:
- Severe diarrhea may be a sign of a serious side effect.

Side effects of this medicine
Along with its needed effects, a medicine may cause some unwanted effects. Although not all of these side effects may occur, if they do occur they may need medical attention.

Check with your doctor immediately if any of the following side effects occur:

Less common or rare: Abdominal or stomach cramps

and pain (severe); abdominal tenderness; diarrhea (watery and severe, which may also be bloody); fever; unusual bleeding or bruising (more common for cefamandole, cefoperazone, and cefotetan)

NOTE: Some of these side effects may also occur up to several weeks after you stop taking this medicine.

Rare: Blistering, peeling, or loosening of skin; convulsions (seizures); decrease in urine output; hearing loss (more common with cefuroxime treatment for meningitis); joint pain; loss of appetite, nausea, or vomiting (more common with ceftriaxone); pain, redness, and swelling at place of injection; skin rash, itching, redness, or swelling; trouble in breathing; unusual tiredness or weakness; yellowing of the eyes or skin rash.

CLARITIN
(loratadine)

Description

Antihistamines are used to relieve or prevent the symptoms of hay fever and other types of allergy. They work by preventing the effects of a substance called histamine, which is produced by the body. Histamine can cause itching, sneezing, runny nose, and watery eyes. Also, in some persons histamine can close up the bronchial tubes (air passages of the lungs) and make breathing difficult.

Some antihistamine preparations are available only with your doctor's prescription. Others are available without a prescription. However, your doctor may have special instructions on the proper dose of the medicine for your medical condition.

Before using this medicine

Allergies

Tell your doctor if your child has ever had any unusual or allergic reaction to antihistamines. Also tell your health-care professional if you are allergic to any other substances, such as foods, preservatives, or dyes.

Breastfeeding

Small amounts of antihistamines pass into the breast milk. Use is not recommended since babies are more susceptible to the side effects of antihistamines, such as unusual excitement or irritability. Also, since these medicines tend to decrease the secretions of the body, it is possible that the flow of breast milk may be reduced in some patients. It is not known yet whether loratadine can cause these same side effects.

Children

Serious side effects, such as convulsions (seizures), are more likely to occur in younger patients and would be of greater risk to infants than to older children or adults. In general, children are more sensitive to the effects of antihistamines. Also, nightmares or unusual excitement, nervousness, restlessness, or irritability may be more likely to occur in children.

Proper use of this medicine
Dosing

For oral dosage forms (tablets or liquid):

- Adults and children 6 years of age and older: 10 milligrams (mg) once a day.

- Children 2 to 5 years of age: 5 mg once a day.

Side effects of this medicine

Less frequent or rare: Fast or irregular heartbeat

Less common or rare: Sore throat; unusual bleeding or bruising; unusual tiredness or weakness

Symptoms of overdose: Clumsiness or unsteadiness; convulsions (seizures); drowsiness (severe); dryness of mouth, nose, or throat (severe); feeling faint; flushing or redness of face; hallucinations (seeing, hearing, or feeling things that are not there); shortness of breath or troubled breathing; trouble in sleeping

Other side effects:

More common: Drowsiness; dry mouth, nose, or throat; gastrointestinal upset, stomach pain, or nausea; increased appetite and weight gain; thickening of mucus

Less common or rare: Blurred vision or any change in vision; confusion; drowsiness; dryness of mouth, nose, or throat; fast heartbeat; increased sensitivity of skin to sun; loss of appetite; skin rash; gastrointestinal upset; unusual excitement, nervousness, restlessness, or irritability; thickening of mucus

CORTISPORIN (neomycin, polymyxin B, and hydrocortisone) Otic (ear) form

Description

Neomycin, polymyxin B, and hydrocortisone (nee-oh-MYE-sin, pol-i-MIX-in bee, and hye-droe-KOR-ti-sone) is a combination antibiotic and cortisone-like medicine. It is used to treat infections of the ear canal and to help provide relief from redness, irritation, and discomfort of certain ear problems.

Before using this medicine

Allergies

Tell your doctor if your child has ever had any unusual or allergic reaction to this medicine or to any related antibiotic, such as amikacin (e.g., Amikin), colistimethate (e.g., Coly-Mycin M), colistin (e.g., Coly-Mycin S), gentamicin (e.g., Garamycin), kanamycin (e.g., Kantrex), neomycin by mouth or by injection (e.g., Mycifradin), netilmicin (e.g., Netromycin), paromomycin (e.g., Humatin), polymyxin B by injection (e.g., Aerosporin), streptomycin, or tobramycin (e.g., Nebcin). Also tell your health-care professional if you are allergic to any other substances, such as preservatives or dyes.

Pregnancy

Neomycin, polymyxin B, and hydrocortisone otic preparations have not been studied in pregnant women. However, studies in animals have shown that topical corticosteroids (such as hydrocortisone) cause birth defects. Before using this medicine, make sure your doctor knows if you are pregnant or if you may become pregnant.

Breastfeeding

Neomycin, polymyxin B, and hydrocortisone otic preparations have not been reported to cause problems in nursing babies.

Children

Although there is no specific information comparing use of otic neomycin, polymyxin B, and hydrocortisone preparation in children with use in other age groups, this preparation is not expected to cause different side effects or problems in children than it does in adults.

Proper use of this medicine

• Lie down or tilt the head so that the infected ear faces up. Gently pull the earlobe up and back for adults (down and back for children) to straighten the ear canal. Drop the medicine into the ear canal. Keep the ear facing up for about 5 minutes to allow the medicine to coat the ear canal. (For young children and other patients who cannot stay still for 5 minutes, try to keep the ear facing up for at least 1 or 2 minutes.) Your doctor may have inserted a gauze or cotton wick into your ear and may want you to keep the wick moistened with this medicine. Your doctor also may have other directions for you, such as how long you should keep the wick in your ear or when you should return to your doctor to have the wick replaced. If you have any questions about this, check with your doctor.

• To keep the medicine as germ-free as possible, do not touch the dropper to any surface (including the ear). Also, keep the container tightly closed.

Dosing

For otic (ear drops) dosage forms for ear-canal infection:

• Children: Use three drops in the ear three or four times a day.

Side effects of this medicine

More common: Itching, skin rash, redness, swelling, or other sign of irritation in or around the ear not present before use of this medicine

DEXAMETHASONE

Sold under these brand names

Decadron
Decadron Elixir
Decadron-LA
Decadron Phosphate

Description

Corticosteroids (kor-ti-koe-STER-oyds) such as dexamethasone (cortisone-like medicines) are used to provide relief for inflamed areas of the body. They lessen swelling, redness, itching, and allergic reactions. They are often used as part of the treatment for a number of different diseases, such as severe allergies or skin problems, asthma, or arthritis. Corticosteroids may also be used for other conditions as determined by your doctor.

Your body naturally produces certain cortisone-like hormones that are necessary to maintain good health. If your body does not produce enough, your doctor may have prescribed this medicine to help make up the difference.

Corticosteroids are very strong medicines. In addition to their helpful effects in treating your medical problem, they have side effects that can be very serious. If your adrenal glands are not producing enough cortisone-like hormones, taking this medicine is not likely to cause problems unless you take too much of it. If you are taking this medicine to treat another medical problem, be sure that you discuss the risks and benefits of this medicine with your doctor.

- Elixir (U.S.)
- Oral solution (U.S.)
- Tablets (U.S. and Canada)

Before using this medicine

Allergies

Tell your doctor if your child has ever had any unusual or allergic reaction to corticosteroids. Also tell your health-care professional if you are allergic to any other substances, such as foods, preservatives, or dyes.

Diet

If you will be using this medicine for a long time, your doctor may want you to:

- Follow a low-salt diet and/or a potassium-rich diet.
- Watch your calories to prevent weight gain.
- Add extra protein to your diet.
- Make certain your health-care professional knows if you are already on any special diet, such as a low-sodium or low-sugar diet.

Pregnancy

Studies on birth defects with corticosteroids have not been done in humans. However, studies in animals have shown that corticosteroids cause birth defects.

Breastfeeding

Corticosteroids pass into breast milk and may cause problems with growth or other unwanted effects in nursing babies. Depending on the amount of medicine you are taking every day, it may be necessary for you to take another medicine or to stop breastfeeding during treatment.

Children

Corticosteroids may cause infections such as chickenpox or measles to be more serious in children who catch them. These medicines can also slow or stop growth in children and in growing teenagers, especially when they are used for a long time. Before this medicine is given to children or teenagers, you should discuss its use with your child's doctor and then carefully follow the doctor's instructions.

Proper use of this medicine

- Take this medicine with food to help prevent stomach upset. If stomach upset, burning, or pain continues, check with your doctor.

Dosing

For oral dosage forms (elixir, oral solution, tablets):

- Children: Dose is based on body weight or size and must be determined by your doctor.

Missed dose

If you miss a dose of this medicine and your dosing schedule is:

- One dose every other day: Take the missed dose as soon as possible if you remember it the same morning, then go back to your regular dosing schedule. If you do not remember the missed dose until later, wait and take it the following morning. Then skip a day and start your regular dosing schedule again.

- One dose a day: Take the missed dose as soon as possible, then go back to your regular dosing schedule. If you do not remember until the next day, skip the missed dose and do not double the next one.

- Several doses a day: Take the missed dose as soon as possible, then go back to your regular dosing schedule. If you do not remember until your next dose is due, double the next dose.

Precautions while using this medicine

Do not stop using this medicine without first checking with your doctor. Your doctor may want you to reduce gradually the amount you are using before stopping the medicine completely.

Avoid close contact with anyone who has chickenpox or measles. This is especially important for children. Tell your doctor right away if you think you have been exposed to chickenpox or measles.

While you are being treated with this medicine, and after you stop taking it, do not have any immunizations without your doctor's approval. Also, other people living in your home should not receive the oral polio vaccine, since there is a chance they could pass the polio virus on to you. In addition, you should avoid close contact with other people at school or work who have recently taken the oral polio vaccine.

Side effects of this medicine

Corticosteroids may lower your resistance to infections. Also, any infection you get may be harder to treat. Always check with your doctor as soon as possible if you notice any signs of a possible infection, such as sore throat, fever, sneezing, or coughing.
Less common: Decreased or blurred vision; frequent urination; increased thirst

Rare: Blindness (sudden, when injected in the head or neck area); burning, numbness, pain, or tingling at or near place of injection; confusion; excitement; false sense of well-being; hallucinations (seeing, hearing, or feeling things that are not there); mental depression; mistaken feelings of self-importance or being mistreated; mood swings (sudden and wide); redness, swelling, or other sign of allergy or infection at place of injection; restlessness; skin rash or hives

Additional side effects may occur if you take this medicine for a long time. Check with your doctor if any of the following side effects occur: Abdominal or stomach pain or burning (continuing); acne; bloody or black, tarry stools; changes in vision; eye pain; filling or rounding out of the face; headache; irregular heartbeat; menstrual problems; muscle cramps or pain; muscle weakness; nausea; pain in arms, back, hips, legs, ribs, or shoulders; pitting, scarring, or depression of skin at place of injection; reddish purple lines on arms, face, groin, legs, or trunk; redness of eyes; sensitivity of eyes to light; stunting of growth (in children); swelling of feet or lower legs; tearing of eyes; thin, shiny skin; trouble in sleeping; unusual bruising; unusual increase in hair growth; unusual tiredness or weakness; vomiting; weight gain (rapid); wounds that will not heal

Other side effects may occur:

More common: Increased appetite; indigestion; loss of appetite (for triamcinolone only); nervousness or restlessness

Less common or rare: Darkening or lightening of skin color; dizziness or lightheadedness; flushing of face or cheeks; hiccups; increased joint pain (after injection into a joint); increased sweating; nosebleeds (after injection into the nose); sensation of spinning

After you stop using this medicine, your body may need time to adjust.

ELOCON, WESTCORT (Mometasone/hydrocortisone valerate)

Description

Topical corticosteroids (kor-ti-ko-STER-oyds) are used to help relieve redness, swelling, itching, and discomfort of many skin problems. These medicines are like cortisone. They belong to the general family of medicines called steroids.

Before using this medicine

Allergies

Tell your doctor if your child has ever had any unusual or allergic reaction to corticosteroids. Also tell your health-care professional if you are allergic to any other substances, such as foods, preservatives, or dyes.

Pregnancy

When used properly, these medicines have not been shown to cause problems in humans. Studies on birth defects have not been done in humans. However, studies in animals have shown that topical corticosteroids, when applied to the skin in large amounts or used for a long time, could cause birth defects.

Breastfeeding

Topical corticosteroids have not been reported to cause problems in nursing babies when used properly. However, corticosteroids should not be applied to the breasts before nursing.

Children

Children and teenagers who must use this medicine should be checked often by their doctor since this medicine may be absorbed through the skin and can affect growth or cause other unwanted effects.

Proper use of this medicine

Do not bandage or otherwise wrap the skin being treated unless directed to do so by your doctor.
For patients using flurandrenolide tape :

• This medicine usually comes with patient directions. Read them carefully before using this medicine.

• Do not use this medicine more often or for a longer time than your doctor ordered.

• Do not use this medicine for other skin problems without first checking with your doctor.

Dosing

Follow your doctor's orders or directions on label.

Precautions while using this medicine

Check with your doctor if your symptoms do not improve within 1 week or if your condition gets worse.

Avoid using tight-fitting diapers or plastic pants on a child if this medicine is being used on the child's diaper area. Plastic pants or tight-fitting diapers may increase the chance of absorption of the medicine through the skin and the chance of side effects.

Side effects of this medicine

Less frequent or rare: Blood-containing blisters on skin; burning and itching of skin; increased skin sensitivity (for some brands of betamethasone lotion); lack of healing of skin condition; loss of top skin layer (for tape dosage forms); numbness in fingers; painful, red or itchy, pus-containing blisters in hair follicles; raised, dark red, wart-like spots on skin, especially when used on the face; skin infection; thinning of skin with easy bruising

Less frequent or rare—usually mild and transient: Burning, dryness, irritation, itching, or redness of skin; increased redness or scaling of skin sores; skin rash

FLOVENT
(fluticasone)

Description

Fluticasone (floo-TIK-a-sone) belongs to the family of medicines known as corticosteroids (cortisone-like medicines). It is used to help prevent the symptoms of asthma. When used regularly every day, inhaled fluticasone decreases the number and severity of asthma attacks. However, it will not relieve an asthma attack that has already started.

Inhaled fluticasone works by preventing certain cells in the lungs and breathing passages from releasing substances that cause asthma symptoms.

This medicine may be used with other asthma medicines, such as bronchodilators (medicines that open up narrowed breathing passages) or other corticosteroids taken by mouth.

This medicine is available only with your doctor's prescription, in the following dosage form(s):
• Aerosol (U.S. and Canada)
• Powder for inhalation (U.S. and Canada)

Before using this medicine
Allergies

Tell your doctor if your child has ever had any unusual or allergic reaction to fluticasone. Also tell your health care professional if you are allergic to any other substances, such as foods, especially milk, preservatives, or dyes.

Pregnancy

Inhaled fluticasone has not been studied in pregnant women. However, in animal studies, fluticasone given by injection was shown to cause birth defects. Also, too much use of corticosteroids during pregnancy may cause other unwanted effects in the infant, such as slower growth and reduced adrenal gland function.

Breastfeeding

It is not known whether inhaled fluticasone passes into breast milk. However, in animals given fluticasone by injection, the medicine did pass into breast milk.

Although most medicines pass into breast milk in small amounts, many of them may be used safely while breast-feeding. Mothers who are taking this medicine and who wish to breastfeed should discuss this with their doctor.

Children

Corticosteroids taken by mouth or injection have been shown to slow or stop growth in children and cause reduced adrenal gland function. If enough fluticasone is absorbed following inhalation, it is possible it also could cause these effects. Your doctor will want you to use the lowest possible dose of fluticasone that controls asthma. This will lessen the chance of an effect on growth or adrenal gland function. It is also important that children taking fluticasone visit their doctors regularly so that their growth rates may be monitored. Children who are taking this medicine may be more susceptible to infections, such as chickenpox or measles. Care should be taken to avoid exposure to chickenpox or measles. If the child is exposed or the disease develops, the doctor should be contacted and his or her directions should be followed carefully. Before this medicine is given to a child, you and your child's doctor should talk about the good this medicine will do as well as the risks of using it.

Proper use of this medicine

Inhaled fluticasone is used to prevent asthma attacks. It is not used to relieve an attack that has already started. For relief of an asthma attack that has already started, you should use another medicine. If you do not have another medicine to use for an attack or if you have any questions about this, check with your health-care professional. In order for this medicine to help prevent asthma attacks, it must be used every day in regularly spaced doses, as ordered by your doctor.

Inhaled fluticasone is used with a special inhaler and usually comes with patient directions. Read the directions carefully before using this medicine. If you do not understand the directions or you are not sure how to use the inhaler, ask your health-care professional to show you what to do.

Dosing

For bronchial asthma, for inhalation aerosol:
- Children younger than 12 years of age: Use and dose must be determined by your doctor.

  Canadian labeling recommends: For children 4 to 16 years of age: 50 to 100 mcg two times a day. For children up to 4 years of age: Use and dose must be determined by your doctor.

For powder for inhalation:
- Children 4 to 11 years of age: 50 to 100 mcg two times a day.
- Children younger than 4 years of age: Use and dose must be determined by your doctor.

Side effects of this medicine

More common: White patches in mouth and throat

Less common: Diarrhea; earache; fever; lower abdominal pain; nausea; pain on passing urine; redness or discharge of the eye, eyelid, or lining of the eye; shortness of breath; sore throat; trouble in swallowing; vaginal discharge (creamy white) and itching; vomiting

More common: Cough; general aches and pains or general feeling of illness; greenish-yellow mucus in nose; headache; hoarseness or other voice changes; loss of appetite; runny, sore, or stuffy nose; unusual tiredness; weakness

KEFLEX (cephalexin)

Description

Cephalexin is used in the treatment of infections caused by bacteria. They work by killing bacteria or preventing their growth. It will not work for colds, flu, or other virus infections.

Before using this medicine

Allergies

Tell your doctor if your child has ever had any unusual or allergic reaction to any of the cephalosporins, penicillins, penicillin-like medicines, or penicillamine. Also tell your health-care professional if you are allergic to any other substances, such as foods, preservatives, or dyes.

Pregnancy

Studies have not been done in humans. However,

cephalexin has not been reported to cause birth defects or other problems in animal studies.

Breastfeeding
Most drugs of this class pass into breast milk, usually in small amounts. However, they have not been reported to cause problems in nursing babies.

Children
Cephalexin has been tested in children and, in effective doses, have not been shown to cause different side effects or problems than they do in adults.

Proper use of this medicine
Cephalexin may be taken on a full or empty stomach. If this medicine upsets your stomach, it may help to take it with food.

Dosing
For oral dosage forms (capsules, oral suspension, or tablets):

- Children 40 kg (88 pounds) of body weight and over: 250 mg to 1 gram every six to 12 hours.

- Children 1 year of age and older and up to 40 kg (88 pounds) of body weight: 6.25 to 25 mg per kilogram (kg) (2.84 to 11.36 mg per pound) of body weight every six hours, or 12.5 to 50 mg per kg (5.68 to 22.72 mg per pound) of body weight every 12 hours.

- Infants and children 1 month to 1 year of age: 6.25 to 12.5 mg per kg (2.84 to 5.68 mg per pound) of body weight every six hours.

Missed dose
If you miss a dose of this medicine, take it as soon as possible. This will help to keep a constant amount of medicine in the blood or urine. However, if it is almost time for your next dose, skip the missed dose and go back to your regular dosing schedule. Do not double doses.

Precautions while using this medicine
In some patients, cephalexin may cause diarrhea:
- Severe diarrhea may be a sign of a serious side effect.

Side effects of this medicine
Along with its needed effects, a medicine may cause some unwanted effects. Although not all of these side effects may occur, if they do occur they may need medical attention.

Check with your doctor immediately if any of the following side effects occur:

Less common or rare: Abdominal or stomach cramps and pain (severe); abdominal tenderness; diarrhea (watery and severe, which may also be bloody); fever; unusual bleeding or bruising
NOTE: Some of these side effects may also occur up to several weeks after you stop taking this medicine.

Rare: Blistering, peeling, or loosening of skin; convulsions (seizures); decrease in urine output; hearing loss; joint pain; loss of appetite, nausea, or vomiting; pain, redness, and swelling at place of injection; skin rash, itching, redness, or swelling; trouble in breathing; unusual tiredness or weakness; yellowing of the eyes or skin

LURIDE
(sodium fluoride)

Description
Fluoride (FLURE-ide) has been found to be helpful in reducing the number of cavities in the teeth. It is usually present naturally in drinking water. However, some areas of the country do not have a high enough level in the water to prevent cavities. To make up for this, extra fluorides may be added to the diet. Some children may require both dietary fluorides and topical fluoride treatments by the dentist. Use of a fluoride toothpaste or rinse may be helpful as well.

Taking fluorides does not replace good dental habits. These include eating a good diet, brushing and flossing teeth often, and having regular dental checkups.

The daily amount of fluoride needed has been defined in different ways.
- U.S. Recommended Dietary Allowances (RDAs) are the amount of vitamins and minerals needed to provide for adequate nutrition in most healthy

persons. RDAs for a given nutrient may vary depending on a person's age, sex, and physical condition (e.g., pregnancy).

- Daily Values (DVs) are used on food and dietary supplement labels to indicate the percent of the recommended daily amount of each nutrient that a serving provides. DV replaces the previous designation of U.S. Recommended Daily Allowances.

  There is no RDA for fluoride. Daily recommended intakes for fluoride are generally defined as follows:

- Infants and children birth to 3 years of age: 0.1 to 1.5 milligrams (mg).
- Children 4 to 6 years of age: 1 to 2.5 mg.
- Children 7 to 10 years of age: 1.5 to 2.5 mg.

Before using this medicine

Allergies

Tell your health-care professional if your child is allergic to any other substances, such as foods, preservatives, or dyes.

Pregnancy

It is especially important that you are receiving enough vitamins and minerals when you become pregnant and that you continue to receive the right amount of vitamins and minerals throughout your pregnancy. The healthy growth and development of the fetus depend on a steady supply of nutrients from the mother. However, taking large amounts of a dietary supplement in pregnancy may be harmful to the mother and/or fetus and should be avoided. Sodium fluoride occurs naturally in water and has not been shown to cause problems in infants of mothers who drank fluoridated water or took appropriate doses of supplements.

Breastfeeding

It is especially important that you receive the right amounts of vitamins and minerals so that your baby will also get the vitamins and minerals needed to grow properly. However, taking large amounts of a dietary supplement while breastfeeding may be harmful to the mother and/or baby and should be avoided. Small amounts of sodium fluoride pass into breast milk.

Children

Problems in children have not been reported with intake of normal daily recommended amounts. Doses of sodium fluoride that are too large or are taken for a long time may cause bone problems and teeth discoloration in children.

Proper use of this medicine

Take this medicine only as directed by your health-care professional. Do not take more of it and do not take it more often than ordered. Taking too much fluoride over a period of time may cause unwanted effects.

Dosing

For oral dosage form (lozenges, solution, tablets, or chewable tablets) to prevent cavities in the teeth (where there is not enough fluoride in the water):

- Children: Dose is based on the amount of fluoride in drinking water in your area. Dose is also based on the child's age and must be determined by your health-care professional.

Precautions while using this medicine

Do not take calcium supplements or aluminum hydroxide-containing products and sodium fluoride at the same time. It is best to space doses of these two products 2 hours apart, to get the full benefit from each medicine.

Inform your health care professional as soon as possible if you notice white, brown, or black spots on the teeth. These are signs of too much fluoride in children when it is given during periods of tooth development.

Side effects of this medicine

Sores in mouth and on lips (rare)

Sodium fluoride in drinking water or taken as a supplement does not usually cause any side effects. However, taking an overdose of fluoride may cause serious problems.

Black, tarry stools; bloody vomit; diarrhea; drowsiness; faintness; increased watering of mouth; nausea or vomiting; shallow breathing; stomach cramps or pain; tremors; unusual excitement; watery eyes; weakness

Pain and aching of bones; stiffness; white, brown, or

black discoloration of teeth occur only during periods of tooth development in children

MYCOSTATIN
(Nystatin)
Oral form

Description

Nystatin (nye-STAT-in) belongs to the group of medicines called antifungals. The dry powder, lozenge (pastille), and liquid forms of this medicine are used to treat fungus infections in the mouth.

Before using this medicine
Allergies
Tell your doctor if your child has ever had any unusual or allergic reaction to nystatin. Also tell your health-care professional if you are allergic to any other substances, such as foods, preservatives, or dyes.

Pregnancy
Studies in humans have not shown that oral nystatin causes birth defects or other problems.

Breastfeeding
Oral nystatin has not been reported to cause problems in nursing babies.

Children
This medicine has been tested in children and has not been reported to cause different side effects or problems in children than it does in adults. However, since children up to 5 years of age may be too young to use the lozenges (pastilles) or tablets safely, the oral suspension dosage form is best for this age group.

Proper use of this medicine
Dosing

For the lozenge (pastille) and tablet dosage forms:
- Adults and children 5 years of age and older: 1 or 2 lozenges or tablets three to five times a day for up to 14 days.
- Children up to 5 years of age: Children this young may not be able to use the lozenges or tablets safely. The oral suspension is better for this age group.

For the suspension dosage form:
- Adults and children 5 years of age and older: 4 to 6 milliliters (mL) (about 1 teaspoonful) four times a day.
- For older infants: 2 mL four times a day.
- For premature and low-birth-weight infants: 1 mL four times a day.

Side effects of this medicine

Diarrhea; nausea or vomiting; stomach pain

MYCOSTATIN
(nystatin)
Topical form

Description

Nystatin (nye-STAT-in) belongs to the group of medicines called antifungals. Topical nystatin is used to treat some types of fungus infections of the skin.

Nystatin is available in the U.S. only with your doctor's prescription. It is available in Canada without a prescription; however, your doctor may have special instructions on the proper use of this medicine for your medical problem.

Before using this medicine
Allergies
Tell your doctor if your child has ever had any unusual or allergic reaction to nystatin. Also tell your health-care professional if you are allergic to any other substances, such as preservatives or dyes.

Pregnancy
Nystatin topical preparations have not been shown to cause birth defects or other problems in humans.

Breastfeeding
It is not known whether nystatin passes into breast milk. Although most medicines pass into breast milk in small amounts, many of them may be used safely while breastfeeding. Mothers who are using this medicine and who wish to breastfeed should discuss this with their doctor.

Children
Although there is no specific information comparing

use of topical nystatin in children with use in other age groups, this medicine is not expected to cause different side effects or problems in children than it does in adults.

Proper use of this medicine

- Topical nystatin should not be used in the eyes.
- Apply enough nystatin to cover the affected area.
- Sprinkle the powder between the toes, on the feet, and in socks and shoes.
- To help clear up your infection completely, keep using this medicine for the full time of treatment, even if your condition has improved. Do not miss any doses.

Dosing

For topical dosage forms (cream or ointment):

- Adults and children: Apply to the affected area(s) of the skin two times a day.

For topical dosage form (powder)

- Adults and children: Apply to the affected area(s) of the skin two or three times a day.

Side effects of this medicine

Skin irritation not present before use of this medicine.

PATANOL
(Olopatadine)
Opthalmic (eye) form

Description

Olopatadine (oh-loe-pa-TA-deen) ophthalmic (eye) solution is used to temporarily prevent itching of the eye caused by a condition known as allergic conjunctivitis. It works by acting on certain cells, called mast cells, to prevent them from releasing substances that cause the allergic reaction.

Before using this medicine
Allergies

Tell your doctor if your child has ever had any unusual or allergic reaction to olopatadine. Also tell your health-care professional if you are allergic to any other substances, such as certain preservatives.

Pregnancy

Olopatadine has not been studied in pregnant women. However, studies in animals have found that this medicine given in extremely high doses results in a decreased number of live births; it has not been found to cause birth defects. Before using this medicine, make sure your doctor knows if you are pregnant or if you may become pregnant.

Breastfeeding

It is not known whether olopatadine passes into human breast milk. However, it does pass into the milk of animals with nursing young. Discuss with your doctor whether or not to breast-feed while using this medicine.

Children

Studies on this medicine have been done only in adult patients, and there is no specific information comparing use of olopatadine in children up to 3 years of age with use in other age groups.

Proper use of this medicine
Dosing

For ophthalmic dosage form (eye drops):

- Adults and children 3 years of age and older: Use one drop in each affected eye two times a day, with each dose being at least six to eight hours apart.
- Children up to 3 years of age: Use and dose must be determined by your doctor.

Side effects of this medicine

More common: Headache

Less common: Burning, dryness, itching, or stinging of the eye; change in taste; eye irritation or pain; feeling of something in the eye; redness of eye or inside of eyelid; runny or stuffy nose; sore throat; swelling of eyelid; unusual tiredness or weakness

PREDNISOLONE, PREDNISONE

Sold under these brand names:
Prednisone Intensol
Pred-Pak 79

Description

Corticosteroids (kor-ti-koe-STER-oyds) (cortisone-like medicines) are used to provide relief for inflamed areas of the body. They lessen swelling, redness, itching, and allergic reactions. They are often used as part of the treatment for a number of different diseases, such as severe allergies or skin problems, asthma, or arthritis. Corticosteroids may also be used for other conditions as determined by your doctor.

Your body naturally produces certain cortisone-like hormones that are necessary to maintain good health. If your body does not produce enough, your doctor may have prescribed this medicine to help make up the difference.

Corticosteroids are very strong medicines. In addition to their helpful effects in treating your medical problem, they have side effects that can be very serious. If your adrenal glands are not producing enough cortisone-like hormones, taking this medicine is not likely to cause problems unless you take too much of it. If you are taking this medicine to treat another medical problem, be sure that you discuss the risks and benefits of this medicine with your doctor.

- Oral solution (U.S. and Canada for prednisolone; U.S. for prednisone)
- Syrup (U.S.)
- Tablets (U.S. for prednisolone; U.S. and Canada for prednisone)

Before using this medicine

Allergies

Tell your doctor if your child has ever had any unusual or allergic reaction to corticosteroids. Also tell your health-care professional if you are allergic to any other substances, such as foods, preservatives, or dyes.

Diet

If you will be using this medicine for a long time, your doctor may want you to:

- Follow a low-salt diet and/or a potassium-rich diet.
- Watch your calories to prevent weight gain.
- Add extra protein to your diet.
- Make certain your health-care professional knows if you are already on any special diet, such as a low-sodium or low-sugar diet.

Pregnancy

Studies on birth defects with corticosteroids have not been done in humans. However, studies in animals have shown that corticosteroids cause birth defects.

Breastfeeding

Corticosteroids pass into breast milk and may cause problems with growth or other unwanted effects in nursing babies. Depending on the amount of medicine you are taking every day, it may be necessary for you to take another medicine or to stop breastfeeding during treatment.

Children

Corticosteroids may cause infections such as chickenpox or measles to be more serious in children who catch them. These medicines can also slow or stop growth in children and in growing teenagers, especially when they are used for a long time. Before this medicine is given to children or teenagers, you should discuss its use with your child's doctor and then carefully follow the doctor's instructions.

Proper use of this medicine

- Take this medicine with food to help prevent stomach upset. If stomach upset, burning, or pain continues, check with your doctor.

Dosing

For oral dosage forms (oral solution, syrup, tablets):

- Children: Dose is based on body weight or size and must be determined by your doctor.

Missed dose

If you miss a dose of this medicine and your dosing schedule is:

- One dose every other day: Take the missed dose as soon as possible if you remember it the same morning, then go back to your regular dosing schedule. If you do not remember the missed dose until later, wait and take it the following morning. Then skip a day and start your regular dosing schedule again.
- One dose a day: Take the missed dose as soon as possible, then go back to your regular dosing schedule. If you do not remember until the next day, skip

the missed dose and do not double the next one.

- Several doses a day: Take the missed dose as soon as possible, then go back to your regular dosing schedule. If you do not remember until your next dose is due, double the next dose.

Precautions while using this medicine

Do not stop using this medicine without first checking with your doctor. Your doctor may want you to reduce gradually the amount you are using before stopping the medicine completely.

Avoid close contact with anyone who has chickenpox or measles. This is especially important for children. Tell your doctor right away if you think you have been exposed to chickenpox or measles.

While you are being treated with this medicine, and after you stop taking it, do not have any immunizations without your doctor's approval. Also, other people living in your home should not receive the oral polio vaccine, since there is a chance they could pass the polio virus on to you. In addition, you should avoid close contact with other people at school or work who have recently taken the oral polio vaccine.

Side effects of this medicine

Corticosteroids may lower your resistance to infections. Also, any infection you get may be harder to treat. Always check with your doctor as soon as possible if you notice any signs of a possible infection, such as sore throat, fever, sneezing, or coughing.

Less common: Decreased or blurred vision; frequent urination; increased thirst

Rare: Blindness (sudden, when injected in the head or neck area); burning, numbness, pain, or tingling at or near place of injection; confusion; excitement; false sense of well-being; hallucinations (seeing, hearing, or feeling things that are not there); mental depression; mistaken feelings of self-importance or being mistreated; mood swings (sudden and wide); redness, swelling, or other sign of allergy or infection at place of injection; restlessness; skin rash or hives

Abdominal or stomach pain or burning (continuing); acne; bloody or black, tarry stools; changes in vision; eye pain; filling or rounding out of the face; headache; irregular heartbeat; menstrual problems;

muscle cramps or pain; muscle weakness; nausea; pain in arms, back, hips, legs, ribs, or shoulders; pitting, scarring, or depression of skin at place of injection; reddish purple lines on arms, face, groin, legs, or trunk; redness of eyes; sensitivity of eyes to light; stunting of growth (in children); swelling of feet or lower legs; tearing of eyes; thin, shiny skin; trouble in sleeping; unusual bruising; unusual increase in hair growth; unusual tiredness or weakness; vomiting; weight gain (rapid); wounds that will not heal

More common: Increased appetite; indigestion; loss of appetite (for triamcinolone only); nervousness or restlessness

Less common or rare: Darkening or lightening of skin color; dizziness or lightheadedness; flushing of face or cheeks; hiccups; increased joint pain (after injection into a joint); increased sweating; nosebleeds (after injection into the nose); sensation of spinning

After you stop using this medicine, your body may need time to adjust. The length of time this takes depends on the amount of medicine you were using and how long you used it.

PULMICORT
(budesonide)
respules for nebulizer

Before using this medicine
Allergies

Tell your doctor if your child has ever had any unusual or allergic reaction to corticosteroids. Also tell your health-care professional if you are allergic to any other substances, such as foods, preservatives, or dyes.

Pregnancy

Although studies in animals have shown that inhaled corticosteroids cause birth defects and other problems, in humans these medicines, when used in regular daily doses during pregnancy to keep the mother's asthma under control, have not been reported to cause breathing problems or birth defects in the newborn. Also, corticosteroids may prevent the effects of poorly controlled asthma, which are known to be harmful to the baby. Before taking an inhaled corti-costeroid, make sure your doctor knows if you are pregnant or if you may become pregnant.

Breastfeeding

It is not known whether inhaled corticosteroids pass into breast milk. Although most medicines pass into breast milk in small amounts, many of them may be used safely while breastfeeding. Mothers who are using this medicine and who wish to breastfeed should discuss this with their doctor.

Children

Inhalation corticosteroids have been tested in children and, except for the possibility of slowed growth, in low effective doses, have not been shown to cause different side effects or problems than they do in adults.

Studies have shown that slowed growth or reduced adrenal gland function may occur in some children using inhaled corticosteroids in recommended doses. However, poorly controlled asthma may cause slowed growth, especially when corticosteroids taken by mouth are needed often. Your doctor will want you to use the lowest possible dose of an inhaled corticosteroid that controls asthma. This will lessen the chance of an effect on growth or adrenal gland function. It is also important that children taking inhaled corticosteroids visit their doctors regularly so that their growth rates may be monitored.

Regular use of inhaled corticosteroids may allow some children to stop using or decrease the amount of corticosteroids taken by mouth. This also will reduce the risk of slowed growth or reduced adrenal function.

Children who are using inhaled corticosteroids in large doses should avoid exposure to chickenpox or measles. When a child is exposed or the disease develops, the doctor should be contacted and his or her directions should be followed carefully.

Before this medicine is given to a child, you and your child's doctor should talk about the good this medicine will do as well as the risks of using it. Follow the doctor's directions very carefully to lessen the chance that unwanted effects will occur.

Proper use of this medicine

Inhaled corticosteroids will not relieve an asthma attack that has already started. However, your doctor may want you to continue taking this medicine at the usual time, even if you use another medicine to relieve the asthma attack.

Use this medicine only as directed. Do not use more of it and do not use it more often than your doctor ordered. To do so may increase the chance of side effects. Do not stop taking this medicine abruptly. This medicine should be discontinued only under the supervision of your doctor.

In order for this medicine to help prevent asthma attacks, it must be used every day in regularly spaced doses, as ordered by your doctor.

Gargling and rinsing your mouth with water after each dose may help prevent hoarseness, throat irritation, and infection in the mouth. However, do not swallow the water after rinsing. Your doctor may also want you to use a spacer device to lessen these problems.

For patients using budesonide powder for inhalation:
To prime the inhaler:
• Unscrew the cover of the inhaler and lift it off.

• Hold the inhaler upright with the brown piece pointing downward. Turn the brown piece of the inhaler in one direction as far as it will go. Then twist it back until it clicks. Repeat this step one more time and the inhaler will be primed.

• Prime each new inhaler before using it the first time. After it has been primed, it is not necessary to prime it again, even if you put it aside for a long period of time.

To load the inhaler:
• Unscrew the cover of the inhaler and lift it off.

• Hold the inhaler upright with the brown piece pointing downward. Turn the brown piece of the inhaler in one direction as far as it will go. Then twist it back until it clicks.

To use the inhaler:
• Hold the inhaler away from your mouth and breathe out slowly to the end of a normal breath.

• Place the mouthpiece in your mouth and close your lips around it. Tilt your head slightly back. Do not block the mouthpiece with your teeth or tongue.

• Breathe in quickly and evenly through your mouth until you have taken a full deep breath.

- Hold your breath and remove the inhaler from your mouth. Continue holding your breath as long as you can up to 10 seconds before breathing out. This gives the medicine time to settle in your airways and lungs.

- Hold the inhaler well away from your mouth and breathe out to the end of a normal breath.

- Replace the cover on the mouthpiece to keep it clean.

- This inhaler delivers the medicine as a very fine powder. You may not taste, smell, or feel this medicine.

- This inhaler should not be used with a spacer.

- When the indicator window begins to show a red mark, there are about 20 doses left. When the red mark covers the window, the inhaler is empty.

For patients using budesonide suspension for inhalation:

- This medicine is to be used in a power-operated nebulizer equipped with a face mask or mouthpiece. Your doctor will advise you on which nebulizer to use. Make sure you understand how to use the nebulizer. If you have any questions about this, check with your doctor.

- Any opened ampul should be protected from light. The medicine in an open ampul must be used promptly after the ampul is opened. Ampuls should be used within 2 weeks after the envelope containing them is opened.

- To prepare the medicine for use in the nebulizer:

- Remove one ampul from the sheet of five units and shake it gently.

- Hold the ampul upright. Open it by twisting off the wing.

- Squeeze the contents of the ampul into the cup of the nebulizer. If you use only half of the contents of an ampul, add enough of the sodium chloride solution provided to dilute the solution.

- Gently shake the nebulizer. Then attach the face mask to the nebulizer and connect the nebulizer to the air pump.

- To use the medicine in the nebulizer:

- This medicine should be inhaled over a period of 10 to 15 minutes.

- Breathe slowly and evenly, in and out, until no more mist is left in the nebulizer cup.

- Rinse your mouth when you are finished with the treatment. Wash your face if you used a face mask.

- To clean the nebulizer:

- After each treatment, wash the cup of the nebulizer and the mask or mouthpiece in warm water with a mild detergent.

- Allow the nebulizer parts to dry before putting them back together again.

Dosing

For powder for inhalation: for bronchial asthma:

- Children 6 years of age and older: At first, 200 mcg two times a day. Then your doctor may increase the dose to 400 mcg two times a day, depending on your condition. A lower dose of 200 mcg or 400 mcg once daily, either in the morning or in the evening, may sometimes be used for mild to moderate asthma when the symptoms are well controlled.

- Children up to 6 years of age: Use and dose must be determined by the doctor.

For suspension for inhalation: for bronchial asthma:

- Children 12 months to 8 years of age: 250 to 500 mcg mixed with enough sterile sodium chloride solution for inhalation, if necessary, to make 2 to 4 mL. This solution is used in a nebulizer for a period of 10 to 15 minutes. The medicine should be used two times a day.

- Children up to 12 months of age: Use and dose must be determined by the doctor.

Precautions while using this medicine

Check with your doctor if:
- You go through a period of unusual stress to your body, such as surgery, injury, or infection .

- You have an asthma attack that does not improve after you take a bronchodilator medicine.

- You are exposed to viral infections, such as chickenpox or measles.

- Signs of infection occur, especially in your mouth, throat, or lung.

- Your symptoms do not improve or if your condition gets worse.

Your doctor may want you to carry a medical identification card stating that you are using this medicine and that you may need additional medicine during times of emergency, a severe asthma attack or other illness, or unusual stress.

Before you have any kind of surgery (including dental surgery) or emergency treatment, tell the medical doctor or dentist in charge that you are using this medicine.

- Do not stop taking the corticosteroid taken by mouth without your doctor's advice, even if your asthma seems better.

Side effects of this medicine

Rare: Shortness of breath, troubled breathing, tightness in chest, or wheezing; signs of hypersensitivity reactions, such as swelling of face, lips, or eyelids

Less common: Bruising; burning or pain while urinating, blood in urine, or frequent urge to urinate; chest pain; creamy white, curd-like patches in the mouth or throat and/or pain when eating or swallowing; dizziness or sense of constant movement or surroundings; general feeling of discomfort or illness; irregular or fast heartbeat; itching, rash, or hives; sinus problems; stomach or abdominal pain; swelling of fingers, ankles, feet, or lower legs; unusual tiredness or weakness; weight gain

RITALIN
(methylphenidate)

Description

Methylphenidate (meth-il-FEN-i-date) belongs to the group of medicines called central nervous system (CNS) stimulants. It is used to treat attention-deficit hyperactivity disorder (ADHD), narcolepsy (uncontrollable desire for sleep or sudden attacks of deep sleep), and other conditions as determined by the doctor.

Methylphenidate works in the treatment of ADHD by increasing attention and decreasing restlessness in children and adults who are overactive, cannot concentrate for very long or are easily distracted, and are impulsive. This medicine is used as part of a total treatment program that also includes social, educational, and psychological treatment.

Before using this medicine
Allergies

Tell your doctor if you have ever had any unusual or allergic reaction to methylphenidate. Also tell your health-care professional if you are allergic to any other substances, such as foods, preservatives, or dyes.

Pregnancy

Studies on effects in pregnancy have not been done in either humans or animals.

Breastfeeding

It is not known whether methylphenidate passes into breast milk. Although most medicines pass into breast milk in small amounts, many of them may be used safely while breastfeeding. Mothers who are taking this medicine and who wish to breastfeed should discuss this with the doctor.

Children

Loss of appetite, trouble in sleeping, stomach pain, fast heartbeat, and weight loss may be especially likely to occur in children, who are usually more sensitive than adults to the effects of methylphenidate. Some children who used medicines like methylphenidate for a long time grew more slowly than expected. It is not known whether long-term use of methylphenidate causes slowed growth. The doctor should regularly measure the height and weight of children who are taking methylphenidate. Some doctors recommend stopping treatment with methylphenidate during times when the child is not under stress, such as on weekends.

Proper use of this medicine

- Take this medicine with or after a meal or a snack.
- To help prevent trouble in sleeping, take the last dose of the short-acting tablets before 6 p.m., unless otherwise directed by your doctor.

Dosing

For attention-deficit hyperactivity disorder:

• Children up to 6 years of age: The dose must be determined by the doctor.

Precautions while using this medicine

Your doctor should check your progress at regular visits and make sure that this medicine does not cause unwanted effects, such as high blood pressure.

Methylphenidate may cause dizziness, drowsiness, or changes in vision.

Side effects of this medicine

More common: Fast heartbeat; increased blood pressure

Less common: Chest pain; fever; joint pain; skin rash or hives; uncontrolled movements of the body

Rare: Black, tarry stools; blood in urine or stools; blurred vision or other changes in vision; convulsions (seizures); muscle cramps; pinpoint red spots on skin; uncontrolled vocal outbursts and/or tics (uncontrolled and repeated body movements); unusual bleeding or bruising

Symptoms of overdose

Agitation; confusion (severe); convulsions (seizures); dryness of mouth or mucous membranes; false sense of well-being; fast, pounding, or irregular heartbeat; fever; hallucinations (seeing, hearing, or feeling things that are not there); headache (severe); increased blood pressure; increased sweating; large pupils; muscle twitching; overactive reflexes; trembling or shaking; vomiting

TOBREX (tobramycin)
Opthalmic form

Description

Ophthalmic tobramycin (toe-bra-MYE-sin) is used in the eye to treat bacterial infections of the eye. Tobramycin works by killing bacteria.

Either the drops or the ointment form of this medicine may be used alone during the day. In addition, both forms may be used together, with the drops being used during the day and the ointment at night.

Before using this medicine
Allergies

Tell your doctor if your child has ever had any unusual or allergic reaction to ophthalmic tobramycin or to any related medicines, such as amikacin (e.g., Amikin), gentamicin (e.g., Garamycin), kanamycin (e.g., Kantrex), neomycin (e.g., Mycifradin), netilmicin (e.g., Netromycin), streptomycin, or tobramycin by injection (e.g., Nebcin). Also tell your health-care professional if you are allergic to any other substances, such as preservatives.

Pregnancy

Studies have not been done in humans. However, tobramycin ophthalmic preparations have not been shown to cause birth defects or other problems in animals even when given at high doses.

Breastfeeding

Tobramycin ophthalmic preparations may be absorbed into the eye. However, tobramycin is unlikely to pass into the breast milk in large amounts and little would be absorbed by the infant. Therefore, this medicine is unlikely to cause serious problems in nursing babies.

Children

This medicine has been tested in children and, in effective doses, has not been shown to cause different side effects or problems than it does in adults.

Proper use of this medicine

For patients using tobramycin ophthalmic solution (eye drops) :

• First, wash your hands. Tilt the head back and with the index finger of one hand, press gently on the skin just beneath the lower eyelid and pull the lower eyelid away from the eye to make a space. Drop the medicine into this space. Let go of the eyelid and gently close the eyes. Do not blink. Keep the eyes closed for 1 or 2 minutes, to allow the medicine to come into contact with the infection.

• If you think you did not get the drop of medicine into your eye properly, use another drop.

• To keep the medicine as germ-free as possible, do not touch the applicator tip to any surface (including the eye). Also, keep the container tightly closed.

- If your doctor ordered two different ophthalmic solutions to be used together, wait at least 5 minutes between the times you apply the medicines. This will help to keep the second medicine from "washing out" the first one.

For patients using tobramycin ophthalmic ointment (eye ointment):

- First, wash your hands. Tilt the head back and with the index finger of one hand, press gently on the skin just beneath the lower eyelid and pull the lower eyelid away from the eye to make a space. Squeeze a thin strip of ointment into this space. A 1.25-cm (approximately ½-inch) strip of ointment usually is enough, unless you have been told by your doctor to use a different amount. Let go of the eyelid and gently close the eyes and keep them closed for 1 or 2 minutes, to allow the medicine to come into contact with the infection.

- To keep the medicine as germ-free as possible, do not touch the applicator tip to any surface (including the eye). After using tobramycin eye ointment, wipe the tip of the ointment tube with a clean tissue and keep the tube tightly closed.

- To help clear up your eye infection completely, keep using tobramycin for the full time of treatment, even if your symptoms have disappeared. Do not miss any doses.

Dosing

For ophthalmic ointment dosage forms for mild to moderate infections:

- Adults and children: Use every eight to twelve hours.

For severe infections:

- Adults and children: Use every three to four hours until improvement occurs.

For ophthalmic solution (eye drops) dosage forms for mild to moderate infections:

- Adults and children: One drop every four hours.

For severe infections:

- Adults and children: One drop every hour until improvement occurs.

Side effects of this medicine

Less common: Itching, redness, swelling, or other sign of eye or eyelid irritation not present before use of this medicine

Symptoms of overdose: Increased watering of the eyes; itching, redness, or swelling of the eyes or eyelids; painful irritation of the clear front part of the eye

Less common: Burning or stinging of the eyes

ZANTAC, ZANTAC 75, ZANTAC 150 GELDOSE, ZANTAC 300 GELDOSE
(ranitidine)

Description

Histamine H_2-receptor antagonists, also known as H_2-blockers, are used to treat duodenal ulcers and prevent their return. They are also used to treat gastric ulcers and for some conditions, such as Zollinger-Ellison disease, in which the stomach produces too much acid. In over-the-counter (OTC) strengths, these medicines are used to relieve and/or prevent heartburn, acid indigestion, and sour stomach. H_2-blockers may also be used for other conditions as determined by your doctor.

H_2-blockers work by decreasing the amount of acid produced by the stomach.

- Capsules (U.S.)
- Effervescent granules (U.S.)
- Syrup (U.S. and Canada)
- Tablets (U.S. and Canada)
- Effervescent tablets (U.S.)

Before using this medicine
Allergies

Tell your doctor if your child has ever had any unusual or allergic reaction to cimetidine, famotidine, nizatidine, or ranitidine.

Pregnancy

H_2-blockers have not been studied in pregnant women. In animal studies, famotidine and ranitidine have not been shown to cause birth defects or other problems. Make sure your doctor knows if you are pregnant or if you may become pregnant before taking H 2 -blockers.

Breastfeeding

Ranitidine passes into the breast milk and may cause unwanted effects, such as decreased amount of stomach acid and increased excitement, in the nursing baby. It may be necessary for you to take another medicine or to stop breastfeeding during treatment. Be sure you have discussed the risks and benefits of the medicine with your doctor.

Children

This medicine has been tested in children and, in effective doses, has not been shown to cause different side effects or problems than it does in adults when used for short periods of time.

Proper use of this medicine

For patients taking the nonprescription strengths of these medicines for heartburn, acid indigestion, and sour stomach:

- Do not take the maximum daily dosage continuously for more than 2 weeks, unless directed to do so by your doctor.

- If you have trouble in swallowing, or persistent abdominal pain, see your doctor promptly. These may be signs of a serious condition that may need different treatment.

Dosing

The dose of histamine H 2 -receptor antagonists (also called H 2 -blockers) will be different for different patients. Follow your doctor's orders or the directions on the label. The following information includes only the average doses of these medicines. If your dose is different, do not change it unless your doctor tells you to do so.

For oral dosage forms (capsules, effervescent granules, syrup, tablets, effervescent tablets) to treat duodenal ulcers:

- Children: 2 to 4 mg per kilogram (kg) (1 to 2 mg per pound) of body weight two times a day. However, your dose will not be more than 300 mg a day.

To prevent duodenal ulcers:
- Children: Dose must be determined by your doctor.

To treat gastric ulcers:
- Children: 2 to 4 mg per kg (1 to 2 mg per pound) of body weight two times a day. However, your dose will not be more than 300 mg a day.

To treat heartburn, acid indigestion, and sour stomach:
- Children: Dose must be determined by your doctor.

To prevent heartburn, acid indigestion, and sour stomach:
- Children: Dose must be determined by your doctor.

To treat some conditions in which the stomach produces too much acid:
- Children: Dose must be determined by your doctor.

To treat gastroesophageal reflux disease:
- Children: 2 to 8 mg per kg (1 to 3.6 mg per pound) of body weight three times a day. However, most children usually will not take more than 300 mg a day.

For injectable dosage form to treat duodenal or gastric ulcers:
- Children: 2 to 4 mg per kg (1 to 2 mg per pound) of body weight a day, injected slowly into a vein.

Precautions while using this medicine

Remember that certain medicines, such as aspirin, and certain foods and drinks (e.g., citrus products, carbonated drinks, etc.) irritate the stomach and may make your problem worse.

Side effects of this medicine

Rare: Abdominal pain; back, leg, or stomach pain; bleeding or crusting sores on lips; blistering, burning, redness, scaling, or tenderness of skin; blisters on palms of hands and soles of feet; changes in vision or blurred vision; confusion; coughing or difficulty in swallowing; dark-colored urine; dizziness; fainting; fast, pounding, or irregular heartbeat; fever and/or chills; flu-like symptoms; general feeling of discomfort or illness; hives; anxiety, agitation, nervousness, shortness of breath; slow heartbeat; swelling of face, lips, mouth, tongue, or eyelids; unusual bleeding or bruising; wheezing; yellow eyes or skin

Less common or rare: Constipation; trouble in sleeping

ZITHROMAX
(azithromycin)

Description

Azithromycin (az-ith-roe-MYE-sin) is used to treat bacterial infections in many different parts of the body. It works by killing bacteria or preventing their growth. However, this medicine will not work for colds, flu, or other viral infections.

Before using this medicine

Allergies
Tell your doctor if your child has ever had any unusual or allergic reaction to azithromycin or to any related medicines such as erythromycin. Also tell your health-care professional if you are allergic to any other substances, such as foods, preservatives, or dyes.

Pregnancy
Azithromycin has not been studied in pregnant women. However, azithromycin has not been shown to cause birth defects or other problems in animal studies.

Breastfeeding
It is not known whether azithromycin passes into breast milk. Although most medicines pass into breast milk in small amounts, many of them may be used safely while breastfeeding. Mothers who are taking this medicine and who wish to breastfeed should discuss this with their doctor.

Children
This medicine has been tested in a limited number of children up to the age of 16. In effective doses, the medicine has not been shown to cause different side effects or problems than it does in adults.

Proper use of this medicine

Azithromycin capsules and pediatric oral suspension should be taken at least 1 hour before or at least 2 hours after meals. Azithromycin tablets and adult single dose oral suspension may be taken with or without food.

Dosing

For the capsule dosage form for bronchitis, strep throat, pneumonia, and skin infections:

- Children up to 16 years of age: Use and dose must be determined by your doctor.
- Children 6 months to 12 years of age: Use and dose must be determined by your doctor.

For otitis media and pneumonia:

- Children 6 months to 12 years of age: 10 milligrams (mg) per kilogram (kg) (4.5 mg per pound) of body weight once a day on the first day, then 5 mg per kg (2.2 mg per pound) of body weight once a day on days two through five.

For strep throat:

- Children 2 to 12 years of age: 12 mg per kg (5.4 mg per pound) of body weight once a day for five days.
- Children up to 2 years of age: Use and dose must be determined by your doctor.

For the tablet dosage form for bronchitis, strep throat, pneumonia, and skin infections:

- Children up to 16 years of age: Use and dose must be determined by your doctor.
- Children up to 16 years of age: Use and dose must be determined by your doctor.

Missed dose

If you miss a dose of this medicine, take it as soon as possible. However, if it is almost time for your next dose, skip the missed dose and go back to your regular dosing schedule. Do not double doses.

Side effects of this medicine

Stop taking this medicine and get emergency help immediately if any of the following side effects occur:

Rare: Abdominal or stomach cramps or pain (severe); abdominal tenderness; diarrhea (watery and severe, which may be bloody); difficulty in breathing; fever; joint pain; skin rash; swelling of face, mouth, neck, hands, and feet

Other side effects:
Less common: Diarrhea (mild); nausea; stomach pain or discomfoomiting

Rare: Dizziness; headache

ZOVIRAX
(acyclovir)

Description

Acyclovir (ay-SYE-kloe-veer) belongs to the family of medicines called antivirals, which are used to treat infections caused by viruses. Usually these medicines work for only one kind or group of virus infections.

Acyclovir is used to treat chickenpox, shingles, herpes virus infections of the genitals (sex organs), the skin, the brain, and mucous membranes (lips and mouth), and widespread herpes virus infections in newborns.

Before using this medicine

Allergies

Tell your doctor if your child has ever had any unusual or allergic reaction to acyclovir, ganciclovir, or valacyclovir. Also tell your health-care professional if you are allergic to any other substances, such as foods, sulfites or other preservatives, or dyes.

Pregnancy

Acyclovir has been used in pregnant women and has not been reported to cause birth defects or other problems. However, studies have not been done in humans. Studies in rabbits have shown that acyclovir given by injection may keep the fetus from becoming attached to the lining of the uterus (womb). However, acyclovir has not been shown to cause birth defects or other problems in mice given many times the usual human dose, or in rats or rabbits given several times the usual human dose.

Breastfeeding

Acyclovir passes into breast milk. However, it has not been reported to cause problems in nursing babies.

Children

A limited number of studies have been done using oral acyclovir in children, and it has not caused different effects or problems in children than it does in adults.

Proper use of this medicine

If you are taking acyclovir for the treatment of chickenpox, it is best to start taking acyclovir as soon as possible after the first sign of the chickenpox rash, usually within one day.

Acyclovir capsules, tablets, and oral suspension may be taken with meals or on an empty stomach.

If you are using acyclovir oral suspension, use a specially marked measuring spoon or other device to measure each dose accurately. The average household teaspoon may not hold the right amount of liquid.

Acyclovir is best taken with a full glass (8 ounces) of water.

Dosing

For oral dosage forms:

- Children up to 12 years of age: Use and dose must be determined by the doctor.

For treatment of chickenpox:

- Children 2 years of age and older and weighing 88 pounds (40 kilograms) or less: Dose is based on body weight and must be determined by the doctor. The usual dose is 20 mg per kilogram (kg) of body weight, up to 800 mg, four times a day for five days.

- Children up to 2 years of age: Use and dose must be determined by the doctor.

Precautions while using this medicine

If your symptoms do not improve within a few days, or if they become worse, check with your doctor.

The areas affected by herpes, chickenpox, or shingles should be kept as clean and dry as possible. Also, wear loose-fitting clothing to avoid irritating the sores (blisters).

It is important to remember that acyclovir will not keep you from spreading herpes to others.

Side effects of this medicine

For both oral acyclovir and acyclovir injection blistering, peeling, or loosening of skin; changes in facial skin color; changes in vision; confusion; convulsions (seizures); coughing; difficulty in breathing or swallowing; dizziness or feeling faint, severe; fast heartbeat; muscle cramps, pain, or weakness; nausea or vomiting; red or irritated eyes; seeing, hearing, or feeling things that are not there; sense of agitation or uneasiness; skin rash, itching, or hives; sore throat, fever, or chills; sores, ulcers, or white spots in mouth or on lips; swelling of eyelids, face, feet, hands, lower legs or lips; swollen, painful, or tender lymph nodes (glands) in neck, armpit, or groin

More common: General feeling of discomfort or illness

Less common: Diarrhea; headache

Frequency not determined: Agitation; loss of hair; burning, prickling, or tingling sensations; drowsiness

ZYRTEC
(cetirizine)

Description

Antihistamines are used to relieve or prevent the symptoms of hay fever and other types of allergy. They work by preventing the effects of a substance called histamine, which is produced by the body. Histamine can cause itching, sneezing, runny nose, and watery eyes. Also, in some persons histamine can close up the bronchial tubes (air passages of the lungs) and make breathing difficult.

Some antihistamine preparations are available only with your doctor's prescription. Others are available without a prescription. However, your doctor may have special instructions on the proper dose of the medicine for your medical condition.

Before using this medicine
Allergies
Tell your doctor if your child has ever had any unusual or allergic reaction to antihistamines. Also tell your health-care professional if you are allergic to any other substances, such as foods, preservatives, or dyes.

Breastfeeding
Small amounts of antihistamines pass into the breast milk. Use is not recommended since babies are more susceptible to the side effects of antihistamines, such as unusual excitement or irritability. Also, since these medicines tend to decrease the secretions of the body, it is possible that the flow of breast milk may be reduced in some patients. It is not known yet whether astemizole, cetirizine, loratadine, or terfenadine cause these same side effects.

Children
Serious side effects, such as convulsions (seizures), are more likely to occur in younger patients and would be of greater risk to infants than to older children or adults. In general, children are more sensitive to the effects of antihistamines. Also, nightmares or unusual excitement, nervousness, restlessness, or irritability may be more likely to occur in children.

Proper use of this medicine
For oral dosage forms (syrup and tablets):
- Children younger than 2 years of age: Use and dose must be determined by your doctor.
- Children 2 to 6 years of age: 2.5 mg once a day, up to a maximum of 5 mg once a day or 2.5 mg twice a day.
- Children 6 years of age and older: 5 to 10 mg once a day.

Side effects of this medicine
Less frequent or rare: Fast or irregular heartbeat

Also, check with your doctor as soon as possible if any of the following side effects occur:

Less common or rare: Sore throat; unusual bleeding or bruising; unusual tiredness or weakness

Symptoms of overdose: Clumsiness or unsteadiness; convulsions (seizures); drowsiness (severe); dryness of mouth, nose, or throat (severe); feeling faint; flushing or redness of face; hallucinations (seeing, hearing, or feeling things that are not there); shortness of breath or troubled breathing; trouble in sleeping

Other side effects
More common: Drowsiness; dry mouth, nose, or throat; gastrointestinal upset, stomach pain, or nausea; increased appetite and weight gain; thickening of mucus

Less common or rare: Blurred vision or any change in vision; confusion; drowsiness; dryness of mouth, nose, or throat; fast heartbeat; increased sensitivity of skin to sun; loss of appetite; skin rash; gastrointestinal upset; unusual excitement, nervousness, restlessness, or irritability; thickening of mucus

Product recalls

Contents

Product recalls

The majority of baby products are regulated by two federal agencies. The National Highway Traffic Safety Administration oversees child car-seat safety, and the Consumer Product Safety Commission administers mandatory federal standards for cribs, seats, pacifiers, rattles, and toys. There are also general regulations, applicable to all products, that cover small parts that a baby could ingest, sharp edges and sharp points that can cut, and lead in paint. The regulations require manufacturers of baby products to report consumer complaints about injuries or deaths.

The agencies monitor consumer complaints and injuries, and issue a recall when there's a safety problem. Sometimes manufacturers will recall products voluntarily. You may never hear about a recall unless you stay informed. Mail in all product-registration cards for car seats so the manufacturer can contact you. (If you lose your car-seat registration card, call the NHTSA hotline at 800-424-9393 for a new one.) And check product-safety information sources yourself.

This book includes a category-by-category list of products recalled since early 1999. We go over the typical things that go wrong with each type of product, as well as applicable standards and safety advice. You'll find company contact information within each listing. If you discover an item you've purchased or received as a gift has been recalled, follow the remedial-action advice.

You can find additional product-recall listings monthly in CONSUMER REPORTS and on its online service at *www.consumerreports.org*. These sources list the most far-reaching recalls.

If you have questions about a specific car-seat model, you can call the

NHTSA auto safety hot line, 888-327-4236, or check its web site (*www.nhtsa.dot.gov*) for recalls. To report an unsafe product or get recall information, call the CPSC hotline, 800-638-2772. Consult its web site (*www.cpsc.gov*) for up-to-date recall data.

Should your child have a mishap that's clearly a product's fault, such as hardware that fails or parts that cause harm or entrap, check the manufacturer web site for the address, then report the problem in writing to the manufacturer (with a copy to the CPSC or NHTSA), giving the model number and all the details you can supply about the model (usually on a manufacturer's sticker or label somewhere on the product). It's possible that a company may try to put the responsibility of the injury on you. By law, manufacturers must report injury data to the CPSC or face being sued and fined. You might want to follow up with the appropriate federal agencies to make sure this occurred, and, if needed, to help get satisfaction from the manufacturer.

Product certification

The Juvenile Products Manufacturers Association (JPMA) sponsors and administers a voluntary certification program for juvenile products. Programs are currently in effect for full- and non-full-sized cribs, toddler beds, high chairs, portable hook-on chairs, play yards, strollers, gates, and walkers. A voluntary standard for soft carriers was being considered in Spring 2001.

The JPMA retains an independent laboratory to periodically perform or witness tests of sample units. Products are certified if they meet the minimum safety performance standards developed by the American Society for Testing and Materials (ASTM). They may then carry a sticker reading "CERTIFIED: This model tested by an independent laboratory for compliance with ASTM safety standard." But certification isn't fail safe, so don't view the sticker as a safety guarantee. Voluntary standards cover only major hazards and require only minimum safe-performance levels. Standards vary in strictness from one product category to another. Plus, tests are conducted on brand-new products, not those that have sustained the daily wear and tear of baby use. For specifics on test standards, see the separate product categories throughout the book and in the following recalls.

In this book, we note the certification status of each product category. Or you can obtain the most recent directory of certified products by contacting JPMA. See the Parenting and Health Resources on page 203.

Baby carriers

Typical problem: Leg openings allow small children to slip through.

Safety standards: Baby carriers are covered by basic federal requirements, such as having no small parts. There are no specific federal standards, but a voluntary standard for soft carriers was being developed as of Spring 2001.

Safety advice: Read instructions carefully so you use carrier correctly. Never leave a child unattended in framed carrier. Do not use as a self-standing seat.

EVENFLO
Snugli Front & Back Pack soft infant carriers

Recall: Small infants can slip through the leg openings of these carriers and fall—especially infants under 2 months of age.

Models: 327,000 models were sold in retail stores nationwide from 1/96-05/99 for about $40. Affected model numbers begin with 075 and 080 and can be found on a tag inside that reads, "SOFT CARRIER/" followed by the model number. The brand name, "Snugli"®, is located on the outside of the carrier. These carriers were designed for use as both a front carrier and a backpack and feature a unique vertical strap for adjusting seat height. Color combinations include royal blue with magenta trim, teal with navy blue trim, and navy blue with purple trim.

What to do: Immediately stop using it and call Evenflo at 800-398-8636 anytime to receive instructions on how to exchange the carrier for a free, new version with smaller leg openings.

HUFCO-DELAWARE
Gerry Trailtech Backpack baby carriers

Recall: Small infants can slip through the leg openings and fall.

Models: 111,000 backpack baby carriers sold from 1/96-7/00 in department and baby-products stores nationwide for about $65. Affected models have black, plastic, contoured frames in color combinations of slate blue with teal trim, green with black trim, navy blue and purple with green trim, and blue and purple with silver trim. A tag on the outside of the carrier reads "GERRY®." A long tag, originally inside the carrier when sold, reads, "GERRY TRAIL TECH/TRAIL TECH HP." Writing imprinted on the plastic frame reads, "GERRY."

What to do: Stop using immediately and call Hufco-Delaware at 800-881-9176 anytime for a free repair kit that replaces the seat of the carrier with one that has smaller leg openings.

KELTY K.I.D.S.
Backpack child carriers

Recall: Child could fall out of carrier and suffer serious injury.

Models: 26,000 backpack child carriers sold 3/99-12/99 at specialty and sporting goods retailers such as L.L. Bean, REI, and Eastern Mountain Sports for $100 to $250. Affected models bear the following names: Expedition, Trek, Explorer, Country, and Elite and Town. Model name appears on side of carrier. Carriers are blue and have Kelty K.I.D.S. logo on backrest of seat. Kelty is also recalling carrier that L.L. Bean sold under its "L.L. KIDS" label; it bears Kelty logo on black frame hinge that connects kickstand to main frame. Kelty and L.L. KIDS carriers bought before 3/99 have different type of seat adjustment strap and are not subject to corrective action. Seat-height adjustment strap could slip out of buckle and allow child to slide downward and fall out of carrier.

What to do: Call Kelty at 800-423-2320 or go to *www.kelty.com* for free repair kit.

L.L. BEAN
Backpack child carrier

Recall: Child could wriggle out and fall.

Models: 13,000 child carriers, model W695, sold 1/93-3/95 for about $95 through catalog and web site and at company's retail stores in Del., Maine, N.H., and Ore. Carrier is teal with gray harness; kickstand holds device upright. Model number is on tag on upper-left side of rear storage compartment. L.L. Bean label is on back of carrier. In December, company recalled 10,000 backpack carriers, model AC25 (sold 1/97-10/98), because child could fall out or because harness could entangle child's neck.

What to do: Call 800-555-9717 for instructions on getting refund.

Bassinets

Typical problems: Legs accidentally fold or collapse, entrapping infants between the bedding and the rigid side—in some cases causing suffocation. Soft mattresses or bassinet sides may also pose a suffocation danger.

Safety standards: Bassinets are covered by basic federal requirements, such as having no small parts. There are no specific federal standards, but a voluntary standard was being developed as of Spring 2001.

Safety advice: When buying, inspect the model for sturdy legs with safety locks to prevent accidental folding; avoid using a soft or poorly fitting mattress. Check legs frequently to see that they are locked in the open position and keep siblings from playing with or under the bassinet while baby is inside.

KIDS LINE
Le Cradle Bassinets

Recall: Infants can become entrapped in an opening between the bassinet's side and mattress platform and suffocate. Additionally, fabric can separate from the metal frame. Infants can be injured when they scrape against or become caught in the frame.

Models: 46,000 bassinets sold in children's products stores nationwide between 01/89–05/00 for between $100 and $200. The recalled bassinets sold under the name Le Cradle Bassinette have a white metal base with wheels and removable canopy. The oval bassinet portion consists of a wire frame with a wooden baseboard that rests on the metal base. A sticker on the mattress platform gives instructions for use of the bassinet and says, "Le Cradle, Kids Line, Los Angeles, California." A fabric-covered foam mattress covers the wooden board. Matching fabric covers the bassinet frame, and comes in various colors and designs.

What to do: Stop using the bassinet and contact Kids Line toll-free at 866-LECRADL (532-7235) anytime to obtain a free in-home repair kit.

Bath items

Typical problems: Suction cups on bathtub seats release, allowing baby to go facedown into water and drown. Squeakers on rubber duckies work loose and cause choking. Compressible soft toys and sponges also may become jammed in a baby's throat.

Safety standards: Bath toys are covered by basic federal requirements for toys, such as having no small parts. There is no specific federal standard, but there is a voluntary ASTM standard. Consumer groups, including Consumers Union, advocate a ban on or federal regulation for bath seats.

Safety advice: Don't purchase or use a suctioned bath seat. Always supervise babies and toddlers in the tub, and don't allow them to chew on bath toys.

GRACO AND CHILDREN ON THE GO
Activity trays and bath seats with suction cups

Recall: Suction cups could detach and pose choking hazard to small child.

Models: 100,000 devices sold 1/98-8/99 at discount, department, and juvenile-product stores nationwide, including Toys "R" Us and Sears, for $10 to $15. Recall involves the Graco and Children on the Go brand Stroller Snack and Activity Tray, Bathtime Activity Tray, and Bathtime Toy Netting products. Activity trays attach with suction cups to tiled or smooth surfaces, and four toys are affixed to each tray. Toys are removable and interchangeable with other Mix 'N Move toys, which can be bought separately. Stroller Snack and Activity Tray toys include toucan, rolling ball, star, and dog. Bathtime Activity Tray's toys include octopus, U-tube, spinning ball, and paddle wheel. "Graco" or "Children on the Go" appears on underside of tray. Bathtime Toy Netting consists of clam soap holder and fish washcloth holder that attaches with suction cups to various surfaces. A net, used to store toys, hangs between clam and fish. "Graco" is on the back of the clam and fish.

What to do: Consumers should stop using these products immediately. To receive a free repair kit, call Graco anytime at 800-446-1366. Consumers can also visit the company's web site, *www.gracobaby.com*, or write to Graco Children's Products, Attention: Consumer Affairs, P.O. Box 100, Elverson, PA 19520.

Car seats

Typical problems: Harnesses, buckles not designed well and result in seats being installed incorrectly or child being restrained improperly.

Safety standards: All car seats sold in the U.S. must pass a simulated front-end crash test. Tests do not assess effect of rear-enders or side crashes, or how varying types of adult belts affect performance. Car seat should have a sticker indicating it meets "Federal Motor Vehicle Safety Standard (FMVSS) No. 213." Since September 1999, all front-facing seats with an internal harness come with a tether for attaching the top of the car seat to the vehicle. The federal government also announced new rules that require an anchoring system that doesn't rely on safety belts, but on lower seat anchors to attach to the vehicles. Tether anchors will be required in most new vehicles beginning in September 1999 for passenger cars and September 2000 for light trucks (including SUVs and minivans). By September 2001, all front- and rear-facing car seats must be able to be attached to lower anchors in the vehicle while maintaining the ability to be secured in cars without lower-anchor systems by using the vehicles own safety belts.

Safety advice: Follow instructions in the vehicle's owner's manual and those that come with seat. Don't place in front of front or side air bags. Be sure seat is correctly anchored so it does not move either side to side or front to back. Check harnesses and buckles to be sure child is well secured. Use harnesses every time.

CENTURY
Infant car seats/carriers

Recall: More than 2,700 reports of handle-related problems, including handles breaking, cracking, or not being locked while the seat is being used as a carrier with more than 200 reports of baby injury, including concussions, skull fractures, lacerations, broken bones, bruises, and scratches as a result of falls and handle-related problems.

Models: The 10/00 recall involves all Century rear-facing infant car seats/carriers with one-piece handles, approximately 4 million, manufactured between 01/91 through 07/97 and sold in juvenile-product, mass-merchandise, and major discount stores nationwide for about $40 when sold alone to about $130 when sold with a stroller. The date of manufacture, written as month, day, year (010191 through 073197), can be found on a label on the side of the seat. The recalled car seats/carriers have a molded, one-piece, one-color plastic handle colored white, gray, or tan. The seats can continue to be used in the car.

What to do: Don't carry the baby using the handle and contact Century toll-free at 800-865-1419 or by using their web site *(www.centuryproducts.com)* to obtain a free replacement handle.

COSCO
Arriva and Turnabout infant car seats/carriers

Recall: When used as an infant carrier, handle locks on each side of the seat can unexpectedly release, causing the seat to flip forward and an infant to fall to the ground and suffer serious injuries. (Seat can still be used as a car restraint.)

Models: A 07/99 recall of 670,00 seats sold in juvenile-product, mass-merchandise, and major discount stores nationwide, beginning 03/95 for about $29 to $59 when sold alone, or $89 to $139 when sold with strollers. The manufacture date and model number are written on a label located on the side of the seat. The car seat/carriers have the following model numbers preceded by the digits 02: 665, 729, 731, 732, 733, 751, 756, 757, 758, 759, 760, 761, 762, 763, 764, 765. (If the car seat/carrier does not have the model name written on it, the unit can be identified by the model number and manufacturing date.)

What to do: Don't carry the seat by the handle and contact Cosco's toll-free number, 800-221-6736, between 8 a.m. and 4:30 p.m. EDT Monday through Friday, or visit Cosco's web site, *www.coscoinc.com* to get a free repair kit to make the handle stronger.

EVENFLO
Joyride infant car seats/carriers

Recall: When the car seat is used as an infant carrier, the handle can unexpectedly release, causing the seat to flip and allowing the baby to fall to the ground with possible serious injuries.

Models: 3.4 million models found in juvenile-product, mass-merchandise, and major discount stores nationwide between 01/88 and 12/98 for about $30; $48 when sold as a Travel Tandem (with a detachable convenience base); and $89 when sold with a matching stroller. Affected seats have model numbers beginning with 203, 205, 210, 435, or 493 found on a label underneath or on the side. The seat/carriers are white or gray plastic with seat pads of various colors and patterns. "Evenflo Joyride Car Seat/Carrier" is written on the outside of the handle locks.

What to do: Order a free repair kit by calling Evenflo toll-free at 800-557-3178 anytime, or by visiting *www.joyridecarseat.com*. Have the car seat in front of you when you make the contact.

EVENFLO
On My Way Position Right child safety seat

Recall: Over time, infant carrier might not latch securely to its base, resulting in inadequate protection in crash.

Models: 164,144 carriers/bases made 1/26/99–2/10/00. Date of manufacture appears on white label on underside of base. Base bears words "Position Right" and has large red knob in front. Base was sold individually, with On My Way Position Right safety seat, or as part of Easy Comfort Premier or Trendsetter Advantage travel system (with safety seat and matching stroller). Hazard exists because alignment posts in base could bend. If so, consumer could encounter difficulty installing carrier onto base or in latching components together. According to Evenflo, consumers may still use carrier as a safety seat without the base, using the built-in safety-belt guides.

What to do: Call Evenflo at 800-316-4779 or visit its web site, *www.evenflo.com*, for free repair kit consisting of metal clip, which is designed to keep posts in base from bending.

KOLCRAFT
Infant car seats/carriers

Recall: More than 3,000 reports of handle-related problems when the handle unexpectedly moved from the intended carrying position, causing the seat to suddenly rotate and pitching the baby to the ground, sometimes resulting in serious injuries. (Seat can still be used as a restraint in the car.)

Models: 754,000 infant car seat/carriers (a total of 50 Model/Style numbers) sold in juvenile-product, mass-merchandise, and major discount stores nationwide 01/93–7/99 for about $30 to $60 when sold alone, or $100 to $150 when sold with strollers. (Recall excludes models made after 07/99 and Rock N Ride seats.) The five-digit model/style number and manufacture date, written as month/day/year and possibly the model name, are written on a label on the side of the seat. Model numbers include: 1312X, 1382X, 1383X, 1384X, 1385X, 368XX, 43XXX, 7700X. Names include: Infant Rider, Secura, Travel-About, Plus 4, Plus 5, Kolcraft Infant Restraint, Kolcraft Infant Car Seat, and Playskool Infant Car Seat.

What to do: Stop using the seat's handle to carry your baby and contact Kolcraft toll-free at 877-776-2609, 24 hours a day, seven days a week for a free repair kit.

Clothing

Typical problems: Decorative parts or fasteners can be chewed off, posing a choking hazard: Strings on hoods or jackets create a strangulation risk.

Safety standards: The CPSC regulates flammability of sleepwear and revised its standard in 1996 to allow tight-fitting sleepwear in sizes under 9 months to be made without added flame-retardants. In 1995, the CPSC issued guidelines to help prevent strangulation from strings on hoods, waists, mittens, or other children's clothing parts that become entangled on protrusions. Most major clothing manufacturers have agreed to remove or sew down and shorten strings on clothing.

Safety advice: Do not buy clothing with strings that could capture baby's neck or get caught on crib posts, doors, or other protrusions. Or cut strings on such clothing as hoods, jackets, parkas, and mittens. Do not buy clothing with small parts—buttons, bows, etc.—that might come off and pose a choking hazard.

GAP AND OLD NAVY
Chidren's pajamas

Recall: Garments may be neither flame-resistant nor self-extinguishing if fabric ignites, in violation of federal flammability standards.

Models: 231,000 garments sold 8/99-12/99 at GapKids, babyGap, Gap Outlet, and Old Navy stores for about $20 to $40. Six styles of pajamas are subject to recall, including the following: Style 353558: 2-piece flannel pajama sets with long sleeves and pants, and buttons in front. Sets came in yellow with penguin print or navy with bear print. Labeled "Gap" and "100% polyester." Sold in sizes 2 through 14. Style 353554: Like 353558, but in fleece material. Came in white, blue, and pink with snowflake print.

Style 466291: 1-piece fleece footed pajama with zipper front and long sleeves. Came in navy with white star print. Labeled "babyGap" and "100% polyester." Sold in infant and toddler sizes XS through 3XL.

Style 674060: 2-piece button-front top with long sleeves and long pants. Came in lavender or blue with white piping around pant cuff; shirt has piping around collar, front placket, and cuff. Labeled "Old Navy" and "100% polyester." Sold in infant sizes 6 to 12 months through toddler sizes 2T to 3T.

Style 733002: 1-piece fleece footed pajama with zipper front and long sleeves. Came in blue with white snowflake print. Labeled "babyGap" and "100% polyester." Sold in infant and toddler sizes XS through 4XL. Style 733032: Like 733002, but in black-and-white pony print and cheetah print. Labeled "babyGap" and "100% polyester." Sold in infant and toddler sizes XS through 3XL.

What to do: Return garment to any Gap or Old Navy store for refund plus $10 gift certificate. For information, call Gap Inc. at 800-427-7895 or 800-653-6289, or visit *www.gap.com*.

GYMBOREE
Baby Boy Bodysuits

Recall: The wheel-shaped zipper pull can twist off and become a choking hazard to young children.

Models: 5,500 Baby Boy Body suits sold on the Gymboree website and stores nationwide from 3/01-5/01 for about $17. The recalled baby bodysuits are short-sleeved, one-piece outfits for toddlers sizes 0-3T. The bodysuits come in green and red, and have a wheel-shaped zipper pull. On the left arm of the outfit is a patch that says "1st Place Soap Box Derby." A white care label inside of the outfit reads, "Made in Thailand" and "2000 Gymboree."

What to do: Consumers should stop using these outfits and return them to any Gymboree store for a full refund. For more information, call Gymboree toll-free at (800) 222-7758 between 9 a.m. and 5 p.m. PT Monday through Friday, or log on to the company's website at *www.gymboree.com*.

NIKE
Little Air Jordan XIV infants' and children's sneakers

Recall: Paint in red trim contains lead, toxic if ingested.

Models: 110,000 pairs of white sneakers, in sizes 2C to 10C, sold 1/99-3/99 for about $40. "JORDAN" appears on outside of tongue. Model number 132549 102 is on label on inside of tongue, above UPC code.

What to do: Return sneakers to store for replacement or store credit.

SPIEGEL
Navy blue stretch-knit velvetlike baby garments sold by Spiegel

Recall: Metal snaps could come off and choke child.

Models: 4,200 garments sold 11/98-2/99 including the following: cardigan with snap front, item number 82-5609, sold for about $15; coveralls with long sleeves and snaps at shoulder, legs, and crotch, item number 82-5604, sold for about $20; and long-sleeve T-shirt with snaps at shoulder, item number 82-5610, sold for about $13. Collar tag on garments says "elements baby... exclusively spiegel." Clothes were sold through various Spiegel catalogs and at Spiegel Ultimate Outlet stores.

What to do: Return garment to Spiegel Ultimate outlet store for refund.

TOMMY HILFIGER
Infant cardigans

Recall: Snaps could come off and pose choking hazard.

Models: 3,800 long-sleeve fleece sweaters, in sizes 3 mo. to 24 mo., sold 8/98-10/98 at department stores for about $36. Sweater came in red or navy and has four plastic snaps and two pockets on front.

What to do: Call Tommy Hilfiger Consumer Relations Dept. toll-free at 877-866-6922 for refund or exchange.

TOMMY HILFIGER
White socks for infants and children

Recall: Heat-sealed Tommy Hilfiger flag logo could come off and pose choking hazard to small child.

Models: 360,000 pairs of socks sold 1/99-1/00 in two-pair packages at department and specialty stores for about $10. Recalled socks came in sizes "S/M" for 6-12 months; "L/XL" for 12-24 months; and toddler shoe sizes 7-11½. Each sock has a red, white, and blue Tommy Hilfiger flag logo applique on its side. Writing on sock reads "TOMMY HILFIGER."

What to do: Call distributor, Mountain High Hosiery Ltd., at 877-729-4916 or visit *www.mtnhighinc.com* to learn how to get refund or replacement socks.

Cribs

Typical problems: Bars separate from railings; hardware on dropsides and mattress supports breaks or malfunctions.

Safety standards: The JPMA/ASTM certification sticker on the crib's frame pertains to the manufacturer, not the individual model, which certifies all its products met the standard. Tests evaluate overall construction; corner-post protrusions (a strangulation hazard if posts catch clothing or strings worn around the neck); interior dimensions and spacing of components such as bars; and sturdiness of mattress-support attachments, latching mechanisms, and teething rails. Cribs must also carry a safety-warning label advising frequent inspection for missing or broken parts; placement away from windows and drapery cords; and regular latch checks. The label also warns buyers and others about mattress dimensions and age limits on use.

Safety advice: Watch for problems caused by wear or assembly. Very hot, humid, or cold storage conditions cause wood to swell or split and glues to deteriorate. Disassembling and reassembling cribs can damage screw holes, weakening crib's frame. If screws are changed or any crib parts altered, the manufacturer is no longer responsible for safety or performance.

NEXT GENERATION
Pisces crib

Recall: Slats on endboards could come loose and create space wide enough to trap infant's head, possibly resulting in strangulation.

Models: 6,600 cribs, model 67-8100, made 3/4/97-3/10/98 and sold through 12/98 for about $200. Model no. and date of manufacture appear on sticker on bottom of headboard. Crib comes in natural-wood finish and has high-arched headboard and footboard with middle slats joined in small arch underneath top rails. Drop siderail bears "NEXT GENERATION" stamped in gold-colored letters. Fully assembled, crib measures around 30 inches wide, 54 inches long, and 50 inches high. Model 67-8102 Pisces cribs are not involved in recall.

What to do: Call manufacturer at 800-736-1140, ext. 224, for replacement endboards.

SIMMONS
"Little Folks" cribs

Recall: Mattress could collapse and trap baby, possibly causing suffocation.

Models: 68,600 ash or maple cribs sold 1/98-12/00 at mass-merchandise, juvenile-product, and department stores for $200-$600. Most cribs were made in 1998. Those sold at Sears were made from '98-00. "Simmons" and two-digit year of manufacture appear on label attached to headboard. "Little Folks" is written on a second label on headboard. Cribs come in more than a dozen colors, including natural, golden, and white. "Simmons" name appears on top rail. Bracket hooks used to position mattress height could break. In the past four months, Simmons has received more than 800 reports of broken bracket hooks.

What to do: Call Simmons at 800-421-2951 or visit *www.simmonsjp.com* for free replacement brackets.

Feeding items

Typical problems: Formula has been recalled because of consistency problems, missing or problematic ingredients, or the black marketing of mislabeled brands. Baby foods may be recalled for contamination.

Safety standards: Although uniform federal small-parts standards are administered by the CPSC for bottles, nipples, nursers and bottle proppers, product recalls in this category are rare. Baby formula and baby foods are regulated by the U.S. Food and Drug Administration, and formula recalls are rare and usually confined to a specific region. Baby foods containing meat are regulated by the U.S. Department of Agriculture.

Safety advice: Inspect nipples frequently for tears and deterioration and replace them every few months. Don't microwave baby bottles or nursers. Throw out formula when it passes its "use by" date. Don't use unopened baby-food jars that have lost their vacuum or are past the expiration date. Immediately report formula and baby-food contamination and other problems to the appropriate federal agency (remember to save the offending product).

PLAYSKOOL
Spillproof plastic drinking cups

Recall: Flexible spout may tear, creating small parts that can choke young child.

Models: 273,000 two-handled cups, for children ages 6 months and older, sold nationwide 1/98–7/99 for $3 to $6. Cup includes twist-on lid with flexible yellow spout. Lid comes in various colors and bears word "Playskool." Bottom of cup reads "MADE IN CHINA" and "HASBRO." The following models are subject to recall: the Spillproof (in 6- and 8-oz. sizes); Spillproof Trainer (6 oz.); Easy Grip Spillproof (7 and 10 oz.); and Spillproof Trainer (8 oz.) and Spillproof (6 oz.) with Teletubby character decals imprinted on them. Cups came in packages of one or two.

What to do: Call Playskool toll-free at 888-690-6166 of visit company's web site at *www.hasbro.com* for additional information and form for obtaining free replacement lid.

High chairs

Typical problems: Restraint bar may break or seat belt may malfunction, allowing baby to slip through leg holes: Chair legs may lack secure folding mechanism, allowing for accidental collapse. Trays may capture fingers.

Safety standards: JPMA certification program. The requirements of the ASTM standard cover: a locking device to prevent accidental folding; secure caps and plugs; sturdy, break-resistant trays; no springs or dangerous scissoring actions that could entrap a baby's fingers. Safety belts have to pass loading tests. A "crotch post," so babies cannot slip under a tray, is required whenever the tray is used.

Safety advice: Check the folding mechanism on legs: Rock chair to assess stability: Examine all surfaces for sharp edges or entrapment hazards.

Assess how securely small parts are attached. Always use belts, even when the crotch post is in place.

COSCO
Options 5 high chairs

Recall: In the recline position of these adjustable chairs, the seats can separate from the frame and fall to the ground. In the upright position, the seats can slip from their set height position to the lowest position or can fall to the ground. Additionally, some seats were sold with a metal restraint anchor that can slip through the back of the seat, allowing the child to fall to the ground. Infants and toddlers can suffer head, face, and bodily injuries.

Models: Approximately 1 million models manufactured 12/97–08/00 and sold in mass-merchandise, juvenile-products, and major discount department stores nationwide for about $40 to $50. Affected models can be identified by model number 03-286 and manufacture date, which are located on the bottom of the seat. The name "Cosco" appears on the chair's leg-support bar, tray, and on a sticker on the bottom of the seat.

What to do: Stop using the chair immediately and contact Cosco by calling 800-221-6736 between 8 a.m. and 4:30 p.m. EST Monday through Friday or using the following web address: *www.coscoinc.com* to order a free repair kit and to obtain instructions for proper assembly and use. You will need the model number and four-digit manufacture date located on the bottom of the seat to determine the particular repair kit required.

GRACO
High chairs (various models)

Recall: Legs could come out, causing chair to collapse and child to suffer serious injuries.

Models: 860,000 high chairs with white plastic seat and white metal legs sold 1/95–6/98 at mass-merchandise, juvenile-product, and discount department stores for $30 to $35. To determine whether unit is subject to recall, check the sticker beneath seat, which bears the model and serial numbers. Model number contains 3170, 36051, or 74001 within it. The first six numbers indicate the date of manufacture. Recalled high chairs were made 1/1/95 12/8/97 (code: 010195 through 120897). "Graco" is printed on front of tray. Company has received reports of 105 injuries, such as a concussion, broken noses, cuts, black eyes, bumps, and bruises associated with a high chair collapsing.

What to do: Call Graco at 800-617-7447 for free repair kit. (You'll need to have the highchair nearby when you call.) For more information, visit *www.gracobaby.com* or write to company's consumer-affairs department at Box 100, Elverson, PA 19520.

Infant activity seats

Typical problems: The motion of the baby causes the seat to collapse or "walk" off the edges of tables or counters, resulting in falls and injuries. Or the seat overturns with the baby inside when the it's placed on a bed, waterbed, or couch, resulting in suffocation or entrapment. Safety belts fail to restrain the baby. Toy bars come loose or contain toys that can cause choking if chewed on or parts break loose.

Safety standards: Infant seats are covered by federal regulations involving small parts. A voluntary ASTM safety standard addresses safety of openings, scissoring, shearing, pinching, carrying-handle integrity, and slip resistance, as well as performance of the restraint system.

Safety advice: Follow the manufacturer's weight specifications for babies' use. Choose seats with effective slip-resistant pads on the base. Position the seat on the floor or well away from the edges of tables and counters. Check toy bars to ensure they are securely fastened and avoid bars having toys with small parts that could be swallowed and cause choking.

KIDS II
Bouncer seats

Recall: The removable toy bar that attaches to the seat can suddenly release and cause injuries to babies. (You can continue to use the bouncer seat for the baby to sit in as long as the toy bar is removed.)

Models: 99,000 bouncer seats sold in mass-merchandise and juvenile-specialty stores nationwide between 10/97 and 4/00 for about $25 to $35. Only models with semicircular (not rectangular) toy bars holding three toys were recalled. The seats were sold under the names "Soft Toy Bouncer Seat" or "Comfort Me Bouncer." The Kids II logo is embroidered on each seat's crotch strap. The bouncer seats have a ruffled seat pad in three patterns: a black, white, and red cow print; a teddy bear, rocking horse, and toy box print; and a nursery rhyme print. Each pattern has certain model and lot numbers, which are found on a tag attached to the seat. The Comfort Me Bouncers feature vibration and soothing sounds, including music, waves, and heartbeat. Some of the recalled seats came with white toy-bar tethers.

What to do: Remove the semicircular toy bar immediately and contact Kids II toll-free at 877-325-7056 between 7:30 am and 4:30 pm EST Monday through Friday for a free in-home repair kit. You can continue to use the bouncer seat as long as the toy bar is removed.

Infant swings

Typical problems: Swing frame is not stable; Frame or seat may have sharp edges; Child may become entangled in harness straps; seat can collapse.

Safety standards: Swings are covered by federal regulations involving small parts. There is no voluntary standard, though one was being developed as of Spring 2001.

Safety advice: Look for a sturdy, stable frame and a secure harness. Follow manufacturer's age and weight specifications.

FISHER-PRICE
Lift 'n Lock swings

Recall: Children can maneuver out of the restraints of these outdoor swings for children 9 months to 3 years and fall out, resulting in serious injuries.

Models: About 2.5 million Lift 'n Lock Swings, outdoor swings sold in mass-merchandise, juvenile-products, and discount department stores 01/91-08/00 for about $19. Recalled models have red or purple plastic seats, yellow "T"-shaped restraint shields, and blue ropes. "Fisher-Price(r)" is written on the front of the restraint shield. The swings have model numbers 2092, 75960, 75970, 75973, or 75980 molded into the back part of the seat.

What to do: Stop using the swing immediately and contact Fisher-Price's toll-free Recall Hotline at 800-343-1502 for a free repair kit with a supplemental waist and crotch restraint belt.

FISHER-PRICE
3-in-1 Cradle Swing with detachable carrier

Recall: When swing is used as carrier, handle locks could suddenly release, causing seat to flip forward and infant to tumble onto ground.

Models: 105,000 cradle swings, models 79321 and 79322, sold 3/97-1/99 nationwide at mass-merchandise, juvenile-products, and major discount stores for about $100. Model number appears on underside of motor housing and on bottom of seat. "Fisher-Price" appears on front of motor housing and on bottom of seat. Only swings with detachable carrier are subject to recall.

What to do: Stop using seat as infant carrier and call company at 800-505-0600 for free repair kit, or visit *www.fisherprice.com/us/help/cradle.asp* for information.

GRACO
Infant swings (various models)

Recall: Under certain conditions, child could fall out or slip down into seat, become tangled in safety belts, and strangle.

Models: 7 million swings made before 11/97 and sold through 1/98 at mass-merchandise, juvenile-products, and major discount department stores for about $70 to $120. Swings are battery-powered or wind up, and are in either the traditional A-frame or open-top design. Date of manufacture appears on label on housing on top of swing. Label bears various information, including model and serial numbers. Date is first six digits of serial number (for instance, 110197, which translates into Nov. 1, 1997). Restraint system on suspect swings consists of waist belt only; a hinged or removable tray on the products also helps restrain baby. Hazard exists if parts are missing, the restraints aren't used, or if tray pops off. There have been six deaths, according to the Consumer Product Safety Commission, and 181 reports of infants falling from swing.

What to do: Call company at 800-934-9082 to learn if swing is subject to corrective action and to obtain free replacement safety restraint. Consumers can also visit the company's web site, *www.gracobaby.com,* or write to Graco Children's Products, Attention: Consumer Affairs, P.O. Box 100, Elverson, PA 19520.

Jumpers

Typical problems: Pressure-mounted tongs that suspend the jumper from the door jamb, support cords, baby-seat seams, or other jumper components break, tear, or release, causing the baby to fall and sustain injuries. Babies crash into the sharp edges of the door jamb or become "seasick" from the jiggling motion.

Safety standards: Jumpers are covered by federal regulations involving small parts. There is no voluntary industry standard.

Safety advice: Follow the manufacturers' recommended baby-weight range and specified door-jamb measurements. Install carefully and inspect components frequently.

COSCO
Bungee Baby Jumpers

Recall: Metal clasps can detach from the bungee cord that suspends the seat, causing the unit to fall to the floor and babies to suffer bumps, bruises, and scratches, primarily to the head.

Models: Recalled were 171,000 jumpers sold in juvenile-product, mass-merchandise, discount department, and specialty stores nationwide,05/96-03/01, for about $40 to $50.The model number 04-461 or 04-468 is located on the bottom of the tray. Model number 04-461 is the Bungee Jumper and model 04-468 is the Bungee Combo Pack, which consists of the Bungee Jumper and parts to convert the Bungee Jumper to a stationary exerciser. (The stationary exerciser, called the Bungee Bouncer Exerciser, is not part of this recall.) Both bungee baby jumper models have a multicolored fabric seat with a white plastic frame with a red foam trim. Three yellow cords connect the seat to a blue plastic strap holder, which says "Cosco." Above the blue plastic strap holder is a thick yellow strap, which connects to a green bungee cord. The bungee cord attaches to a blue door hook.

What to do: Stop using the jumper immediately and contact Cosco at 800-314-9327 between 8 a.m.and 4:30 p.m. EST Monday through Friday or through the web site *www.coscoinc.com* to receive a free repair kit.

FISHER-PRICE
Hop, Skip, Jumpers

Recall: The spring that suspends the jumper seat from the doorway can break. Babies can fall to the ground and suffer serious injuries.

Models: 882,000 jumpers sold by mass-merchandise, juvenile-products, and discount stores from 01/87-01/94 for about $25 were recalled 07/21/00. Only model numbers 9144 and 9146 are being recalled. The model number is molded into the underside of the plastic tray attached to the soft seat. The jumper is red and blue, or all blue, with a bright yellow propeller decoration on the front of the seat. "Fisher-Price" is written on the front of the tray. Fisher-Price will help consumers determine if they have a recalled jumper.

What to do: Stop using the jumpers immediately and contact the Fisher-Price Recall Hotline at 888-821-0077 for a free repair kit with a new suspension strap to support the jumper seat if the spring breaks.

Nursery equipment

Typical problems: Electrical devices such as baby-wipe warmers, bottle warmers, nursery monitors, and night-lights may overheat or pose shock hazards.

Safety standards: Underwriters Laboratories has requirements for electrical safety. Always look for a UL sticker which indicates that an electrical product meets UL requirements.

Safety advice: Keep heat-generating items away from flammable material. Keep all electrical items away from water.

PRINCE LIONHEART
Electric baby-wipe warmer

Recall: Device poses shock hazard.

Models: 152,000 warmers, style number 0224, sold 2/98-12/99 at toy, department, and baby-specialty stores (including Toys "R" Us and Burlington Coat Factory) and by catalog for about $25. Warmers are white plastic boxes, about 9 inches long, 6 inches wide, and 4¾ inches high. Suspect devices bear date codes 9803 through 9901. Style number and date code appear on bottom of unit. "PRINCE LIONHEART" is written on lid, and orange light is located on front to indicate when unit is on. Affected warmers might have cracks in interior tub, which allows water to contact electrical components.

What to do: Unplug warmer, remove wipes, and check interior. If it appears cracked, call distributor, Advance Thermo Control, at 888-843-8718, for free replacement. If tub is not cracked, unit is not subject to recall, and consumers can continue to use product, according to Consumer Product Safety Commission.

Pacifiers

Typical problems: Nipples separate from base; small pieces of nipples break off, posing a choking hazard.

Safety standards: A federal standard requires two ventilation holes in shield to admit air if shield is caught in mouth or throat. Pacifiers must pass a "pull test" after boiling and cooling to ensure they will not come apart. Shield size is regulated to prevent choking. Package must carry warning label advising against hanging pacifier around child's neck due to strangulation risk.

Safety advice: Boil for 5 minutes before first use to remove chemical residues. Never hang from string around baby's neck or tie to crib bars due to strangulation risk. Discard when nipple becomes sticky and crumbly, or when baby starts chewing off pieces.

BINKY
Newborn Orthodontic pacifiers

Recall: Nipple can detach from shield and choke child.

Models: 13,000 pacifiers sold 8/94-8/95 by Target Stores and other stores nationwide and

5/95-8/95 by University Hospitals of Oklahoma City, individually or in sets of two, for about $1 each. Pacifier has red, mint-green, blue, or white butterfly mouth shield, with star and crescent vent holes on each side. Some white shields have crescent vent holes on each side. Some white shields have crescents, stars, and hearts stenciled on front. Knob on pacifier doesn't move if twisted, and well around knob is ¼ inch deep. Pacifier came in plastic shell with cardboard backing. Label on back of package reads, in part, "Made***in Malaysia*** Griptight Malaysia Ltd." English-made pacifiers whose knob moves when twisted and whose well is ⅜ inch deep aren't recalled.

What to do: Return pacifier to store for replacement or mail it to Binky-Griptight, Inc., P.O. Box 3307, Wallington, NJ 07057 for replacement and reimbursement of postage.

PLAYTEX
Classic Patterns Cherubs and Soft Comfort latex pacifiers

Recall: Because the latex ages faster than normal, the nipple can detach from the shield, presenting a choking hazard to babies.

Models: About 1.8 million Classic Patterns "Cherubs" and Soft Comfort latex pacifiers sold in stores nationwide prior to 06/00 for about $2 (single pack) to $4 (double pack). pack. The Classic Patterns pacifiers have the word "Cherubs" embossed in bold block letters on the colored knob of the pacifier shield. The Soft Comfort pacifiers have a soft, butterfly-shaped shield, available with or without a swivel handle. The word "Playtex" is embossed on the pacifier's swivel handle. The pacifiers come in a variety of colors and designs. UPC Codes are as follows: 078300-05448-1 (Soft Comfort Pacifier-1 Pack); 078300-05442-9 (Soft Comfort Angled Orthodontic Pacifier-1 Pack); 078300-05528-0 (Soft Comfort Pacifier-2 Pack); 078300-05529-7 (Soft Comfort Angled Orthodontic Pacifier-2 Pack); 078300-01023-4 (Classic Patterns/Cherubs Oval Pacifier-1 Pack); 078300-01118-7 (Classic Patterns/Cherubs Angled Orthodontic Pacifier-1 Pack); 078300-01024-1 (Classic Patterns/Cherubs Oval Pacifier-2 Pack); 078300-01128-6 (Classic Patterns/ Cherubs Angled Orthodontic Pacifier-2 Pack); 078300-01041-8 (Classic Patterns/Cherubs Pacifier & Holder Set).

What to do: Stop using the recalled pacifier immediately and return the pacifier by mail directly to the company: Playtex Pacifiers, Playtex Products Inc., 20 Troy Road, Whippany, NJ 07981 to receive a free replacement pacifier or a $3 coupon toward the purchase of another Playtex infant feeding or soothing product. For more information, call Playtex toll-free at 800-522-8230 or visit their web site: *www.playtexbaby.com*.

Strollers

Typical problems: Children fall from strollers when they are not properly belted in or the belts fail to hold, or injured in falls into the stroller from outside. Locking mechanisms holding the frame open fail, causing the stroller to collapse, ejecting the baby, or entrapping fingers or hands in the stroller frame. Strollers used in the reclining position and some legholes allow small babies' bodies to slip through, trapping the neck and head and sometimes causing strangulation.

Safety standards: Strollers are covered by federal regulations involving small parts, sharp points and edges, as well as a voluntary ASTM standard that includes tests for safety of the seat-belt system, brakes, leg openings, locking devices to prevent accidental folding as well as stability. If a stroller's backrest can be reclined to form an angle greater than 150 degrees, the standard requires that the gap be measured to ensure it's safe for small infants.

Safety advice: Purchase a certified model, and always check safety latches to see that they have engaged so the stroller can't collapse. Always use the stroller's restraining belts and never leave a child unattended in or around a stroller.

BABY TREND
Road Runner jogging strollers

Recall: Strollers were shipped without straps attached to the frame to secure the seat. Unless the frame straps are attached, a child in the seat of the stroller can lean forward and fall out.

Models: About 1,500 aluminum, three-wheeled strollers with hand brakes sold in Baby's "R" Us stores 01/99-04/99 for about $200. The affected strollers have a seat and seatback made from a blue canvas-type fabric. The stroller has a three-strap harness that secures the child in the seat. Two additional straps snap together and secure the back corners of the seat to the stroller frame. "Baby Trend" is written on the aluminum frame. The recalled stroller is model number 9592T. The model number is written on a label located in the center of the rear axle.

What to do: Stop using these strollers immediately and examine the stroller to determine if the seat is strapped to the stroller frame. For more information, consumers should call Baby Trend toll-free at 800-328-7363 between 8:30 a.m. and 4:30 p.m. PST Monday through Friday, or write to Baby Trend Inc., 2019 S. Business Pkwy., Ontario, CA 91761. Consumers also can visit the company's web site at *www.babytrend.com.*

BOB TRAILERS INC.
Sport Utility Stroller and Sport Utility Stroller D'lux

Recall: The stroller's front-wheel connector can crack during use, causing the wheel to separate from the frame. A jogger could lose control of the stroller or the stroller could suddenly collapse, resulting in injury to a child.

Models: About 3,700 jogging strollers sold through bike, baby, and outdoor-product stores and web sites from 11/98–03/00 for about $280 to $370. The involved strollers have three wheels and are pacific blue and black, or hunter green and black. Each stroller has a canopy. The "BOB" logo is on the stroller's frame, canopy, and seat back.

What to do: Stop using the stroller immediately, and return it to the store where purchased for repair. Consumers also can return the strollers to BOB Trailers for repair. For more information, call the company's toll-free number, 800-893-2447, between 9 a.m. ST Monday through Friday or access the company's web site at *www.bobtrailers.com*.

CENTURY
Take 2, Travel Solutions, Pioneer, Travelite, and Pro Sport 4-in-1 Strollers

Recall: The strollers can unexpectedly collapse or the car seat/carrier adapter can unexpectedly detach. When this happens, an infant or young child inside the stroller or an attached car seat/carrier can fall to the ground and suffer serious injuries.

Models: 650,000 Take 2, Travel Solutions, Pioneer, Travelite, and Pro Sport 4-in-1 strollers sold in mass merchandise, juvenile-products, and discount department stores nationwide from 12/96-3/01 for between $100 and $200.

The recalled strollers are for toddlers when used alone and for infants when a car seat/carrier is connected to the stroller. The model names for the recalled strollers can be found on the footrest, the seat pad, the legs of the frame or on a white label on the side locks. The Take 2 was manufactured in 2000; Travel Solutions 1999-2000; Pioneer 1998-2000;Travelite 1997-1998; Pro Sport 1996-1999.

What to do: Consumers should stop using these strollers and call Century toll-free at 800-766-9998 anytime to order a free repair kit. Consumers should have their strollers available, as Century will help consumers determine if they have one of the recalled models. Consumers also can log on to the company's website at *www.centuryproducts.com* or write to Consumer Affairs, Century Products, Box 100, Elverson, PA 19520. Parents should continue to use these carriers as car seats.

INSTEP
InSTEP and HEALTHRIDER brand single and double jogging strollers

Recall: The stroller's brake can fail, causing the stroller to unexpectedly roll away, resulting in injury to a child.

Models: About 44,000 jogging strollers manufactured 12/98–07/99 and sold in Burlington Coat Factory, J.C. Penney, Healthrider, The Sports Authority, and Target stores nationwide, among others, between 12/98-07/99 for about $100 for a single jogger and $250 for a double jogger. Affected strollers have model numbers: ZS100, ZD200, ZS100WS, ZD200WS, ZS100HR, ZD200HR, PR100, or PR200. The manufacturing date, written as

T "month" R "year" I, is located on a sticker on the lower cross tube (for example, T01R99I is January 1999). "InSTEP" and the model number also are on the sticker. InSTEP model numbers ZS100, ZD200, ZS100WS, ZD200WS, PR100, and PR200 have a blue and green seat and green canopy. "ZII" is on the top and "InSTEP" is on the front of the stroller. HEALTHRIDER model numbers ZS100HR and ZD200HR have a blue and gray seat and blue canopy. "HEALTHRIDER" is on the top and front of the stroller.

What to do: Stop using the strollers immediately and contact InSTEP LLC to receive a free, easy-to-install repair kit. To order the repair kit or for more information, call InSTEP LLC's toll-free number, 800-242-6110, between 8 a.m. and 5 p.m. CST Monday through Friday, or access the company's web site at *www.instep.net*.

KOLCRAFT
Ranger and Ranger Quattro strollers

Recall: Lock mechanisms, found on both sides of the stroller, can break and create a pinch-point hazard. Young children can be injured when their fingers, arms, or hands are pinched between parts of the locking mechanism.

Models: About 25,500 strollers manufactured from 12/99–06/00 and sold by mass-merchandise and juvenile-products stores nationwide 01/00 through 11/00 for about $80. The model number can be found on a sticker on the back-leg frame of the stroller with the manufacture date below it. Models include the Kolcraft Ranger and Ranger Quattro with model numbers 46720 and 46721. The strollers have a sticker with "Ranger" or "Ranger Quattro" on the front of the footrest, and "Kolcraft" sewn into the safety-belt harness material in the stroller's seat. The strollers also have a reversible handle that allows consumers to push the stroller while either facing the child or from behind the child. (Ranger and Ranger Quattro strollers manufactured after 06/00 have different side-lock mechanisms, and are not included in this recall.)

What to do: Stop using the stroller immediately and call Kolcraft's toll-free number anytime, 800-757-4770, to receive a free repair kit.

Toys

Typical problems: Small parts break off or are bitten off, posing choking hazard; toys crack or break, creating sharp edges that can cut; toys can break, spilling out small parts that can choke; crib mobiles strung across crib pose strangulation hazard.

Safety standards: The voluntary ASTM standard for toys stipulates that squeeze toys and teethers must be large enough to preclude a choking hazard; crib-toy strings must be short enough not to wrap around a child's neck; and crib gyms and mobiles must be labeled so parents know to remove them when the child can pull up on hands and knees (about age 6 months). Under the Federal Hazardous Substance Act, all toys sold in the U.S. must meet low lead levels for paint and have smooth surfaces rather than sharp points and edges. Rattles must be large enough not to lodge in a baby's throat and cannot separate into small pieces. No small parts that could pose a choking hazard (this includes small balls and marbles) are allowed on toys intended for children under 3.

Safety advice: Don't buy toys small enough to slip through the center tube of a toilet-paper roll. Avoid any with small parts that can be broken or chewed off; strings or cords that can strangle; sharp edges; and finger-pinching lids and hinges. Check regularly for loose parts, cracks, tears, and sharp edges. Supervise your child's play.

BATTAT
Soft Landing Beanbag Cushion

Recall: Infant pillows and cushions have been banned under the Federal Hazardous Substances Act since 1992 because they pose a suffocation hazard to infants. In addition, two 8- to 9-inch cords, which attach toys to the cushions, pose strangulation hazards.

Models: 1,500 Parents™ magazine-brand Soft Landing Beanbag cushions sold in Target stores nationwide from 9/00-5/01 for about $24. The airplane-shaped cushions, measuring approximately 27 inches long by 21 inches wide, are covered in various solid-colored cloth panels, and are filled with plastic foam pellets. They have a "smiley face" on the front with a propeller that spins and makes clicking sounds, and a plush nose. The back of the cushion has a circular target design. Side pockets on the wings have a "My First Passport" book with circle teether and a heart-shaped rattle attached. The cushions' hang tag reads in part, "Parent's PLAY + LEARN ...Fun and safe for all ages...Battat Inc... Made in Thailand." Writing on the packaging states that the product can be used for infants 6 months and up to nap, and that the cushions are "not considered a safe sleeping area for babies."

What to do: Consumers should take the cushions away from children immediately and return them to a Target store for a refund. Consumers also can send their cushions to Battat Incorporated, Attention: Valinda Cayetano, Quality Assurance, 44 Martina Circle, Plattsburgh, NY 12901 for a refund plus mailing costs. For more information, consumers should call Battat Incorporated at 800-247-6144 between 8 a.m. and 5 p.m. ET Monday through Friday, or visit the Battat web site at *www.battat-toys.com* or the Target web site at *www.target.com*.

THE BETESH GROUP
John Lennon musical crib mobiles

Recall: The screws that connect the mobile's arm assembly and crib clamp can become loose if overtightened. The arms can detach and fall into the crib, injuring the baby inside.

Models: 47,000 mobiles sold in department and specialty stores from 06/99-08/00 for about $39. John Lennon Musical Mobiles hang from white wooden dowels that attach to cribs with white clamps. "John LennonTM" and "MADE IN CHINA" is written on the wind-up music box that turns the mobile. The music box plays the song, "Imagine." The mobile has colorful wooden cutouts of a rhinoceros, two elephants, a giraffe, and a bird hanging from yellow ribbons. Below each animal is a round disk with a drawing of the animal it hangs from on the bottom.

What to do: Immediately stop using the mobile and contact The Betesh Group toll-free, 877-810-4264, or write to: The Betesh Group, One East 33rd Street, New York, NY 10016, to receive a free replacement plastic mobile with stuffed animals.

BRIO
Baking Set and Small Baking Set

Recall: The sets include a hand mixer with a knob that can break off, posing a choking hazard to young children.

Models: 6,450 baking sets sold in specialty stores, Internet retailers, and mail-order catalogs from 3/99-4/01 for $15 to $25. The yellow, blue and red hand mixers are 5.5 inches long, and are sold along with toy utensils, rolling pin, mixing bowl, and baking molds. The BRIO Small Baking Set and BRIO Baking Set are labeled for children ages 2 years and older and are packaged in a clear-plastic tote. Inside of the tote, a label reads, "PARENTS: ENSURE THE ITEMS ARE WASHED THOROUGHLY BEFORE USE." The recalled baking sets have a model number of either 31798 or 31795.

What to do: Consumers should take the hand mixer away from children immediately and call BRIO toll-free at 888-274-6869 between 8:30 a.m. and 5 p.m. CT Monday through Friday, for a refund or replacement item. Consumers also can send the mixer to BRIO Corp., SAFETY RECALL, N120 W18485 Freistadt Road, Germantown, WI 53022, for a refund or replacement. For more information, consumers can log on to the company website at *www.briotoy.com.*

FISHER-PRICE
Bounce 'n Play Activity Dome

Recall: Nylon bands that keep play area level could detach and cause surface to tilt. That could cause infant to slide into one end, become trapped, and possibly suffocate.

Models: 235,000 activity domes, model 79534, sold since 12/98. Dome is portable play-and-nap space for infants. To determine if product is subject to recall, check the model number and six-character code on tag on bottom of unit. All codes that end with 8 are subject to recall, as are those with codes ending in 9 and beginning with numbers 001 through 286. "Fisher-Price" appears on canopy. Note: Activity domes with a green dot on bottom (and a "quality approved" label on sticker on box) have been repaired and are not subject to corrective action.

What to do: Call Fisher-Price at 800-505-0600 to obtain free repair kit and installation instructions or visit w*ww.fisherprice.com* for information.

FISHER-PRICE
Intelli-Table toys

Recall: Two red knobs on the toy can break off, creating small parts that can pose a choking hazard for young children.

Models: About 20,000 of the toy tables sold in mass-merchandise and discount stores nationwide 10/00–03/01 for about $70. The recalled model is a round, plastic activity table with a blue, removable top with a Fisher-Price logo on the top and a date code from 269(0) through 281(0) molded into the underside. The base of the unit is red with three legs that are blue, yellow, and teal green. Model number 77148 and the words, "Mattel, Inc." and "China" are molded into the bottom of the red base. Only models manufactured from 09/25/00–10/07/00 are being recalled. The red knobs that break off are located on the yellow and white interchangeable play rings.

What to do: Remove the toy from young children and contact Fisher-Price's toll-free Recall Hotline, 800-220-7137, anytime, to order a free repair kit with two replacement knobs and new screws. Consumers can also visit the Fisher-Price web site at *www.fisher-price.com* for more information.

GRACO AND CHILDREN ON THE GO
Activity trays and bath sets with suction cups

Recall: Suction cups could detach and pose choking hazard to small child.

Models: 100,000 devices sold 1/98-8/99 at discount, department, and juvenile-product stores nationwide, including Toys "R" Us and Sears, for $10 to $15. Recall involves the Graco and Children on the Go brand Stroller Snack and Activity Tray, Bathtime Activity Tray, and Bathtime Toy Netting products. Activity trays attach with suction cups to tiled or smooth surfaces, and four toys are affixed to each tray. Toys are removable and interchangeable with other Mix 'N Move toys, which can be bought separately. Stroller Snack and Activity Tray toys include toucan, rolling ball, star, and dog. Bathtime Activity Tray's toys include octopus, U-tube, spinning ball, and paddle wheel. "Graco" or "Children on the Go" appears on underside of tray. Bathtime Toy Netting consists of clam soap holder and fish washcloth holder that attaches with suction cups to various surfaces. A net, used to store toys, hangs between clam and fish. "Graco" is on the back of the clam and fish.

What to do: Consumers should stop using these products immediately. To receive a free repair kit, call Graco anytime at 800-446-1366. Consumers can also visit the company's web site, *www.gracobaby.com*, or write to Graco Children's Products, Attention: Consumer Affairs, P.O. Box 100, Elverson, PA 19520.

KB TOYS
Electronic Light N' Learn Activity Gym

Recall: Five detachable hanging rattle toys have small round pegs at the top of the toys that can break off, posing a choking hazard to young children.

Models: 115,000 activity gyms sold in KB Toy stores, KB Toy Works, KB Toy Outlet, Big Lots, Odd Lots, Pic N Save, and MacFrugals from 9/00-1/01 for $20 to $30. The Electronic Light N' Learn activity gym is a multi-colored toy that converts into three different toys, including a crib toy, a floor gym, and a musical keyboard. The gyms' main console has five buttons with numbers that make music when pressed and automatically light up when the continuous song play option is selected. Five detachable rattles in the shape of a bear, snail, star, half-moon and horse hang from the bottom of the console. A label under the handle on the gyms' main console reads in part "ELECTRONIC LIGHT N' LEARN ACTIVITY GYM MODEL: 8735, MADE IN CHINA."

What to do: Remove the toy from children immediately and return it to the store where purchased for a refund. Consumers who purchased the toy online should return the toy to the closest KB Toy store or contact KB Toys for return information. For additional information, contact KB Toys at 800-279-5066 between 8 a.m. and 1 a.m. ET Monday through Saturday and between 10 a.m. and 10 p.m. ET Sunday. Consumers also can visit the firm's web site at *www.kbkids.com*.

PLAYSKOOL
Busy Poppin' Pals Toys

Recall: Small springs inside these toys can break loose, posing a choking and laceration hazard to young children.

Models: 590,000 Busy Poppin' Pals toys and Sesame Street Busy Poppin' Pals toys recalled in two different actions. Busy Poppin' Pals were sold in mass-merchandise stores and toy stores 1/96-8/00. Sesame Street Busy Poppin' Pals were sold 11/94-12/96 in merchandise and toy stores, including Toys "R" Us. Both toys sold for about $10. Busy Poppin' Pals is a 13-inch-long white plastic toy with blue, yellow, and red buttons, levers, and knobs of various shapes that, when activated, make animal characters pop up from under the toy's base. The animals are hidden under blue, yellow, or red lids that have the numbers 1 through 5 on top. The lid colors match the color of the buttons, levers, and knobs that activate them. The pop-up animals are a giraffe, elephant, panda bear, lion, and monkey. The toy has a white carry handle and has the Playskool logo on the front. The model number 5415 and "MADE IN CHINA" are imprinted on the bottom of the toy. Sesame Street Busy Poppin' Pals toy is similar toy, but with a green button instead of red. Sesame Street characters pop up from under the toy's base. The characters—Elmo, Ernie, Big Bird, Bert, and Cookie Monster—are hidden under corresponding blue, yellow, or green lids that have the numbers 1 through 5 imprinted on top. The model number, "5446," "MADE IN CHINA," and "C-023B" are imprinted on the bottom of the toy. (Busy Poppin' Pals with model number 6205 have different springs, and are not part of the recalls.)

What to do: Remove from children immediately and contact Playskool, toll-free, at 877-518-9743 anytime or visit their web site at *www.hasbro.com* to receive a free, redesigned replacement toy.

PLAYSKOOL
Klackeroo toys

Recall: The toy's brightly colored end knobs can detach and allow small, geometric-shaped pieces to come loose, posing a choking hazard to infants and young children.

Models: About 550,000 toys sold in toy and mass-merchandise stores, including Toys "R" Us and Wal-Mart 10/97–9/00 for about $8. Klackeroo is a brightly colored toy with orange plastic rods and small geometric shapes that move through a center purple ball. Solid-colored knobs of green, yellow, blue, and red have animal faces or the sun and moon imprinted on them and cap both ends of each orange rod. When shaken, the rods move through the ball and the geometric shapes slide along each rod, making a "clacking" sound. The Playskool logo is imprinted on one end knob and "MADE IN CHINA" is imprinted on the center ball.

What to do: Take the toy away from infants and young children immediately, and contact Playskool toll-free anytime at 888-671-9764 to receive a free, redesigned replacement Klackeroo toy (model number 5542), which features a red center ball with no sliding geometric shapes.

PRECIOUS MOMENTS
Tender Tails plush toys

Recall: Pom-poms could come off and pose a choking hazard to small child.

Models: 472,000 stuffed toys sold 5/98-8/99 nationwide at gift, card, and collectible stores for about $7. Recalled toys include Lady Bug (item number 476080), Bee (464295), Butterfly (482234), and Reindeer (381969). Item number appears on purple "adoption registration" attached to toy. Toys are about 6 inches long and bear label that reads, in part: "TENDER TAILS," "by ENESCO," and "MADE IN CHINA." Pom-poms are antennae on head of ladybug, bee, and butterfly. On reindeer, they appear as holiday ornaments on antlers.

What to do: Cut off pom-poms and return them, with your name, address, and phone number, to Enesco for free Tender Tails Hippo toy (another Tender Tails toy will be substituted when hippo supply is exhausted). Write to Enesco, P.O. Box 499, Itasca, IL 60143-0499. For information, call 800-632-7968, *visit www.enesco.com,* or e-mail company at *ttpompoms@enesco.com.*

SAFARI LTD.
Shapes or Peek Inside wooden toy puzzle

Recall: Small parts could choke child.

Models: 10,200 puzzles sold 4/98-1/99 for about $5. Puzzle has 10 different-shaped pieces with colorful laminated paper veneer and plastic knob handles. Lifting piece reveals name of shape underneath. Oval and rhombus pose choking hazard. Puzzle is labeled "SHAPES... SAFARI... No.9536-12 ... 1997 SAFARI LTD." Card insert in plastic packaging says "SAFARI LTD ... PEEK INSIDE PUZZLE, Made in Taiwan, NO. 9536-12 SHAPES."

What to do: Call 800-615-3111 for refund or replacement. (Redesigned puzzle, model 9549-12, isn't being recalled.)

SASSY
Scoop Pour 'N Squirt and Bath Time Pals bath sets

Recall: The fish's size, texture, shape, and easy compressibility make it possible for an infant to compress the toy and place it in his or her mouth. If the toy reaches the back of the mouth and expands, it may block the child's airway.

Models: 370,000 squirting fish found in the Scoop Pour 'N Squirt and Bath Time Pals bath toy set sold in mass-merchandise stores and toy stores 02/99-12/00 for about $5. The Scoop Pour 'N Squirt bath toy set has a large plastic fish-shaped scoop with a green textured handle and a spout for pouring water and two small plastic squirting fish. The Bath Time Pals bath toy set comes with one squirting frog, two squirting pearls, and two squirting fish.

What to do: Remove the squirting fish from young children and throw them away. For additional information or to receive replacement squirt toys, contact Sassy, toll-free, at 800-764-8323 or visit their web site at *www.sassybaby.com.*

PLAYGO
Airplanes, cars, dump trucks, trains, and fire engines

Recall: Small parts can break off of the toy vehicles, posing a choking hazard to young children.

Models: About 290,000 toy vehicles sold in drug, grocery, variety stores, and discount department stores, including Wal-Mart, 06/95-12/98 for about $5. The recalled toys are made of multicolored plastic with red, blue, green, and yellow parts. Each vehicle has a battery-operated, detachable remote control with a 40-inch cord. Enclosed in the cab of each vehicle are small multicolored balls about ¼ inch in diameter. A label on the vehicles and the remote reads "PLAYGO." The words, "PLAYGO LTD (HONG KONG) MADE IN CHINA" are imprinted on the bottom of each toy.

What to do: Take the toy vehicles away from children immediately and cut the remote-control cord off the toy, discard the vehicle, and mail just the cord to Supreme at 8348 C, Olive Road, St. Louis, MO 63132 for a $5 refund plus the cost of postage. For more information, call Supreme Toys toll-free at 800-567-1774 Monday through Friday between 9 a.m. and 5 p.m. CST.

VEGGIETALES
Dave and the Giant Pickle playset

Recall: Figures pose choking hazard for young children.

Models: 44,000 playsets with 10 figures, including asparagus, grape, gourds, French peas, pickle, sheep, and tents, sold 9/98-2/99 at major Christian bookstores and by catalog for about $20. Six figures have plastic plug in base that could come out, and French peas figure poses choking hazard because of size and shape. Toys came in mostly blue box showing scenes from animated video. Product number SPCN 9834501358 appears under UPC code on back of box.

What to do: Call 800-743-2514 for replacement figures.

Walkers

Typical problems: Wheels allow walkers to move faster than parents can keep up with them. Babies plummet down staircases, over curbs, and into pools and sustain serious injuries. Toys work loose from consoles, exposing small parts. Seats may tear or unsnap, allowing babies to fall.

Safety standards: Walkers are covered by federal regulations involving small parts, sharp edges, and sharp points. An ASTM voluntary standard issued in April 2000 covers occupant retention; the latching/locking mechanism to prevent accidental folding or collapse; stability; and the requirement that a walker can't pass through doors or openings up to 36 inches wide.

Safety advice: Limit the time a child uses the walker to less than a half hour and stay nearby. Keep the child away from stairs or steps.

FISHER-PRICE
Get Up & Go Walkers

Recall: This three-sided push toy, which looks like a car, is designed for children to support themselves as they are learning to stand and walk. Young children leaning forward on the front of the toys can tip them over and fall, and windshield wipers on some models stick out, injuring young children when they fall.

Models: 246,000 push-behind walkers sold in mass-merchandise and discount stores 07/97-08/00 for about $30. Fisher-Price will help consumers determine if they have a recalled product. The recalled units are white with blue sides with activities such as a rotating mirror/phone, toy windshield wiper, and steering wheel with yellow horn. The back wheels of the walker can be locked into place to prevent rolling as babies learn to stand. The Fisher-Price logo is located on the outside of the toy between the headlight decorations. Models with a front bar for babies to grasp and/or a green windshield wiper are included in the recall.

What to do: Stop using the toy immediately and call Fisher-Price's Recall Hotline, 800-343-1502, for a free repair kit that will eliminate the front bar and windshield wiper.

GRACO
Tot Wheels Entertainer infant walkers

Recall: Walkers can collapse unexpectedly during use and injure infants.

Models: About 31,000 walkers sold in mass-merchandise, juvenile-products, and major discount department stores nationwide, including Wal-Mart and Toys "R" Us from 09/99-02/00 for about $50. The multicolor walker has a removable, green play tray with 12 activities, including a steering wheel, ball spinner, and flashing lights, and it has an animal-print fabric seat. Model numbers 4032LN or 4032BLA are located underneath the front of the walker's tray. "Graco Lights & Sounds" is written on a label on the walker tray. "Tot Wheels® Entertainer® Activity Center with Bounce" is written on a label on the walker's base. (Similar models with different model numbers have not been recalled.

What to do: Stop using immediately, and call Graco's toll-free number, 800-345-4109, anytime for a free repair kit which includes a replacement tray. Or visit the Graco web site at *www.gracobaby.com*, or write to Consumer Affairs, Graco Children's Products Inc., Box 100, Elverson, PA 19520.

KOLCRAFT
Tot Rider walkers

Recall: Cover on walker's removable music center could break off and pose choking hazard to small child.

Models: 3,356 walkers, model 14302, sold 2/00-1/01 at mass-merchandise and juvenile-product stores for $40 to $50. Model number and date of manufacture appear on base of walker. "Tot Rider," "Music Center," and "Kolcraft" appear on front of device. Music center tray has steering wheel, gear shift, buttons, and speaker that plays music.

What to do: Remove music center and call Kolcraft at 800-453-7673 for free replacement tray. Note: Kolcraft Tot Rider, model 14303, is not subject to recall.

SAFETY 1ST
Mobile 4 Wheelin walkers

Recall: Babies can lose their lower teeth when the teeth are caught in parts of the three-spoke steering wheels. The telephone could break apart on some models, releasing small parts and posing a choking hazard.

Models: 170,000 models shaped like cars and sold in mass-merchandise, juvenile-products, and major discount department stores nationwide from 04/98-04/99 for about $50. The recalled unit has a green body, and includes a three-spoke steering wheel with squeaking horn, clicking keys, two rearview mirrors, and a phone with electronic ring. Model numbers 45701, 45701A, or 45701B are written underneath the walker tray. Other writing under the body includes, "Made in the U.S.A., 1997," and "Safety 1st, Inc." (Only walkers with these model numbers are part of the recall, not models with model number 45701C, 45701D, 45704, or 45705, which have different steering wheel and phone designs).

What to do: Stop using these walkers immediately and order repair kits from Safety 1st by calling their toll-free hotline at 800-964-8489 between 9 a.m and 5 p.m. EST Monday through Friday, or write to Consumer Relations Dept., Safety 1st Inc., 45 Dan Road, Canton, MA 02021.

Index